A Season for That

A Season
for That

*Lost and Found in the
Other Southern France*

Steve Hoffman

CROWN
NEW YORK

All rights reserved.
Published in the United States by Crown, an imprint of the Crown Publishing
Group, a division of Penguin Random House LLC, New York.
crownpublishing.com

Scene 78 was originally published in different form in *Food & Wine*.

CROWN and the Crown colophon are registered trademarks of
Penguin Random House LLC.

Library of Congress Cataloging-in-Publication Data
Names: Hoffman, Steve, 1965 October 17- author. Title: A season for that /
Steve Hoffman. Identifiers: LCCN 2023056106 (print) | LCCN 2023056107 (ebook) |
ISBN 9780593240281 (hardcover) | ISBN 9780593240298 (ebook) Subjects: LCSH:
Hoffman, Steve, 1965 October 17—Travel—France—Languedoc. | Hoffman, Steve,
1965 October 17—Friends and associates. | Food writers—United States—Travel. |
Wine and wine making—France—Languedoc. | France—Social life and customs.
Classification: LCC TX649.H64 A3 2024 (print) | LCC TX649.H64 (ebook) |
DDC 641.5944/8092—dc23/eng/20240407
LC record available at https://lccn.loc.gov/2023056106
LC ebook record available at https://lccn.loc.gov/2023056107

ISBN 978-0-593-24028-1
Ebook ISBN 978-0-593-24029-8

Printed in the United States of America on acid-free paper

Editor: Francis Lam
Editorial assistant: Darian Keels
Production editor: Natalie Blachere
Text designer: Andrea Lau
Production manager: Philip Leung
Copy editor: Diana Drew
Proofreaders: Alison Miller and Rob Sternitzky
Publicist: Bree Martinez
Marketer: Mason Eng

9 8 7 6 5 4 3 2 1

First Edition

Book design by Andrea Lau
Jacket design by Christopher Brand
Jacket photograph: Mary Jo Hoffman
Author photograph: Taylor Hall O'Brien

To Mary Jo, Eva, and Joseph

Sorry this took so long

This book was written over a several-year period, several years after the events themselves. I relied on contemporaneous journals and my own memory to reconstruct the story's scenes and their relationship to one another. I relied on subsequent visits to the same locations to deepen some physical descriptions. Though some dialogue was captured in journals, I reconstructed other conversations to the best of my recollection. All characters are actual people, and all scenes are based on actual events. Throughout, I used the writing process and the narrative that emerged from it as an effort to understand the truth, as I felt it, of an experience that affected me profoundly and irreversibly.

PART I

1

"What do you think?" asked Mary Jo.

"About what?"

"About everything. The village."

We had just completed our first tour of Autignac, population eight hundred, burrowed deep in rural Languedoc. This was home for the next six months. This is where our two kids—Eva, fourteen, and Joseph, nine—would go to school. This is what we had picked, of all the options available.

A knife edge of Mediterranean sunlight sliced the central square in two. To our right, in a hot wedge of shade, the white plastic tables and green plastic chairs outside the Café du Commerce were talkatively half-occupied. Two bikes leaned against the nearest table. A pair of men sat across from each other in tight jerseys and half shorts, with two glasses of white wine sweating on the table between them.

"I think it's a perfectly beautiful village," I said. "It's just not a particularly beautiful village, is all."

"What's *seiche*?" asked Joe.

"What's what?"

"*Seiche.*"

He was pointing to the first of four dishes the Café du Commerce was proposing for lunch.

"*Seiche Farcie à la Sétoise,*" I said thoughtfully, as if deciding how best to explain it to him. But I had no idea what a *seiche* was, nor what the stuffing in a *seiche farcie* might be, nor what it meant to be *à la Sétoise*.

I did not know what a *Gardiane* was either—item two on the laminated menu. Nor, in fact, did I know what number three, *Daurade*, was, or whether it would taste good *grillée*.

I did recognize item number four—rather a classic—referred to in this part of France, it appeared, as *Cheeseburger avec Frites*.

The owner of the café, who doubled as the waiter, had a hint of James Dean prettiness, with sandy hair swept back, and sandy stubble along a remarkable shelf of jaw. But the bruised hollows around his eyes and his dingy teeth spoke of a pack or two a day, too much coffee, and not enough sleep.

Something about our group, whether it was our flushed, Nordic skin, our two cameras, or simply the ineffable scent of *touriste américain* we must have given off in spite of ourselves—something about us had evidently triggered something in him, and his sunken eyes had glared at me as he first approached our table, as if, after all these years, he finally found himself face-to-face with the bastard who had run off with his wife.

Our two kids had received their elementary education at a public school called L'Étoile du Nord French Immersion, where the curriculum had been taught in French. As a result, we had spent a good chunk of the prime of our lives commuting more than an hour a day, five days a week, nine months a year, from a perfectly good suburban school district to the east side of Saint Paul, so our kids could speak French, like their father.

As that era of our lives had drawn to a close, Mary Jo and I had decided that eight years of Raffi songs, multiplication cards, and French vocabulary quizzes on the morning commute would feel more worthwhile, in retrospect, were it capped by a semester in France, and (we hoped) by some pretty spanking good French emanating from the mouths of our two children.

One of the very first things American students of French learn is how to order *un Coca* at a restaurant, although you would not have guessed that from Joe's and Eva's blank and disbelieving stares when I had ordered two beers, and invited them, in French, to order their Cokes from Monsieur. He had stood there, looking back and forth, apparently as irritated with my turning this into a teachable moment as with their refusal to speak.

He returned now, carrying a tray, in T-shirt and Adidas sweats, walking on the collapsed heels of his espadrilles.

He set two glasses of Kronenbourg—that ubiquitous, inoffensive, thoroughly quaffable Parisian café standard—in front of Mary Jo and me, and poured each of the kids a Coke.

"Can you ask for some ice for the kids?" asked Mary Jo.

The café owner stood waiting to hear something in his own language.

"They never serve ice in France," I said.

"Sure they do," she said.

"No, they don't," I said.

And what I meant was that, sure, you could ask for ice in France, and they might even have some, but it was not normal, and it made you into that person—in my case, the tall American, wearing hiking shoes, at a table with two cameras on it, speaking English to my family—who asks for ice. Nobody wants to be that person.

"*Merci,*" I said to the owner, and smiled. He notched the serving tray under his armpit, and stalked off.

Eva took a sip. "It's warm," she said.

"It's not warm. It's cool," I said.

"It is warm," said Joe.

"It's not warm. It's not a thirty-two-ounce Slurpee, but it's not warm."

"This is what I was talking about," said Mary Jo. "Weren't we literally just talking about this?"

"Guys, we're in France," I said. "Things are going to be different. That's part of why we're here."

The church bell rang out the noon hour as I took a sip of beer. Across from us, the doors of a municipal library stood open, blasted by sunshine. I tried leaning back in my plastic chair, then, feeling a suspicious amount of give, sat back up.

The talk around us was blessedly free of the English, German, Swedish, and Dutch that seem to breed in those popular places that are in the process of changing, or have already changed, from themselves into painted and tourist-hungry imitations of themselves. But the French I was hearing was a rapid-fire singsong that sounded more Spanish or Italian in many ways than French, and, despite the near French fluency on which I had long prided myself, I struggled to follow much of anything that was said around us.

James Dean returned, and stood hipshot beside our table, as if resigned to get through this cruddy little episode so he could resume staining his teeth with dark roast and tar.

I asked him what a *Gardiane* was, and he explained that it was like a *daube de boeuf*, but made with the meat of bulls from the Camargue. I think I had a notion at that point of what *daube de boeuf* was. A beef stew. Red wine. But my awareness of it was like my awareness of haggis, or stockfish, or Krumkake—something exceptionally regional and distant, more tradition than food.

And what was *Seiche Farcie*, I wondered.

He puffed his cheeks and blew. It was a fruit of the sea, like an *encornet*. My blank smile revealed that I did not know what an *encornet* was any more than a *seiche*, and, as he absently described a stuffing made of breadcrumbs, sausage, and aromatics, he scanned the tables surrounding us, and skipped over to a bald man in a tracksuit sitting by the door, confiscated his partially eaten plate, and placed it under my nose.

"*Seiche Farcie*," said the waiter.

On the plate were two and a half ghostly white inflated ovoids smothered in tomato sauce. The half-eaten one resembled the ivory-colored stomach of a good-sized largemouth bass that had been stuffed tight with bratwurst, and the steam rising into my face was a rich perfume of mingled tomato, sausage, onion, garlic, and saltwater pier.

"Some kind of shellfish?" I asked Mary Jo as the waiter returned the plate to its rightful owner.

"Squid?" she asked.

The waiter returned now to display a whole fish, like a huge bronze sunfish, branded with grill marks. "*Daurade*," he said, and swept away again as the attention of our fellow diners gravitated toward us.

He returned once more, with a plate from the baker's table, and—whether knowingly insulting or simply thorough—explained to us that the meat patty with melted cheese on it, sandwiched between two slices of brioche, was a *sheese-boor-GARE.*

"I will take the *Seiche Farcie,*" I said when the waiter had rejoined us.

Despite my introvert's tendency toward social reticence, I was, and always had been, a broad-minded and rather swashbuckling eater, willing to find room in my heart and my palate for anything that any fraction of the human population had, at some time, found to be edible fare.

I asked the kids, in French, what they would like.

They sat uncomfortably for a second or two, and Joe looked imploringly at Mary Jo.

"Dad," said Eva.

"Stevie," said Mary Jo.

"What?" I asked.

"You know what they want, just order it."

"And for you, Madame?" asked the waiter.

Mary Jo appeared, for a time, willing to wait me out.

"Madame?" asked the waiter.

"Cheeseburger avec frites," said Mary Jo in unselfconscious American Franglais.

"We are not eating cheeseburgers," I said.

The kids both nodded at her.

Mary Jo held up three fingers. "*Trois,*" she said, and the waiter nodded.

"And," said Mary Jo. She pointed to the kids' glasses. "*Glace?*" she asked.

He nodded again, and disappeared through the stone doorway into the café.

"I've got an idea," I said. "Let's ask if they have Doritos."

"It's the first day," she said. "Give the kids a break."

I took another sip of beer. Attempted to lean back again, and changed my mind.

"Joe, let's go check out the library," I said.

It turned out to be a short visit.

"The library is closed, Monsieur," said a fiftyish woman in wire spectacles and a sleeveless blouse.

"My apologies, the doors were open," I said.

"The doors are open, but according to the sign we are closed at noon, therefore we are closed."

"It's closed," I said when we were back at the table.

"The doors are wide open," said Mary Jo.

"The doors are wide open, but the sign says they are closed at noon. Therefore, I'm told, they are closed."

And it had turned into the kind of day in which even such a logical and evidence-backed statement came out sounding evasive and weak.

Our host returned with three plates of cheeseburgers, and one plate of what I would eventually learn were stuffed cuttlefish.

There was mustard and vinegar, but not ketchup, for the fries. The cheese on the cheeseburger was not cheddar, or American, or Monterey Jack, but Emmenthal, which I could smell, along with the waiter's armpits, as the plates were set down. And when the kids lifted their buns there was a sauce on the burgers that might have been fresh mayonnaise or possibly aioli, and they examined this new form of burger as if it had been fished from the trap in the bathroom sink, while I tried my first slice of stuffed cuttlefish, tasting like an ocean-infused dumpling.

Mary Jo tucked more or less contentedly into her *sheese-boor-gare,* and Joe gave it a shot.

But in the end, due to the particular perfume of the Emmenthal, and the French tendency to cook burgers on the rare side of medium rare, both kids abandoned their meals, pushing the smell of ripe Swiss cheese and mystery sauce to my side of the table, where the gibbous moons of their partly nibbled buns went gradually soggy in pools of blood.

I decided that whatever we were trying to accomplish on this trip, it would not be to indulge more of this, whatever this had been. We had some work to do, we Hoffmans, if we were going to fit in around here, and with this thought, and with a practiced Parisian, I suppose the word is "insouciance," I took a sip of beer, lifted my chin, and leaned back into my chair, which snapped with the sound of a belly flop in a quiet pool, and I went over backward with it, baptizing myself on the way down with the dregs of my Kronenbourg, before the glass slipped from my hand and shattered on the pavers near my head.

After a dazed second or two, I began swimming up from the puddle of myself as the diners around me exclaimed and asked after my well-being, and attempted to help, and as mortifying as all of that was, it was as nothing to the sight of the café owner, already armed with broom and dustpan, cheered on in machine-gun patois by the bald man in the tracksuit, making his way across the terrace to sweep up after the new American in town.

On the way home, with the kids still hungry, we stopped by the bakery, which had just closed for lunch, then the greengrocer's called Le Jardin de Marie, also closed for lunch, and finally the *tabac* (a combination newsstand, deli, and bodega), where a rolled steel curtain drawn in front of the entrance announced, in so many words, "Closed for lunch."

As we descended Avenue de la Liberté, toward our new home at number 42, we passed several other pedestrians, including an attractive young couple with suggestively white teeth. Before I could make out the words they were saying, their intonation marked them as inescapably American, and so, as we passed, I made sure to greet them first, not with a "Hello," or even a "Bonjour," but, because it was past noon and that was the rule, and because I was in that kind of mood, driven by visions of Coca-Cola with ice, and plates of uneaten cheeseburgers, to say nothing of the miasma of spilled beer accompanying my every step—I made sure to greet them, as I say, with an intentionally snooty "*Bon après-midi*," to which they grinned in that ingratiatingly confused, insipid, and apologetic way of all lost American tourists, and I discovered, to my satisfaction, that I hated them.

2

My love for France had been established early, during a sixth-grade summer class in which I discovered that my mouth and throat accepted fairly naturally the demands put on them by French pronunciation. The experience of not just sounding like, but in some sense inhabiting, a person who was not myself intoxicated me, and led me to imagine living in France someday, and speaking its language, like a spy undetected. From then on, France—the idea of France—served, in various incarnations, as an escape hatch, both from the distressing ordinariness of American suburbia, and, to a degree I didn't entirely understand, from my own person.

I was twenty-one when my idea of France was finally replaced by the real thing.

I was one month into a nine-month hiatus from my junior year of college, in Paris's unglamorous 17th arrondissement, or district.

I had been rehearsing a role for the first month of my stay: that of a young sophisticate, an intellectual in training, an aspiring polyglot, speaking nearly unaccented French, working on his ancient Greek, thinking of taking up modern Greek. A citizen of Paris—naturalized not by the requirements of residency but by the studied correctness of his manner—whose faint aloofness was softened by a reflexive kind of surface charm.

Maybe it should have unnerved me how much better I already liked whoever I was becoming than whoever I had supposedly always been. How without cost it felt to let so much of what had defined me for two-plus decades simply fall away. How much hatred I had discovered in myself for largely inoffensive Roseville, Minnesota, home of early-morning golfers, and the very first Target store in the USA. As if there had been something intolerable about occupying the physical and psychic confines known as Steve Hoffman for all these years, and from which I was in the process of being liberated.

Behind me, one of those massive, wrought-wood Parisian apartment doors crashed shut, and I joined the commuters flowing past number 9 rue Dautancourt, lent to me by Les Petits Frères des Pauvres (The Little Brothers of the Poor) in exchange for the rather dubious currency of my services.

I wore the gray wool herringbone overcoat I had adopted as a uniform, believing it projected something convincingly Continental, although in photos from that time, the nationality of the young man in the crêpe-soled Hush Puppies, the boot-cut Levis, the plaid flannel shirt, the center-part '80s hair, could not be more evident.

The mission of Les Petits Frères was to offer comfort and company to elderly people, whose medical and financial needs were seen to by the French Republic, but whose isolation and loneliness were not. My job description was to spend five afternoons a week visiting the dim apartments of aging Parisians, listening and talking—but mostly listening—and, as a by-product of all of this, inhaling and exhaling great lungfuls of the French language, in what amounted to the most accelerated and comprehensive French conversation course that could reasonably be imagined.

My arrival here had been the result of a snap decision (standing before a study-abroad poster in the modern and classical languages department of Saint John's University, in Collegeville, Minnesota) that if I really wanted to learn French, I should go there by myself, rather than spend a semester in Aix-en-Provence among ballcap-wearing, flaxen-haired SJU undergrads, speaking conspicuous English in small coveys around town. Rating Frenchwomen's backsides. Padding MBA applications.

It also happened that the Little Brothers of the Poor, founded in Paris, had a satellite office in Minneapolis, Minnesota. My parents had volunteered there for years. Had served on the board.

When I announced that I wanted to live in France for a year, a sort of familial commotion ensued. Phone calls made. A lunch or two scheduled. My parents' network queried. And in a process I had very little to do with, and understood on some level I could not have pulled off on my own, a name in Paris rose to the surface. An American named Scott Walker. Muckety-muck of some kind in the executive offices of Les Petits Frères des Pauvres, Paris.

An airmailed letter came back: Internship available. Lodging plus monthly stipend. Office at 12 rue Bridaine, 17th arrondissement. How is his French?

Not good, it turned out. After nearly a decade in American classrooms, I arrived in Paris as a barely passable French technician, able, with a laborious sort of precision, to apply half-mastered rules of grammar and usage to a murky collection of vocabulary words.

I could still re-create the hot-faced, intestine-wringing sense of shameful, unfolding disaster as on my arrival at 12 rue Bridaine for my first day of work, full of the unearned confidence that mere talent had given me among American students of French. I had entered the Little Brothers' office, and offered a nicely enunciated "Bonjour, Madame" to the receptionist at the front desk, who corrected me with the word "Mademoiselle." She then repeated something, over and over, each time more slowly and emphatically, as I, with a sickly smile and a furious, disbelieving effort at concentration, demanded, "*Répetez, s'il vous plaît*" (Repeat please), until finally she was forced to abandon her native tongue and ask, "Arrrh. Yooh. Zeh. Neeew. Eentairn?"

In the weeks since that day, I had reached a low base camp on the ascent toward French conversational competence, although there were still lingering stretches during my working afternoons when, sitting across the room from a stately White Russian emigré, or a derby-capped widower with a face like a pecan, I would smile, nod, and, understanding nothing that was being said to me, guided by blind intuition, deploy my three emergency conversational weapons: "*Comment?*" (What's that?), "*Vraiment?*" (Really?), and "*Voilà*" (Exactly!).

At the first stoplight, one fellow pedestrian and I drew flaring matches into our cupped hands and shook them out as we exhaled.

Like my overcoat, smoking was a personal symbol, recent and intentionally perverse, representing a rejection of, among other things, my life as a summer tennis pro teaching the entitled children of rich parents, my clean-cut jock/brain high school persona, the insufferable Norman Vincent Peale optimism of Reagan's America. My smoking provoked in my parents a sad and slightly panicky disgust, and though I could not quite purge the guilt I felt about this, still, in a confused way, I relished the unfamiliar outlaw feeling of courting disapproval. I had begun to sense a short-of-breath something about the tightness of my family's inner circle. Had begun to smoke too hungrily in what was still, at the time, the greatest city in the Western world in which to smoke.

Work was a snaking, two-cigarette walk across the 17th arrondissement. About halfway there, a line of customers spilled out the door of my morning bakery on Rue Legendre, which is what convinced me to skip my habitual sachet of rock-sugared *chouquettes*, and kept me on schedule to cross paths with the man who would define much of the rest of my stay in Paris, and some part of the next couple of decades of my life.

I maneuvered around the queue, holding my left forearm horizontally across my sternum, cigarette cradled loosely, angling downward from two curled fingers, the way Frenchmen hold their cigarettes. A man a little older than my father approached in a dark suit and bright flannel scarf. He wore the lozenge-shaped wire spectacles of a kindly doctor. Held his cigarette the same way I did. Had a pair of those protective metal taps embedded into the heels of his shoes that made a sound as if he were performing a slow, ceremonial tap dance through the streets.

A stern set to his features. Something resolute about his gait. Not in a hurry, but not willing to be late. Someone you would hesitate to interrupt. An unbothered, paternal, very French self-possession.

As we passed, he did not so much smile as allow his face to soften. There was a friendly and nearly imperceptible slitting of his eyes. He nodded and said, "Bonjour, Monsieur." That was it. A nothing encounter. A courtesy.

On this particular morning, with no other prompting than that, the casualness of the man's greeting felt as if it carried with it some invitation to belong. To be accepted in an unshakable and tribal way that I craved instantly, and so powerfully that as his ringing steps faded in my wake, I felt an ache behind my eye sockets, and the street blurred in front of me. I had to stop and remove my glasses, palming my eyes clear, but as I continued on my way, they brimmed and spilled, like buckets under a slow faucet. I wiped, and snuffled, horrified at this display, but unable to hold it back. At an empty street corner, I stood against the wall to compose myself, before walking the final block to work.

The man stayed with me for the rest of the day. The energy he gave off was almost audible. The powerful hum of a man whose personal melody pleased him, and harmonized effortlessly with his culture. I felt a desperate wish to pull free from the jangle of myself, and be a part of that.

"Bonjour, Monsieur."

I wanted him to accept me as his compatriot, in that offhand way, over and over, for the rest of my life.

For the remainer of those nine months, and for a long time afterward, what I wanted most in life was to be Parisian. To earn and re-earn that badge of belonging, like an inheritance, like the passing down of an heirloom, that had been granted to me, however unconsciously, by a single look, from a stranger I would never see again, amid the sounds of jackhammers and car horns on Rue Legendre, in the unremarkable 17th arrondissement.

More even than simply to be Parisian, I wanted to be *that man*. To be sufficient. To be finished. I imagined him as someone who knew which wine to uncork at home, and which to order at a restaurant, and for which course. I imagined a library and a comfortable chair. A familiarity with Homer, Virgil, Molière, Hugo. A man confident in the office, the kitchen, the bedroom, and the nursery. A father and grandfather at ease with the softer virtues of comforting and care because he had mastered the hard virtues of discipline and command. I wanted, as I imagined he was, to be invulnerable in my completeness. And I understood that Paris was where such a thing might be possible for me. Where I had a chance to atone for the original sin of being Steve Hoffman, from Roseville, Minnesota.

I spent the next several months on an ardent, solitary, and somewhat humorless campaign to perfect my French.

It might have been one of those occasions when, working beside people of goodwill with a vested interest in my speaking well, I could have let go. Could have allowed myself to make forgivable mistakes.

Could have plunged into the language, messily, openheartedly, endearingly, and made great intuitive bounds in the direction of fluency.

But I could not. I could not find my own mistakes endearing or imagine anyone else finding them so. Somewhere between birth and twenty-one, the healthy human instinct for embarrassment had turned ingrown and unnatural in me, associated not with minor social discomfort, but with fear and an inexcusable sort of wrongness. Imperfections were something one denied, or hid, or else overcame in the privacy of some personal hermitage, before reemerging into the waiting judgment of the world. Nobody wanted to watch Steve Hoffman fumble his way toward French conversational proficiency. Nobody wants to watch the cast yodel and declaim through all the interminable rehearsals. What people want is a ticket on opening night.

And so I made it a priority of my self-administered French education to commit as few public mistakes as possible. I marched stiffly through spoken exchanges that often elicited admiration for my pronunciation and largely blemish-free syntactical surface, but lacked the fluidity and spontaneity, the human contours, of conversation because I would so rarely risk an exposed and improvised verbal dash into the open.

I rehearsed entire multisentence paragraphs in my head, cross-checking them first for proper verb tense and accords of number and gender before spouting them in well-pronounced gushes of authentic-sounding Parisian. I began hearing a comment I would eventually hear a lot in France: "*Mais vous parlez très bien français, Monsieur*" (But your French is very good, sir), praise that singled me out as something other than the bellowing tourist herds of my sneaker-hooved, thick-calved American compatriots who stampeded through Paris every summer. The flattery warmed and encouraged me, without ever dissuading me from my understanding of the truth—that, on a fundamental level, I was still not speaking French, but performing a convincing facsimile of it.

Meanwhile, in my private thoughts, I latched on to every mistake, every correction of vocabulary, grammar, and usage offered me; obsessed over them; consulted dictionary, thesaurus, and conjugation manual; mended their cracks, worked their rough edges into smoothness, buffed them into shine; and placed them, perfected, back into working inventory. And slowly, methodically, by pouring vast reserves of energy into this compulsive self-correction, I stocked my mental shelves with stores of correct, usable, unimpeachable French.

3

Autumn gave way to an overcast, damp, vaguely chilly time of year that was, to a lifelong Minnesotan, a laughable excuse for winter.

In the evenings, I sat at my desk, drank Orangina and cheap red Bordeaux, lit each new cigarette from the cherry of the last, and wrote sheaves of lush, exuberant letters home that served as minor works of propaganda, blurring or omitting any reference to my loneliness and semi-reclusiveness, but drawing elaborate attention to the bright, post-metamorphosis exoskeleton I had begun to display to the world, constructed of social quickness and charm, a sort of literary-colored eloquence, a nose for the proper expressions of elevated taste, and a fascination, and growing facility, with the trappings of high culture. In these letters home, I was the hero of a journey from small-spirited regular at the Burger King on Snelling and County Road B to accomplished and fully functioning young Parisian.

I also continued to make my weekday rounds, and with ebbing conversational friction. I memorized the Paris metro map. And, as the feeblest winter I had ever experienced meekly handed off the baton to spring, I made secret visits to Madame Villatte, always late in the morning, when my absence from the office could be mistaken for an early lunch.

A single bulb, dangling from a twisted cloth wire, spread an indistinct yellowish moonglow around the hallway outside her apartment door. The door, when one stood near enough to it to knock, interfered with, but did not entirely block, a faint and insinuating ammonia smell that was the work of her elderly, blind, and occasionally incontinent pug.

Maybe ten seconds of silence followed my rap on her door, and then at some point whatever was on the other side of the door was no longer quite silence, but an almost subaudible rustling that resolved slowly into the sound of shuffling slippers, the tick and scrape of canine toenails on wood, and the muffled melody of love talk between human and animal.

A quavering "*C'est qui?*"

"*C'est Steve.*"

A jingling of chain, a tock of thrown bolt, a triple thwack of French door lock, and a complaining screigh of hinges revealed two sets of impossibly bulging eyes. At about the level of my breastbone were the magnified eyes of Madame Villatte, widened by two round, rimless, double-convex lenses that gave her the permanently astonished expression of someone who has just been leaped at from behind the kitchen door. At shin height were the two milky bubbles protruding from the smashed features of Albert (ahl-BEAR) the pug, who was breathing with the sound of someone trying to squeeze the dregs from a plastic mustard jar.

"There he is, Albert," said Madame Villatte. "I told you he would come."

"As usual," I said, "it was necessary to escape from the office before lunch."

"Because he is a good boy," she said. "*N'est-ce pas,* Albert?" And she led me through the morning twilight of her lace-curtained apartment to my accustomed seat on the collapsed upholstery of a dining room chair. I hung my overcoat on the chair's slender shoulders, and sat next to the massive, dust-filmed, walnut table piled with books and newspapers. She hobbled toward the kitchen, as slight and bent as a shepherd's crook, flesh-colored hose pooled around the knotty twigs of her ankles, a torn swag of slip dipping below the hem of her housecoat.

"*Une tisane?*" she asked. "There is hot water."

"I can't stay long today," I said.

"*Bof,*" she said, without breaking what there was of her stride.

"*Une verveine,*" I conceded.

I had not known that a *tisane* was an herbal tea, nor that a *verveine* was steeped lemon verbena leaves until I met Madame Villatte. I had not known any number of things that I now knew, thanks to the months I had been coming to see her.

I had been given her phone number one morning, during an intra-office personnel scramble to fill in for a sick colleague. I was expected to see her once or maybe twice, do the best I could, and then, when Jean-Baptiste returned to duty, I was supposed, in a manner of speaking, to give her back.

But after my first two visits, she decided she didn't wish to be given back. Jean-Baptiste returned to health, then returned to the office. Madame Villatte called the office, then called again. She did not wish to see Monsieur Jean-Baptiste. She wished to see Monsieur Steve, who, she assured them, wished, in turn, to see her.

Except that it was not convenient for the office to send Monsieur Steve east to the 18th arrondissement to see Madame Villatte, only to have him travel back west, to the 16th, to visit the others on his route. Monsieur Steve was ordered, politely but unequivocally, to knock it off.

At what should have been our final meeting, she made me promise I would keep calling on her, and several surreptitious visits later, I discovered that I did not wish to give her back either, and we had carried on like this throughout the rest of my Paris sojourn.

She set a tray beside me on the table, and from it served one tremoring china cup and saucer to me, and one to herself, then a cup of mixed nuts, a shallow dish of olives, a fan of sliced *saucisson* on a cutting board.

"*Alors,*" she said, backing into her chair across from me. I stood up to help her fall slowly into her seat. Folded a wing of her collar flat. Sat back down.

Albert had been walking stiffly and a little aimlessly around the apartment, but at the sound of her voice, he veered in our direction, first bumping gently into the wall and then the leg of a chair.

"*Viens, chouchou,*" she said, and reached down to stroke his back. He lowered himself, frowning, onto one hip, making wet, congested sounds, and aiming a partial erection like a twist of pink lipstick at me as he stared past my knee. "*Oh, que t'es mignon,*" she told him, reassuring him of his inexhaustible adorability.

She asked for my now-habitual update, which I delivered imperfectly but less stiffly than all those months ago. First, there was general news from America, scuttlebutt from the Little Brothers' office, updates on the old people I had visited this week, highlights of my wanderings around the city, thoughts on what I had been reading.

I had enrolled in an advanced French grammar class a longish metro ride to the south side of Paris and—unheard of for me—early in the morning.

"But, Steve," my office mentor, Stephane, had just lamented the other day when I had told him about the class, "your French is very good. You make almost no faults."

"Almost," I had said.

I relayed this story to Madame Villatte, fishing for a little scrap of compliment.

"Oh, you make plenty of faults, *Ricain,*" she said.

Ricain (ree-CAN) was old World War II slang, as I had also learned from her—an abbreviation of *Américain.* Like Kraut, in English. Or Frog. The Brits were *les rosbifs,* the roast beefs.

From the beginning, she had corrected my French sternly, insistently, exasperatedly, to say nothing of my taste in American food and French authors—"hamburgers and Camus, my God"—all with such dry affection that I was unable to find it in me to retreat from her scolding into my usual self-protective crouch.

However she had done it, she had managed over the months of our—what was it exactly? I had tried off and on to put a word to it. "Relationship" felt too generic. "Friendship" too distant. "Courtship" carried the wrong connotations, although there had been a coy and quasi-flirtatious sort of luring one another out into the unguarded expressions of fondness we now exchanged. I thought of it as something like the months of our "closeness."

During that stretch of time, whatever its proper label, I had discovered in her a quality that I couldn't ever remember sensing in the presence of anyone else. It was as if, intuitively, and without drawing the least attention to it, she had opened up a space between us, and led me to understand that while I was in there, I was—the only word is—safe. There would be some verbal roughhousing. She would thrust an occasional teasing rapier when she saw an opening. But that didn't mean anything. What was important was the establishment, undefined and unreferred to, of something sacred at the core of our exchanges that would not be violated.

And like some stray eyeing an open palmful of food, I crept closer to her, holding up my shield of banter and agile linguistic performance to hide the fooled-too-many-times fear of exposure and shame that I think she sensed, and at the same time, pointedly ignored.

In that stop-and-start way, I approached her with questions of French usage—vocabulary, pronunciation, and simple turns of phrase—that would have felt humiliating to ask of anyone else. Those soon evolved into questions about Parisian mores, manners, and culture, which in turn became questions about life, about music and books, about love, including her long, happy marriage to Georges, who had departed a decade ago. Whose plain gold band she still wore loosely on a knobby left finger.

Here, disorientingly, was something like the opposite of my self-assigned Paris project—the cultivation of a protective, ultra-civilized veneer—and yet in Madame Villatte's living room, I had learned more about speaking French, about living in Paris, about living well generally, than I had learned over all of those months of dedicated solitary study.

And today—already—it was time to talk about my upcoming departure back to the United States.

"No, it is not that moment," she said, pushing herself out of her chair, and sliding her feet back into her slippers.

She returned from the kitchen with two stemmed glasses and a bottle of wine.

"Madame Villatte, I can't. You know I . . ."

"*Tais-toi.*" Shut up.

She poured two glasses.

"Beaujolais nouveau," she announced. "You should probably know about it. Terrible wine, but a pleasant tradition. You Americans adore it, so we send you as much as we can." She raised her glass, huge eyes staring, a smile showing her long teeth and one missing incisor.

I did not know enough to fathom what terrible wine was, and asked her why she thought so. I considered wine to be one of those by-invitation-only cultural realms, like poetry and fly-fishing, full of secrets guarded by a guild of the knowing, who chortled among themselves at the efforts of outsiders to fathom their calling, and who I imagined did not spend much time scouring for new members among the television watchers and dependable voters of Roseville, Minnesota.

She explained that it was the new wine of Beaujolais, a *vin de primeur* bottled each year just after it had fermented. An inconsequential ballerina of a wine. Still, it was nice to look at her tutu.

She took a sip, looking over the edge of her glass at me with as devilish an expression as her telescopic eyeglasses allowed.

Then, while we sipped, she made me read her the first three pages of *Le Figaro,* her newspaper of choice, and interrupted me only once, with a lashing correction of my pronunciation of the French *puis* (then), a tightly coiled, sharp-tipped little word that I had Americanized into a drawling "poo-eeeh," to her intense disapproval.

And then it truly was that moment.

I shrugged into my coat, and told her that I would try to stop by once more before I left—whether cushioning the blow for her or for me, I couldn't tell.

"Who will visit you when I'm gone?" I asked.

"I will continue to receive Monsieur Jean-Baptiste when you are gone," she said, naming my predecessor, unwitting rival, and soon-to-be successor with a wry and agile twist of her mouth.

"Do you have children somewhere?" I wondered, winding on a wool scarf. "Did I already ask you that?"

"Georges and I could not have children," she said.

Albert had risen and was making his way by trial and error through the maze of invisible furniture toward our voices.

"Madame Villatte," I said. "I am sorry to have asked. It was not . . ."

"I am not sorry you asked," she said. "Do you imagine, after all, that I do not like your interminable questions?"

What I said next came out haltingly. I wanted to say it right, and had to think my way through it.

"You would have been a good mother," I said, concentrating hard on my execution of the tricky, conditional perfect construction.

"You would have been a good son," she said.

I smiled and held out my hand, which she ignored, and she reached up to pull my face toward her, then kissed me on both cheeks. The vast globes of her eyes, when I straightened, were swimming behind her glasses.

"*Oh, c'est terrible,*" she said. "Is it not, Albert?"

When I couldn't look anymore, I dropped onto my heels and stroked Albert's head and his rotund, thatched haystack of a back. "Au revoir, Albert."

I stood back up, and said, "Au revoir, Madame Villatte."

She corrected my pronunciation, and I said it again, to her satisfaction, before she would agree to say, "*Au revoir, mon petit* Steve."

I turned and walked into the hallway's yellow gloom. At the booming shut of her door, I paused, and then, to the accompaniment of chain, bolt, and latch, started down the dark stairwell.

I imagined her tiny figure, followed gamely by Albert, shuffling back to the dining room table, to the filigreed serving tray, the gilt-rimmed enameled teacups, the half-empty bottle, the wine dregs like bloodshot eyes looking out from the bottoms of the two empty goblets. Her shuffling back to the kitchen with the loaded tray. The woolly Paris sky pressing feeble light through the filters of lace at her windows. I imagined a week or two of *Le Figaro* piling up before Jean-Baptiste would come again. Wondered if he made time to read to her. Did he accept her offers of herbal tea and mixed nuts? Of coffee and chocolate wafers? Of Porto and ginger crackers? Did he say goodbye to Albert when he left?

Back on the street, I fished for a cigarette, squinted against a faceful of smoke and sulfur, looked up at the blank row of fifth-floor windows, talking myself into the conviction that I would, without fail, see her again. Then, moderately soothed by this thought, I set off generally westerly, threading my way among the cobweb of streets, in search of a restaurant for lunch. Whispering to myself: *Puis.*

Trying it another way: *Puis.*

Trying it again: *Puis.*

Puis.

Puis.

Puis.

4

Shortly before I left Paris, a benefactor and board member of the Little Brothers invited me to dinner with his family.

They occupied the top floor of one of those classic, six-story, mansard-roofed apartment buildings in high Haussmann style.

We talked politely, discussing my experiences, and theirs, as part of the Little Brothers fraternity. We discovered a mutual love for classical music, surprising ourselves with a shared affection for the sacred music of Louis XIV's court composer, Jean-Baptiste Lully.

I don't remember all that was served, except that it was the classic French coursed dinner, *le repas gastronomique français*. Wines were refreshed, if not at every course then nearly so, and the meal concluded with coffee and a digestif—I chose Armagnac because I found its slight obscurity in comparison to Cognac satisfyingly esoteric.

I told them about a trip to Greece I had been planning. I wanted to visit Mycenae, where Homer's Agamemnon may have lived, and then on to Athens—to wander the Acropolis, of course, but mostly to visit the National Archaeological Museum and lay eyes on a hammered gold death mask once touted as the Mask of Agamemnon.

This prompted the daughter-in-law to my left to reveal that she was Greek, and she wondered if I was going to visit the islands. But I wasn't going to visit the islands. I did not plan—or particularly care—to walk a single beach, feel a single ray of Hellenic sunshine on my bare torso, flirt or propose to dance with a single other young person, or get a single whiff of salt water, aside from that furrow of the Ionian Sea plowed by the Brindisi-Patras ferry. I was going to Mycenae and Athens in search of Agamemnon, and this was just the sort of detail that a cultured Parisian family of the upper bourgeoisie would simply eat up, and when I explained that I was taking ancient Greek at school in order, I hoped, to read Homer in his own language, they ate it up still further, and then, when I explained that I had been teaching myself modern Greek at the Pompidou Center via cassette tape—and when I was able, subsequently, to conduct an extremely brief but comprehensible exchange with the Greek daughter-in-law, in modern Greek—the entire family was bedazzled and spent the rest of the meal comfortably and almost gratefully curled in the palm of my hand.

The only other detail I remember from the evening was the son, somewhere around the cheese course, saying, "Stop!" in the middle of one of my answers to their excited questions.

"That was the first time this evening that I have heard you make a *faute de français*" (a grammatical error), he said, and though I feigned surprise and a bit of bashfulness, I was inwardly aglow.

This was my arrival on the stage I had been rehearsing for. This was who Steve Hoffman became when he had shucked off the last tatty rags of Roseville, Minnesota, and stepped into his finished, Parisian form. Speaking three languages. Talking music, antiquity, and literature in a Paris flat. Eating in luxurious sophistication, and knowing what he wished to drink. This. This was the beginning of the life that had crouched inside me, ready to spring.

I knew that I would never see those people again in my life. Not only would I never see them again, but I had no interest in seeing them again.

The performance I had put on, perfectly calibrated, nearly faultless, was all that mattered. I thought of my evening companions with gratitude, but they did not mean anything beyond their roles for that one rapturous evening, as a spellbound audience entranced by Steve Hoffman.

I walked home, overcoat blowing in the winter wind, in as close to a state of bliss as I could remember.

I did go to Greece. I wandered Homer's Mycenae and Plato's Acropolis, feeling as if there were great secrets hidden in the stones around me to which I was not privy. At the National Archaeological Museum in Athens, I stared at the gold mask I had come for, but the impenetrable 1980s modernity of the crush of people around me obscured any glimpse the mask might have given me into the strange and brutal beauty of the Bronze Age and its heroes.

The true casualty of the trip to Greece, however—and of the resulting rush to finish my business in Paris before flying home—was that I did not, despite my veiled promises to her, return to see Madame Villatte. I was in an unaccountable hurry to get back home. I think I was afraid that I had experienced a moment of perfection over dinner in that sixth-floor flat, and that Paris could only be tarnished from there.

I understood this abrupt departure as a betrayal of Madame Villatte—though not, as it also was, a betrayal of that awkward, passionate, wondering, and unguarded part of myself that she had managed briefly to coax into the open, and then been willing to look upon with favor. Those few moments had been the only true triumph of Paris. And finding a way to live more often in that state perhaps the only important lesson to be learned from my time there, though I did not learn it then, despite all of my studying and striving.

Several months after my return to the United States, I sent her a long letter, full of news, gossip, descriptions of Minnesota, questions about Albert, apologies and explanations for why I had not come to see her, and promises that I would return to Paris soon, and would be knocking again on her door.

Two or three weeks later, I received a letter from a Monsieur Camus, no relation. Inside was a letter from him, and my own unopened letter to Madame Villatte, his next-door neighbor, who, he regretted to inform me, was deceased, after several weeks in the Hôpital L'ariboisière. He was looking after her mail, and thought I should be informed.

I arrived back in Minnesota in spring 1987.

That July, I met half-Romanian, half-Scandinavian Mary Jo Lapadat, who would call me to attention with a blazing intelligence, high Swedish cheekbones, a spill of blond hair, a smoky intensity of close-set, dark-rimmed Slavic eyes, an engineer's brain, an artist's soul, and a frank and lusty hunger for life as a sensual celebration and a collaborative art form.

We were set up by her sister, though initially neither of us could imagine what attraction the other might possibly hold—I, a French and ancient Greek major living among Benedictine monks; she, an engineering graduate from UW Madison.

But we discovered, to our surprise, an instant, omnivorous hunger for each other.

We spent that summer nauseating our friends with our greedy togetherness. Our constant touching, sure, but also a kind of mental twinning—a fascination with each other's thoughts, intuitions, and conclusions. We lay naked on damp sheets under an oscillating fan in her apartment—"like they invented it," complained one of Mary Jo's friends—smoking lazy cigarettes and making plans for the remainder of our lives, which, already, after mere weeks, it seemed inevitable we would share.

I had been raised in a family that never quite said exactly what we felt or what we wanted, in which the socially appropriate gesture was encouraged over the straight and often awkward truth. Unspoken wishes and unexpressed resentments drifted like a gas through the house of my late youth, ready to be ignited into accusation and recrimination by a careless word.

Mary Jo's frankness—her refusal to hedge, to mislead, to wait around for what she wanted, or to mope if she didn't get it—was like new and healthy air I got to breathe. I felt for the first time I could remember as if I had been given exactly what I wanted, and had not had to prove I deserved it, and would not have to give it back if I made a mistake.

Mary Jo valued, above all things, a rebellious, tomboyish autonomy—cultivated over a childhood of unsupervised summers spent in woods, lakes, and meadowish empty lots—that meant she got to decide for herself what shape her life should take, and ignore, as completely as she wished, what others might opine, openly or secretly, on the subject.

That fall, she went to work as an aerospace engineer at Honeywell in Minneapolis. Most weekdays, unbeknown to our parents, I would drop her off in the morning, commute an hour and a half to Saint John's for class, and drive back by dinnertime. At night I would read Jane Austen to her while she rested her head on my stomach. The year after that, she got her master's in aeronautics and astronautics at Stanford. I wrote her almost daily letters from my dorm room, wooing her desperately. She returned to Honeywell the next summer, designing guidance systems for hypersonic vehicles. I would join her and her colleagues for late-afternoon pitchers of beer at the Polish Palace in Northeast Minneapolis, where talk was of the unstable longitudinal stability of fighter planes, the application of Newton's $F = ma$ to the acceleration of jet engines, the coming of digital cockpits.

Her father had been a darkly handsome, romantic, and talented Romanian immigrant, a Marine and a pro baseball player, whose profession—selling beer for Hamm's brewery—encouraged the kind of drinking that tends, as it did in his case, to result in outbursts of rage, volatile family relations, and a creeping and ultimately chronic unreliability.

What Mary Jo originally saw in me, I think, was the romance and talent, however raw, of her charismatic father, balanced by a seriousness, an ambitious sort of sobriety, the combination of which looked like an answer to something she had hoped for but not expected to find. She had met an equal.

We dreamed bigger together than we had apart.

I proposed, a little abruptly, less than two years after we met, never imagining that she would say anything but yes.

In September 1989, we were married.

5

I sometimes look back at our first summer—the best summer of my life with no close second, a summer spent falling in love, a summer of sun-stoked heat, of an ecstatic sense of discovery, a summer infused with an almost unbearable feeling of rightness—and I want to go back and intervene, against my own best interests, to warn Mary Jo. Because that was the best of me for a long while.

What followed was an outwardly happy early marriage that was in a number of subtle ways a dispiriting parade of revelations that the romantic and slightly dashing young man that Mary Jo Lapadat had agreed to marry was not the whole Steve Hoffman, but a crafted persona—not intentionally deceitful, but not something, either, that he could quite sustain. His smoking, intriguingly urbane at first, began to look like a simple habit. After he had quit smoking, or claimed to, she found a pack of Marlboro Lights wedged under the front seat of her Honda Civic, and his subsequent, impeccably believable denial revealed him to be a quite accomplished teller of expedient lies. Absent the structure of college coursework and an amateur tennis career, his ambition appeared to deflate like a tent with the poles removed. His academic degrees in modern and classical languages did not offer a straightforward path to a career, and he seemed able to perform neither the gritty networking nor the intricate dreaming that finding a path would have required. He said he wanted to be a writer, but then appeared to lack some deep core out of which to write.

She thought wonderingly to herself, more than once, on the way to her completely stable job as an aerospace engineer, that her new husband might actually believe he could read books, or walk the streets of Paris, for a living. She sat across from him one evening as they paid their bills and saw with consternation that grew into a kind of horror that he was trying and failing to balance their checkbook.

And then he had a kind of breakdown that was a strange hybrid of delayed teenage rebellion and early midlife crisis. They fought for several months, then separated for exactly three days.

She spent those three days ready to be done. This was not what she had signed up for. This was not even the man she had married. They had barely begun. There were no kids. There was not yet a deep shared history linking their fates. She accepted that the brief social humiliation of an early aborted marriage would not outweigh the lifetime of frustration spent trying to discover in the chaos of her new husband's scattered abilities the makings of an equal partner. She had always supported herself. She would be OK.

Three things, in the end, brought her back. He was smart. And working daily with rocket scientists had revealed to her that she liked being surrounded by smart people. He made her laugh, slyly, and often. And somewhere intertwined among his cravings, his evasions, his dreaminess, his short-lived obsessions, his natural gifts, and his infuriating, cloth-headed, lazy betrayals of them, there was a shoot-the-moon enthusiasm, a willingness to dispense with the convenient and ordinary in order to gulp the inconvenient and remarkable, a high-risk, high-reward sort of anti-conventional daring that she realized still thrilled her, and that she was willing to take some risks to join forces with.

On day three, she found him sticking out in several directions from a plaid, sour-smelling comforter on his sister's living room floor.

"Hey," he said, tucking the edge of the comforter under his chin.

"Hey," she said.

Twenty years later, the two of us sat together, watching the unearthly smooth asphalt of the A75 rushing toward us at 130 kilometers per hour. We were about seven hours south of Paris, on our way to the Languedoc, where we had chosen to live for six months with fourteen-year-old Eva and nine-year-old Joseph.

"Little-known fact," said Joe, from the back seat of our brand-new silver-gray Renault Scénic—no less a minivan for being called, in French, a *monospace.*

"Joseph Hoffman," I said like a teacher calling on a student—a schtick we had established over many questions and answers.

"Baby echidnas and baby duck-billed platypuses are both called puggles."

"Why do you know that?" asked Eva.

The jet-lagged kids had spent most of the drive staring out at an ash-gray lid of northern European sky. Eventually, Eva's head fell back, and she began snoring softly. Soon afterward Joseph toppled slowly onto her, like melting ice cream, and for the first time since Minneapolis, Mary Jo and I were, for lack of a better word, alone.

The broken white shoulder stripes of the autoroute flashed at the edge of my vision, and my fingers, tapping the gearshift in rippling waves, as they did when I was anxious or ruminating, took up the same iambic heartbeat: *ba-dum ba-dum ba-dum.*

In Madame Johnson's high school French geography class, we had veered into Languedoc long enough to learn one single fact—that it was the *Langue d'Oc* (the Language of Oc) because there they had once pronounced "yes" as *oc,* which later evolved into Occitan, or Provençal. Northern French was the *Langue d'Oïl,* where *oïl* evolved into the Parisian *"oui,"* which was all I needed to know as a young man in order to dismiss the Languedoc as something on the periphery of the only kind of French civilization I wanted to absorb, namely whatever civilization Paris was the capital of.

And then I hadn't thought about Languedoc for about thirty years.

We had chosen it, in part, because I had settled into an improbably satisfying career as a tax preparer. I had an intense annual earning season between January and July, and, if I planned correctly, an offseason, or at most a client-maintenance season, for the remainder of the year. This meant we could just afford, moneywise and timewise, an academic semester abroad, from late summer into early winter, and southern France, unlike east-central Minnesota, was both Francophone and warm.

Once you have decided on the south, there are really only two options—expensive and exhaustively touristed Provence, or its modest neighbor across the Rhône, Languedoc-Roussillon. From there, we had flung a squadron of electronic darts at a map of southwestern France, and one of them had landed on a tiny pinprick, about fifty minutes north of the Mediterranean and fifty minutes east of the Pyrenees. The name of the pinprick was Autignac, and the name of the owner of the rental home called Olive Tree House was Bill, an Irishman from Ballynure.

Since my short-lived collapse at age twenty-three, there had been an accumulation of mostly good years, some of them very, very good.

After a wandering early professional life—from proofreader, to translator, to handyman, to real estate broker, to manager of several rental properties that Mary Jo and I bought and fixed up—I had eventually taken up tax preparation on the suggestion of my mother-in-law, who was in the business. Against every expectation, I found its linear, rule-based structure congenial to my own rule-seeking worldview, yet also welcomed the surprising intimacy it afforded.

I had five hundred tax clients. Knew all their names. Could break bad news gently. Could face hard news with empathy—divorces, bankruptcies, diagnoses, prognoses, AA, chemo, insulin, Prozac, hospice, deaths of parents, deaths of spouses, deaths of children. I could ask something about each of their lives when they called.

Mary Jo and I had never lost that deep and intuitive connectedness that had flavored our first year together with so much more than just carnality and the first flutterings of young love. We agreed, almost without having to discuss it, that the life we wanted would exist in tension between, on one hand, the comforts and reassurances, the self-restraint and occasional self-sacrifice, of middle-class domesticity, and on the other, the call to adventure, the pull of the impulsive, the ineffable, the extraordinary.

In that spirit, we had made some of our biggest decisions with a deliberate sort of whimsy. An impromptu three months in French Polynesia in our twenties, living in tents and boardinghouses, foraging for mangoes, papayas, breadfruit, and reef fish. A summer in Brittany—memorable if misguided—when Eva was six, and Joe was not yet crawling.

In 2005, we had bought our Minnesota house in the woods much earlier in our lives than we could afford it, blowing up our budget and our retirement savings for years, if not decades, because there was an inarticulable Nordic dreaminess about it that we both agreed made perfectly weird sense.

We had spent more time picking out vacuum cleaners than that house, and the casual bravado it took simply to say, "Fuck it, let's do it" brought out something inspired in us, and made us each excited to be the other's partner. We trusted our mismatched talents and coordinated them well. We could be both disciplined and creative when we had to, and if it all ended in a heaping pile of crap, we would laugh, and have a good story to tell.

There was this spirit behind our trip to Languedoc. We had done this kind of thing. We could do it again.

"Hey, twitchy," said Mary Jo as the dead volcanoes of the Auvergne loomed up from the horizon. She gave my fluttering hand a squeeze. "What you thinking about?"

"Not a thing," I said.

But, in fact, as I signaled my way back into the left lane with a *tick-ah tick-ah tick-ock* sound that my right fingers briefly made their new compulsive rhythm, I was thinking about Paris.

At one point early in the day, trapped at morning rush hour on the drab beltway around the city called the *périphérique,* inching past a backdrop of brutalist greater Paris, we had passed the Porte de Vincennes, and I had vividly imagined turning in, following the Rue du Faubourg Saint-Antoine past café awnings with round marble tables and bentwood cane chairs lined up beneath them. We could drive to the Bastille, amid the familiar diesel fumes and minor-key goose calls, rising and falling, of ambulance vans and gendarmes. We could follow our noses to the Place des Vosges for coffee at Café Victor Hugo, and that most civilized stroll through the arcades of that most civilized square, down through the Marais to the Seine, and a long afternoon of wandering before dinner.

I was thinking that children thrived in Paris. As did I.

So why were we not aiming our new-car-smelling *monospace* through the boulevards of the 11th arrondissement this morning? Why this? This smooth floating southward to a place almost as far from Paris as you can get and not be in Spain?

The definitive rift with the rest of France happened just after crossing the celestial white Millau suspension bridge, looking like a seven-sloop regatta passing through the gates of heaven.

Everything was instantly blunter, scruffier, less dramatic, and lower to the ground. A rough carpet hugging the contours of the land, raggedly bare in places like the forequarters of a bison shedding its winter pelt. No more poplars or firs or great oaks. Just a hilly plain laid out in mottled sage and olive green.

In a hundred square yards, there might be forty shades of that green, among tufts of vegetation that nevertheless managed to look juiceless and brittle as the wind rubbed against them like a palm along a shorn shrub. This was the *garrigue*—the supposedly iconic Mediterranean landscape.

When we finally exited the autoroute, the road narrowed to a strip just wide enough for two cars to pass. Concrete power poles in this land of no trees. Collapsing piles of dry-stacked stones. The round boulders of old retaining walls sticking out like molars from recessed sockets of washed-away mortar.

"What is it?" asked Mary Jo, resting her hand once more over my drumming fingers.

Stone huts bright with graffiti, occasionally missing roofs, stood in the middle of vineyards. We crossed a one-lane bridge over a bone-dry creek bed.

"Nowhere in France isn't pretty," I said. "Except the place we picked to live for the next six months."

Outside her window a stretch of alien, native landscape gave way to rows of vines, flickering past like shuffled cards. "I kind of love it," she said.

As we wound through a hilly town called Faugères, we crept past two men on a bench next to three women on another, who did not interrupt their talking as their eyes followed our passing car. They watched us clump up and down the speed bump in the middle of the street, and as we pulled away, their faces, shrinking in the rearview mirror, were still turned toward us.

There was a final turn onto an unpainted strip of paving. A power line stretched across it, with a cortege of starlings huddled like black buds on a black vine. I pulled over tight to a weedy ditch as a bulbous, dusty pickup rumbled past like some World War II patrol.

At the final intersection before the village proper, there was a flat gravel park, where three wooden benches sat empty in the shade of a row of dusty olive trees. Beside the park was a sign, a rectangle with black lettering that read "Autignac."

"You know there's no 42 Avenue de la Liberté here," I said.

"Mmm," said Mary Jo. "Well, that would suck."

"How much does it take to call yourself 'Bill,' from Ballynure, and post some eye candy of a stone house on a website? Fifteen minutes? Maybe? Bill from Ballynure, my eye."

"You're delirious."

"Our three-thousand-dollar booking fee didn't go to Bill from Ballynure. It went to Yevgeny from Minsk, who is using it right now to buy his girlfriend Veuve Clicquot and caviar, and they are laughing about the American family who are about to show up for six months in a house in southern France that doesn't exist."

We drove through a lane of plane trees growing tight against the edges of the road.

"Then," I said, "they're going back to their hotel room for a night of wonderfully athletic sex."

"How bad can it be when there are plane trees?" Mary Jo asked.

"I hate Yevgeny," I said.

Mary Jo had slipped a hand into the crook of my elbow, and there had been laughter in her voice.

I pulled alongside an arched garage door made of stout planks, once a deep forest green, now peeling, with an old skeleton key lock. Ahead of us, a two-step concrete stoop led to a narrow doorway displaying, on the stone lintel above it, the number 42.

Apparently, it did exist.

"We're here, guys," I said softly, and as the kids roused and stretched, a head poked out of the garage next door, then disappeared.

We stepped out into woolly late-summer heat to a din of cicada song, sounding like endlessly shaken tambourines announcing our arrival.

Our next-door neighbor reappeared, shushing a clamoring pack of dogs clear of the garage door before shutting it.

He was wiry and thin, with the lean musculature of an old rooster. In multipocketed shorts and a button-down, short-sleeved shirt, he would have fit well among the engineering faculty of any Big Ten university. His rectangular wire-rims added to his professorial air, as did his salt-and-pepper mustache, groomed to a point just shy of fussiness.

He could have been your uncle Lou, in a first-ring suburb, done mowing the yard for the second time this week, and about to grill something on the Weber before settling in with a Coors screwed between his thighs.

He approached us with a smile, a bandy-legged stride, a bottle of rosé in one hand and a foil-covered plate in the other.

Bill, our landlord, had informed him that we would be arriving. He pronounced the name *Beel.*

I accepted the cold bottle of rosé, and introduced the family clustered blearily around our new front stoop.

He took stock of me for a second or two. *"Mais vous parlez très bien français,"* he said.

He removed the foil from the plate. "Beignets of eggplants. From Nicole, my wife. You will be hungry."

He held out his hand. *"Je m'appelle Jean-Luc,"* he said.

6

We woke early the next morning. The heat, and our bodies' circadian confusion, hung on us like something heavy and wet.

Our new neighbor, Jean-Luc, had explained that all of the houses on our street had once been *maisons vigneronnes,* or winemaker's houses, with the living quarters located up a flight of stairs, above the most important space in the building—the street-level family *cave,* which, historically, had acted as a combination winery, cellar, barn, and barnyard.

As a result, the "main floor" of our new home was the second story, which our bedroom shared with a single, open, stone-walled room composed of kitchen, living room, and dining room. Three glass doors opened out onto a wide terrace overlooking a rear courtyard. Above us, on the third story, *Beel* the landlord had converted an attic/granary into three more bedrooms and a bathroom.

Joseph quickly annexed the cloister-like, stone-walled backyard, containing a small pool and the olive tree that gave the house its name. He announced his discoveries one by one: lizard sunning on stone wall, swallows' nests of mud and straw, orb-weaving spider, dead some-kind-of-wasp in pool. Then, abruptly, after the words "ant nest" had floated up to us, we didn't hear from him for a while.

Our family had read Gerald Durrell's *My Family and Other Animals*, the first volume of his bucolic Corfu Trilogy, maybe a dozen times, and Joe had gradually adopted the story as a kind of holy book, a depiction of the highest form that boyhood could take. An extended adventure without risk, where nothing ever goes seriously wrong, and what does go wrong goes wrong comically. Where young boys—in blissful solitude and unsupervised—roam a benevolent Mediterranean countryside populated by reptiles, insects, and small mammals offering themselves up for observation and occasional adoption.

In the midst of emailing French school principals, shopping for a house sitter, and putting two businesses and four rental properties to bed, we had let Joe live with the illusion that, upon our arrival in Autignac, we, but especially he, would be stepping into something very like young Gerry Durrell's life on the idyllic Corfu of his preadolescence.

Eva had claimed the nicest upstairs bedroom, and now, with all of her clothes already unpacked and folded, and Joe's toiletries rearranged in their shared bathroom so her more important things were more easily accessible, she wandered the premises, thick chestnut topknot spilling damp tendrils, offering vaguely critical organizing and general life advice, free of charge.

Mary Jo had claimed half of the dining room table, laying out books, Coptic-bound journals, and collections of markers and pens. Her new camera sat at one end of the table, and the camera it had replaced, now Eva's, sat next to it.

Eva had been negotiating the nature of her indebtedness to her mom for a number of years. A lot of Eva's young life had been spent at tables like this one, littered with paper, paint, scissors, markers, glue sticks, and stacks of artworks, completed and in progress. Mary Jo called it "parallel play." She would sit for hours working on a project of her own, sometimes asking for an opinion, while Eva, and later Joe, worked next to her, or across from her, swept by the current of some inner creative river.

Mary Jo had recently started a new discipline, a blog called STILL, and, with that, had committed to posting a photo every day, on a white background, of a natural object found near her, wherever she happened to be.

Her emergence into this new and happily productive stage of life had furthered Eva's own ambitions for herself, and at the same time upset her personal equilibrium. Eva's absolute insistence on her independence had begun to get in the way of an awakening desire to live a life that might express, through some form of art and imaginative work, her uniquely forceful engagement with the world. The problem was that such a life might bear a resemblance to her mother's life, and imply an indebtedness Eva was not yet prepared to concede.

She had recently submitted a photo to a youth *National Geographic* contest, and been named one of three finalists, and I had watched her pride in this bit of self-assertion progressively sour as grandparents exclaimed how excited she must be about following in her mother's footsteps.

"Mom, don't touch my stuff," Eva said at some point, and moved her camera to the other side of the room.

On a map, Autignac was a loose spiderweb of streets.

But now, as we set off on our first walk through the village, it was Autignac, hot and loud with insects. And one filament of the spiderweb, Avenue de la Liberté, had been transformed into a village street, paved with asphalt that showed signs of patching, climbing gently to our left, toward the church and the central square.

The houses formed an uninterrupted stretch of building façade. They did not have porticoes or porches or exterior entryways. They were vertical canyon walls that dropped straight to the edges of the street. Each house was a slightly different height, and a slightly different width, and the façades and window shutters were each a slightly different color from those of their neighbors, giving the street a jumbled sort of unity.

The primary impression, the overwhelming impression, was of stone and iron—stone houses with iron grillwork over their windows. Stone walls flanking iron gates. Stone staircases with iron balustrades. The stone, where it was visible, was a distinctive honey tan, the color of the walls of our house and rear courtyard, and the color, I felt sure, of the stones in the surrounding fields, making Autignac, like villages throughout rural Europe, a soft-spoken advertisement for its native soil.

I was feeling that constant, anxious, and not particularly productive accounting for the moods of others that was like a background accompaniment to most of my life. Were the kids more or less receptive? Were they hot? Was I walking too fast? What was Mary Jo thinking? How hungry was everybody?

Thoughts like these were like my own digestive system. Something that was always in some ruminant form of motion, and that sometimes I became conscious of for short stretches.

What I was most aware of feeling, though, was the simple relief I always felt at being back in France, which was full of a sense of homecoming and reunion that felt like a return to a tonic chord.

An elderly man in a cap and a sport coat, bent so far forward that he had to crane his neck to greet us, emerged from a garage, leaning on a fendered bicycle for support.

"What's that smell?" asked Eva as the flung-open door of the *tabac* breathed a puff of cool air into the street, scented unapologetically with the deliquescent smells of ripe fruit and ripe cheese.

"That's what it smells like when you go to heaven," I said.

Eva walked with a slight limp in her webbed sandals. An insistent summer barefooter, she had driven a sliver of cedar from our ancient Minnesota dock deep into the ball of her right foot, and neither I, with a needle and tweezers, nor a doctor with a scalpel, had managed to extract the entire thing. Her limp was like a constant declaration of frustration at her vulnerability.

I began reflexively practicing phrases. All those niceties that help you glide through a day of interactions. The fact that you always announced yourself with a *bonjour* when you walked into a shop, and said *bonne journée* when you left. Or *bonsoir* and *bonne soirée* if it were evening. The shopkeepers' patter—*ensuite* (next), *avec cela?* (anything else?), *je vous en prie* (you're welcome), which, once you knew them, were like picking a lock and gaining entrance into a particularly gracious stroll through the stations of daily life.

At the same time, I found myself fighting off a rising disappointment, and I wondered if Mary Jo was feeling the same uneasy sense of letdown—that, through our particular brand of impulsive half-planning, we had just disruptively extricated ourselves from our own lives, only to arrive in a village that was—well, it was fine. It was fine.

We turned a corner and passed a greengrocer's called Le Jardin de Marie, promising *fruits et légumes*. One aimless zig and an unavoidable zag later, a green street sign told us we had turned onto the Rue du Plô, a passageway so narrow that in places I could have spread my arms and opened two front doors simultaneously. A hint of a breeze carried the smoke of grilling meat toward us. From a window with shutters thrown wide came the unmistakable breathless cheer of a television commercial, accompanied by the smell of stewing tomatoes and garlic.

I was thinking that the word "Plô" sounded sort of uncongenially un-French, and wondered if the name might be my first encounter with the Langue d'Oc of Madame Johnson's class. In any case, I would always remember the word "Plô" as a result of this thought, and also because what happened next would turn out to be the first identifiable detour leading away from the trip I had imagined and looked forward to and toward the trip this would actually become.

7

The narrow street opened like a tiny river delta, and emptied us into a courtyard, where the shrieks and slapping shoes of five or six mop-haired kids reverberated against faded peach- and lemon-colored walls.

In the center of the courtyard, a stone planter commemorated the old village well. The iron crank with its fretwork wheel stood rusty and resigned among red geraniums.

The kids were playing one of those games that get invented when no ball or stick is handy, and they were shouting under the half-watchful supervision of their dark-haired mothers. If we had approached from a street with a longer view of the courtyard, we might have chosen an alternate route and left the kids to their game. But we had burst onto a stage so intimate and confined that we did not have room to be passersby. We were immediately and intrusively a part of the scene.

A dozen villagers stood, interrupted, looking our way.

I attempted a smile, and said, quietly, "Bonjour."

In ragged unison, everyone in the courtyard who was not American said, "Bonjour, Monsieur."

And the air remained still while I waited for the awkwardness of the moment to pass so we wouldn't look as if we were actually fleeing when we skirted the perimeter of the courtyard and left the kids to resume their game.

At which point Mary Jo said, in English, in a perfectly normal speaking voice that sounded to me under the circumstances as if she were trying to narrate a story into her mother's bad ear, "Why don't you introduce us?"

Mary Jo's tone of voice was so clearly asking me to intervene in some way with the group that they prolonged their silence—a silence that might quite comfortably have ended by now—to wait for the man who could say bonjour passably well to translate what his wife was asking him to convey.

What I said, in the end, was *"Euhh"*—the slightly dopey-sounding French equivalent of "Umm."

"These will be the kids' classmates," Mary Jo said.

I smiled at the group of our new neighbors.

"This isn't urgent," I said.

And still, a little shufflingly now, our uncomprehending audience watched us.

Our kids finally decided that wandering lost and alone through a strange French village was preferable to the agony of what was unfolding in front of them, and they moved off along the same path we had been pursuing when we arrived—those many hours ago that had somehow been compressed into a few short minutes of earth time.

The French kids took this as their cue to resume running after each other, with several heading directly for the stone planter wall, which in the context of their play appeared to be a home base of some sort giving temporary immunity, until they sprinted back into the open field and were once again fair game. They played loudly and happily, effortlessly in tune with each other and all that surrounded them. Their mothers gestured to each other in forceful agreement that looked like dispute.

I felt entirely outside the harmonious bubble of their world. I couldn't imagine their lives, or what our presence in their village could possibly offer them.

And then, the moment seeming to have passed, I drifted out of the square in the kids' wake. Eva was scaling a short stone wall ahead of us, while Joe checked the cracks for lizards. Mary Jo pulled level with me.

"What the fuck was that?" she asked.

We had reached a ring road that appeared to belt the village proper, separating it from the outskirts. It meant that in ten minutes of lazy wandering, we had walked from one side of the village, through its center, to the other side. We were looking over a rolling valley floor, carpeted with vineyards, the stitches of their vine rows meeting at angles along the seams that separated them. The enormous dome of pale blue sky was empty except for a single wisp of cloud poised above a line of dark hills in the distance.

"You are going to speak French at some point while we're here, right?" Mary Jo asked.

"Is that a question?"

"Because I can't do it like you, but at least I'll try."

Three or four turtledoves were calling out in overlapping patterns like songs sung in a round. Two of them slapped their way out of a hedge beside us and flew down the street on whistling wings.

"You know I don't do things that way," I said. "I have no idea who's who, or what the rules are here."

"How are you going to find out, if you won't talk to people?"

"I'll talk to people. Like I always do."

"This isn't like we always do, hon. We've got two kids here at the edge of their capacities."

"I just . . ."

"I know you just," said Mary Jo.

And acknowledging our shorthand for an old and unhelpful verbal habit, I said, "Yeah, I just."

Up ahead, Eva and Joe passed a woman in an orange and rust print dress, wearing leather shoes with blocky heels, a heavy-looking straw bag in one hand. She hauled herself along on legs so bowed they resembled parentheses, rocking to the side with each step.

Although the chances were near zero that she would understand a single spoken word of English, I had an instinct to pause our conversation until we had passed her. But exactly as we overtook her, Mary Jo resumed.

"I'm not interested in the Stevie show this time," she said as I turned to the woman and offered a smiling bonjour and a crisp little bow of the head.

"We've got two sensitive kids going to school in a foreign place, and we need more from Steve Hoffman than perfect French to impress waiters and shopkeepers."

The ring road bent left, continuing its circling embrace of the village. To our right, beyond the vineyards baking in their penitent, immobile ranks, I watched the single plodding cloud on the horizon, like a raptor riding thermals, dragging its slow shadow across the line of hills.

"I get it," I said.

"Do you?"

It was a good question. Did I? Or did I still think that everything really was just going to work out, without particular effort on my part, because we were magically back in France?

The kids stopped and pointed up a narrow street, and we nodded.

We passed an untended hedge, alive with the gabbling and squeaking of a flock of starlings, and turned to climb the street the kids had chosen. The stone wall to our right belonged to the church, which we discovered when we reached the far corner, and found ourselves standing at the edge of the village's main square. A knife edge of Mediterranean sunlight sliced the square in two. Two men in biker's uniforms sat across from each other at a café table, drinking late-morning glasses of white wine.

"What do you think?" asked Mary Jo.

"About what?"

"About everything. The village."

8

It was Thursday evening, and we had laid out a cutting board full of salami, fruit, cheese, and baguette on the long, Moroccan-tiled slab that served as a terrace tabletop. It was the kind of cold collation that Mary Jo and I had gotten good at putting together over many repetitions—rooted in our attempts to introduce some of what we liked about European life into our American routines.

We were seated around the table—wine and Orangina glugging into glasses, knives knocking against the cutting board, torn bread crust crackling—when we heard an approaching vehicle's horn bleating over and over, mixed with a recorded loop, distorted and massively amplified, of what sounded like the exhortations of a carnival barker. The noise swelled, passed beneath our front windows, and faded on its way toward the village center.

"What was that?" asked Joe.

"The circus is in town," I said. "Or possibly the Germans are invading."

We resumed eating, and I was just encouraging the kids to leave behind the relative safety of their wedge of Brie for the craggy shores of a blue cheese from the Auvergne, when a frantic electronic chime rang seven times over the town loudspeaker system, and a female voice called for our attention in a rising and falling cadence: "*ALLÔ? . . . ALLÔ!*"

This was the Biterrois subregion of Languedoc, where the strange anachronism persists of announcing village business over a system of loudspeakers around town, and eventually we would accept it as part of life. Sometimes we would learn that the boules club would be meeting at eighteen hours thirty. Sometimes we would learn that boar-hunting licenses would be sold the following Saturday at the Salle Polyvalente.

From our window, I listened to the announcement pass from one part of town to another before finally arriving at a speaker about fifty feet from my head. I made out perhaps ten words of breakneck French blurred by what sounded like the announcer's insistence on shouting into the microphone through a cardboard tube.

In the relative silence that followed, a sparse procession of my fellow villagers emerged from their front doors, market baskets swinging.

"She's saying something about *coquillages*," I announced. "People are walking to the main square."

I fully intended to return to our table and linger over my glass of Sancerre, letting the inhabitants of the village conduct their business unmolested by American interlopers.

When I turned around, however, Mary Jo had grabbed her camera and was slipping into her sandals. "Let's go, kids," she said.

What we found in the Place de la Mairie was a panel truck parked at one end, with one of its sides now lifted into an awning, and a score of neighbors waiting to place an order with Monsieur Viguier, who kept up a shouted conversation with each in turn as he scooped and weighed kilo after kilo of mussels, oysters, clams, sea snails, and a pile of what looked like warty potatoes, labeled *violets*.

Short and wiry, Monsieur Viguier moved back and forth in a narrow aisle behind his wares, talking constantly in the kind of hoarse baritone that occasionally cracked, like a boy whose voice is changing.

He plunged his scoop into a deep crate of black and purple shells. "How many? Two kilos? *Ah bon?* Guests? Ah, well. It is necessary they not die of hunger."

He laid a plastic sack on the scale before pouring in his scoopful of mussels. He dug a second heaping mound and, with his eyes on the scale, let fall a clattering half scoop, then shook the scoop gently to drop one mussel, then two, then one more.

Ahead of us in line, Jean-Luc caught my eye and offered a polite smile, then leaned close to the woman standing next to him, surely Nicole of the eggplant fritters, and she glanced furtively back at us.

When everyone in line had finished ordering, we drifted toward the truck. Monsieur Viguier bellowed a hoarse greeting and asked what he could do for us.

Eva had a polite frown on her face as she contemplated the barnacled mussels strewn with seaweed, the sea snails with their fingernail-shaped feet drawn into their shells, and the tiny flat clams called *tellines*, with sticky white tongues bulging from half-opened mouths.

"How often do you visit?" I asked.

"Every Thursday at six!" he thundered.

"These are from the Mediterranean?"

"Better than that! From the *Étang de Thau!*"

"The *Étang* . . ."

"*De Thau!* The Oysters of Bouzigues!" he said, and I had the impression I was supposed to snap to attention at this, as if I had been looking over a display of suits and he had just let slip the word "Armani."

"You are . . . Swiss?" he asked.

"American."

"American?"

Mary Jo, on tiptoes trying to get the right angle on a basket of mussels, rolled her eyes at Eva in anticipation of the inevitable.

"*Mais vous parlez très bien français,*" said Monsieur Viguier, and then proceeded to pluck a selection of oysters from his display, which he insisted that *Monsieur l'Américain* and his family of Americans must absolutely try.

It was not until we were outside our front door with our double-bagged plastic sack full of Oysters of Bouzigues, whatever those were—from *L'Étang de Thau,* whatever that was—and a lemon thrown in for "goodwill among nations," that it occurred to me I had no idea how to open an oyster.

"Ask Jean-Luc," said Mary Jo.

One story above us, the lights of Jean-Luc and Nicole's kitchen shone through a curtained window. His doorbell was perhaps five steps away.

"Any ideas other than asking Jean-Luc?" I asked.

"Dad, just look it up on YouTube," said Eva.

"Or," said Mary Jo, "ask your neighbor who's been eating oysters his whole life."

"And who is sitting with his wife right now," I said, "and saying to himself, 'What would make this dinner so much better is if an American tourist stopped by for an impromptu oyster-shucking demo.'"

"We're not tourists, Stevie. We're their neighbors for the next half a year."

Eva, in a dead and hopeless monotone: "Oh my gaahhhd."

"I can figure out how to shuck an oyster," I said. "It can't be that hard."

"Well," she said. "That's one way of living in a village."

Our meal still awaited us on the terrace. The wine, by now well warmed, was lifted from its puddle of condensed drippage and set to rechill in the fridge.

I consulted the iPad, and in my first attempt to wedge a paring knife into what appeared to be the seam between the oyster's top and bottom halves, my knife slipped, and I raked the backs of three fingers across the flint-sharp edge of the shell. A patter of blood began dripping into the aluminum sink with a pleasantly musical, vaguely bossa nova rhythm.

With no bandages to be found, I tied three rolled-up strips of paper towel around my three bleeding fingers before resuming my oyster-shucking apprenticeship.

Eventually, eleven halved oysters lay cocked at odd angles on a dinner plate, the twelfth having been so thoroughly shattered that none of the remaining fragments of its shell were large enough to hold the shreds of its mutilated flesh.

I laid the plate on the table next to the rest of our meal, which, an hour earlier, might have been served in Minnesota, Iowa, or Wisconsin. Now our terrace smelled like the seashore, and we had been joined by strange creatures from a body of water we'd never heard of.

The oysters were deep-shelled and oblong. Their flesh varied from glistening ivory to a light mushroomy tan, ringed by a sutured-looking band of dark pewter. They were beautiful in their way. When, as the elected oyster taster for the group, I tried the first one, it was plump and chewy and rotten-fresh and bitingly salty. And it featured several grains of shell grit as a silent commentary on my shucking technique.

"Incredibly salty," I said. "But, honestly . . . they're good."

Mary Jo, for whom "too salty" does not exist, took her turn, and her eyes opened wide with approval as she lifted the shell to her lips and tipped in the last of the brine.

"Eva?" I asked.

"Nope," said Eva, who was still processing the recent display of snails, clam tongues, and warty sea potatoes.

"You love the ocean," I said. "These taste like that."

I knew I was pushing. Eva's need for autonomy did not just express itself as a drive to impose herself, to be seen, but also as a wish not to be physically dependent. She hated illness and injury. Had a morbid fear of throwing up. And, when it came to food, would occasionally simply refuse to swallow something—not out of rebellion or stubbornness, but because the act of swallowing began a process in her body that was then out of her control. There was no way to take it back.

I sliced a bit of the thin outer edge of one oyster and squeezed a couple drops of lemon juice on it. She held the forked and dangling morsel in front of her nose, examining it from all angles, and then the very tip of her tongue ventured testingly forth, like an antenna probing something unknown and potentially capable of attack. She smacked her mouth a few times to assess the flavor on her tongue, made a face, and finally, resignedly, placed the scrap of oyster between her lips and minced it between her front teeth before swallowing with a "Nyeah" of shivery disgust.

"Another?" I asked.

"Yeah, Dad!" she said.

"Joe?"

Joseph had watched his sister's performance and saw in it both risk and opportunity for himself.

"I'll try it," he said.

I sliced him a piece and squeezed another drop of lemon juice.

He grabbed the fork, tilted his head back, and took in the piece of oyster before he could think too much about it. He chewed and swallowed and considered. His delicate, impossibly long eyelashes closed for a moment as he absorbed the sensation. And then he asked for another bite.

I've thought about the moment a lot since then. I think there was some bravado in it. I think there was some younger-brother satisfaction at making his sometimes-overbearing sister come off a little prissy. I think there was a feeling of joining the adult world in some way that he couldn't make happen in other realms. I also think, given the aftermath, he truly liked the taste, or if not the taste exclusively, then the larger, ambitious experience of the taste—the salty ocean tenderness in his mouth, the strangeness of eating raw wild animal, the recognition that something as big and abstract as the sea could be tasted in a mouthful of food.

He took another larger bite, without lemon juice this time, and then ate a whole oyster.

"Nice job, Joe," said his sister with, to her credit, no undertone expressing anything other than "Nice job, Joe."

The rechilled wine was very cold, and we tasted the Loire Valley and the Étang de Thau in succession. The kids drifted off to watch something in the living room and stopped back occasionally to lean against us and nibble.

A chimney rose above the wall we shared with Jean-Luc and Nicole, and at intervals the shifting breeze cast the smell of woodsmoke and charring meat over us.

We could hear them talking in low voices, somehow both discreet and intimate.

By the time we finished dinner it was dark outside. The kids were giggling at their show. Someone several doors down began playing a harmonica.

I used a phrase we often repeated to each other when life had been turbulent for a while and we needed reminding that we had always gotten through such times, and always would.

"Right now," I said, "everything is OK."

Out beyond the circle of lamp glow, the moon was rising over the stone courtyard walls. Mary Jo said, "This isn't working."

9

I continued looking at the moon, partly rooted by stirrings of alarm I didn't want to telegraph, partly trying to read into her inflection whether she was being serious or just waxing sarcastic about how absolutely right everything so obviously was.

"What isn't working?" I asked.

"You. Us. This whole thing."

"Us?"

"You in France. It's not working."

"How, not working? How could anything not be working right now?"

"Tonight in the street, when you couldn't just knock on our neighbors' door . . ."

"Wait, is this about *oysters*?"

". . . I thought to myself, 'He can't do this. He'll never be able to do this.' And I've never had that thought about you before. About anything."

"Can't do what?"

"Can't . . . can't fucking get over himself. Can't let go. Can't . . . I mean . . . ask for ice for his kids' Cokes for Christ's sake, because it might make him look like an American in France, which is exactly what he fucking is."

"Did you just live through the same evening I did? With the wine, and the food, and the happy kids, and Joe eating an actual Mediterranean oyster on our terrace? In southern France? Were you here for that?"

"We're not here to eat salami and drink wine on the terrace, Stevie."

"Well, what the hell are we here for then?"

"You tell me! We're not here because of me. We're here because of you. France is your thing."

"Our thing."

"It's been our thing. But really it's your thing. I could stand in the middle of Madrid and ask stupid questions in my bad Spanish and not give a shit. I could be happy in California. I could, quite frankly, be happy in Shoreview, Minnesota. But you've got this thing you're after. I don't know. We keep coming here, and I just keep . . . keep waiting for you to . . . to start building something. If you really want France . . ."

"If? If I want France?"

"What are you guys saying?" hollered Eva from the living room.

"Nothing," said Mary Jo.

"Yes, you are," said Eva.

The sound of a window shutting drifted from Jean-Luc and Nicole's side of the wall.

"This," Mary Jo said, waving her palm over the table, "is what you get after you've done the work. But you're not doing the work. You're just playing some character, and I don't even like him."

"Some character? Some . . . you mean the one version of myself I like? The person I have to put on a shelf for years when we're not in France? The guy I wish I were when I'm sitting at my suburban tax desk, adding postal receipts and staring out the window? That character?"

"Well, whoever that is, he's not helping his family become a part of this village, which is the whole reason we're here, spending more money than we—"

"We just got here, hon. You don't barge into a strange village and start trying to choke friendships out of everybody."

"I'm not interested in a practice trip this time. We've done that. We've walked the cute streets and gone to cafés and wondered what it would be like to live there. We're here now. We're living here. Right now. You can . . . I guess you can be anyone you want to be in France. I'm just telling you I'm not interested anymore . . ."

"In what?"

"Not interested in . . ."

"In France? In me? What are we talking about here?"

"In . . . Stevie, I'm not going to leave you."

"Well, that's a relief."

"But I'm not interested in watching you wait for your life to be revealed to you. This is real, Stevie. We've got kids and they're not extras in the Steve Hoffman show. We've got a marriage that doesn't need France in order to be what it needs to be. You say France is something important to you. OK. Make this count. And take us along. Or I'm . . . Honestly. I'm not interested in France anymore."

"I don't believe that," I said.

"You should," she said.

"Wait a minute. I don't even particularly like this place so far. This is just . . . this is just some village where the kids are going to school. I'm not making my stand in Autignac. If I was going to make any kind of stand, it would be in Paris. You know that."

"Then we should be in Paris. And no. I didn't know that. And if it's true you should have told me a long time ago."

"I don't even know what you're asking. What do you want me to be?"

"You say you want to be French, Stevie. Go be French. And help us be French with you. I'm asking you to do what you have always said you want to do."

"So you . . . what? You want me to be another happy American extrovert? The dopey marketing exec who's sure all the neighbors on his cul-de-sac think he's a great guy?"

"Stevie," she said. "You say you want your kids to fall in love with France. Right now you're making sure that won't happen. And I'm on their side."

"Well, if it means selling vacuum cleaners door-to-door in Autignac, then, sorry. I'm not the guy."

I reached for my wineglass, but it was empty.

The thought of losing my connection with France struck me as an unthinkable calamity—a toppling of one of the central pillars under-girding my sense of who I was. And yet, even in the privacy of my own thoughts, I could not swallow down the disgust I felt at the idea of work-ing the village like a showroom salesman.

I sat next to Mary Jo, following the moon's slow climb through the sky. I had a vision of myself walking the streets for the next six months, bare American legs sticking out from my European trench coat, exhibit-ing myself over and over to our horrified neighbors.

When the bats started circling in too close to our heads, we cleared the table and headed in for the night.

10

Later, alone at the dining room table, unable to sleep, I opened my lap-top. Down in the courtyard, a stroke of warm breeze raised a lingering sigh from the olive tree.

Below a continuing-education reminder from the National Associa-tion of Tax Professionals there was an email from Mom and Dad, ad-dressed to me only, which, I knew, could be innocent or could be intended as a deliberate, if deniable, dismissal of Mary Jo.

There was a complicated web of hurt, resentment, defensiveness, and miscommunication binding us all to what we had become to each other.

My mom had inherited from her own brittle and judgmental Catho-lic mother a collection of rigid codes that ordered and civilized the world as they understood it. Grammar, etiquette, table setting, thank-you notes, elevated reading, flowery and fawning politeness were all equated with high and genteel virtue, and enforced by manipulating the two opposing levers of social inclusion and social rejection.

When we had announced our engagement, the initial assumption, I'm quite sure, had been that Mary Jo would fold herself into this new family—would, perhaps more accurately, consent to be elevated into the social and cultural refinements that this new family could offer—so different from life among her own raucous and chaotic Romanian kin.

But Mary Jo did not feel she had been done a favor or granted a higher station. And the arbitrariness of the rule changes that determined her status had initially so confused her, and later so offended her, that she soon gave up trying to play by them, or to be anything, really, other than Mary Jo Hoffman, née Lapadat. And you could take her or leave her.

I felt at first that this rift was a problem of translation—something repairable through painstaking diplomacy. I worked hard for a while to explain Mary Jo to my family, and them to her. Trying not to take sides.

But in the end, Mary Jo's version of the world, and of my family, and of my family's influence on me, kept holding true under examination, and what I had been brought up believing began to show cracks and fall apart. I discovered new joys and freedoms with Mary Jo that I had not often let myself experience as an anxious and fearful kid, struggling to accept himself in any state shy of perfection, the parameters of which were not his to determine.

As I drifted further and further from the island of my original family on the raft of my new marriage, I was eventually encouraged, in a number of subtle and obvious ways, to consider myself a defector. I would be allowed to return, under certain circumstances, to my homeland, but I was no longer a citizen.

What was left was a kind of inversion of the fundamentals of family. Rather than squabbles and fights that did nothing to challenge a durable love and devotion, we maintained a bright, complimentary, intimate-seeming surface that did its best to ignore a fundamental feeling of mutual rejection that lay beneath everything.

Still, despite a certain emptiness, this way of interacting could be comforting in its long familiarity. A tarnished thing that had used to shine.

"Hope the American landing was a success," my parents' email began, "and the invasion of France continues apace."

And like settling into an old couch, I sank into the rules of this familiar world.

"The eagle has landed," I replied.

"We have just finished a meal of charcuterie, assorted French cheese, and Sancerre, looking over the olive tree in our rear courtyard," I said. "The son and heir ate his first raw oyster this evening, delivered to us fresh from the Mediterranean by the village shellfish monger, and shucked, a little bloodily, by yours truly. Apparently, the shellfish merchant will be visiting us every week, and I intend to keep him solvent. Meanwhile, there is a village café serving pretty good lunches, a bakery selling us baguettes and chocolate croissants for breakfast, and a greengrocer called Le Jardin de Marie, which I hope to explore as soon as tomorrow..."

And so on, in that vein.

11

During my final year of college, the year after I lived in Paris, my dad bought one of those round-the-world airline tickets that let you circle the globe on a single fare, as long as you keep moving west. My mom did not go with him and though I never learned the exact reasons, it was no secret that he had been flirting with depression for a year or more, and they had not been getting along.

The trip was framed as a sabbatical, after a quarter century of practicing law, but it appeared from my perspective like a way of fleeing his life for a year, and although in theory I was one element of the life he was fleeing, I found his complicated, somewhat desperate-looking escape—from his law firm, from Roseville, from mown lawns and golf courses, from a house he had begun to hate, and even from us—thrilling and instructive.

I saw it as a reconnaissance mission that would bring him home wise in experiences, and full of ideas about how to live the next act of his life. He loved history and the battlefields of northern France. Maybe we would all live near each other in some quiet Paris *quartier* and raise kids and grandkids in parks, libraries, and museums, floating sailboats in the Jardin du Luxembourg, eating Berthillon ice cream and roasted chestnuts, in season. We would break the genealogical chains that, for several generations, had bound us to the American Upper Midwest for no better reason than that a random assortment of Irish and German Catholics had once settled there and refused to use birth control.

Whether by the letters they exchanged, or by some intuitive mutual softening, Mom and Dad had put their difficulties behind them by the time he got home. He left his law firm, and they sold the house in Roseville, which had come to symbolize, I think, the treadmill of income and status seeking that had ultimately thrown such a dark blanket of melancholy over him.

He went back to work, not as an attorney, but as a self-employed judicial arbitrator and mediator—the same field, give or take, he had just left. They bought a condo in Minneapolis. My sister went to work for him. And he just sort of settled back into this new life that was for all practical purposes the old life with a smaller mortgage and no pressure from law partners.

His was not my life to conduct, or to accept the consequences of, and I could clearly see his contentment with this simpler, less expensive, less beholden new way of living, among colleagues and friends who loved and respected him and whom he knew well. Despite all of this, I never really forgave him.

I told my folks once, on a phone call home from college, with the two of them on separate lines, that I was disappointed with what Dad had decided to do since returning from his big trip.

Shortly after we hung up, I got a call back, from Mom only, her voice muted, but choked with fury and scorn. "How *dare* you say you're disappointed in your father?" she asked. "What have you done that gives you *any* right?"

But I had already decided that I would never repeat his error. Would never merely globe-trot, or stake an ephemeral claim in some foreign place, only to accept a gravitational settling back into what I had always been. One day I would leave Roseville behind and all that it stood for. Except I would never come back.

12

From our living room in Minnesota, integrating into a small French village had looked not just straightforward but more or less inevitable. At first we would be the new, unfamiliar neighbors, and then we would become the old, familiar neighbors. I did not have a plan for this. Or if I did, it was simply to be a presence around town, and, I suppose, to win people over with my ability to speak their language, and then accept whatever hospitality they were willing to offer me in return. We would shop at the shops, and sit in the café, and drop the kids off at school, and soon enough . . . Well, we would be a part of things.

In the days following our moonlit talk on the terrace, I tried to imagine a more pressing and forcible entry into the life of the village, and mostly failed. In a community of only eight hundred people, we were unmistakably new arrivals, but no one appeared interested in us, much less ready to escort us through their front doors and into their inner lives. The café divided itself into regulars who paid us no mind and an occasional tourist or two with whom we didn't particularly care to be associated.

We took a meandering drive around the outskirts of the village one morning, gazing at vines and scrub and half-built new housing developments through the tinted glass of our rented vehicle, and then came home to our pool and our olive tree and our stifling-hot house and each other.

It was early evening, and we were trying once more to slip between the cracks of the posted hours at Le Jardin de Marie.

Not far from our front door, Mary Jo broke from the group and moved toward a soft mound of feathers at the edge of the street.

It was a songbird, intact, with a familiar speckled breast, like a juvenile robin.

"Thrush?" I asked.

"I think so," said Mary Jo.

"Mom," said Eva.

"I run out of images tomorrow," said Mary Jo. She had preloaded enough STILL images to get through our travel days, but it was time to resume posting.

I crouched to roll it over and see if there was blood, or beetles, or worms. I had grown used to this.

"Still a little warm," I said.

"Dad," said Eva.

I lifted the bird by its feet, and it dangled loosely, wings spread wide, head swaying.

Joe agreed it was probably a thrush. "We are not carrying dead birds around," said Eva.

But she was wrong. Mary Jo took the bird from me and we resumed our walk. She had vowed, when she started her STILL project, never to miss a day. And she did not make vows lightly.

The man we had seen earlier walking his bike had now set a straight-backed chair in front of his garage, looking as fixed an element of the village as the stone doorway that framed him. He was sitting, bent but smiling, in wool pants, collared shirt, sweater, and felt cap against the 85°F chill. He greeted us and pointed to the bird dangling from Mary Jo's hand. His black eyes widened.

Where does one start, exactly, if one wishes to bring an octogenarian French villager up to speed on the ins and outs of blogging?

I clicked an imaginary shutter in front of my eye: "She wishes to take a photo."

He made a funny gesture, bunching the fingertips of his right hand together and, like a pecking hen, thrusting them several times toward his mouth. He spoke softly, and though I didn't catch all he had said, I got the main point.

"Good to eat?" asked Joe as we resumed our gentle climb toward the village square.

"No way," said Mary Jo. "You must have heard wrong."

"I mean, there are only so many interpretations to *bon à manger*," I said.

Mary Jo examined the thrush, and I tried to imagine taking a bite of it.

Eva stared at it as if it had suddenly grown fangs.

Below the plate-glass windows on either side of the entrance to Marie's store, arrayed like gourmet flower boxes, were wooden crates filled with pale green grape clusters, pyramids of heavy tomatoes, peaches, plums, nectarines, eggplants, and zucchini. Two framed chalkboards flanking the windows listed, on the left, "*Nos Vins*," and on the right, fresh eggs, "€1 *les 6*."

"You guys go ahead," said Mary Jo, and took her dead treasure for an investigatory stroll around the square.

Inside the shop, we appeared to have walked in on an argument. A woman in her early forties, in a sweater and foulard—presumably

Marie—stood behind the counter to our left, leaning on her fists, and gripping a long knife of a length somewhere between a stiletto and a sword. The knife was aimed a little carelessly across the counter at the abdomen of a woman several decades her senior—a delicate, vibrant woman in clamdiggers and a fitted blouse, who possessed that sort of ageless elegance that stops time for some people, permitting them to look a youngish sixty well into their ninth decade.

If you ignored the knife, it smacked of a confrontation at the retail returns counter that has escalated to the point where someone is asking to see a manager, and possibly mentioning the Better Business Bureau.

Then, abruptly, Marie said, "*Allez, Maman*," and, like that, it was over. She removed her rather stylish horn-rimmed glasses and leaned over the counter, offering a kiss on both cheeks to the other woman, who was not, as it had appeared, an imminent victim, but Marie's mother.

"*A tout à l'heure, Cherie*," said Maman, and, then, with a nod and a perfunctory "*Messieurs-dames*," she made her way past us out the door.

Marie now placed the knife at an angle atop an unwrapped half-cylinder of blue cheese, and looked inquiringly at the other customer in the store, an unsteady gentleman with droopy eyes and thin jowls, who had stood there patiently throughout the drama.

He mumbled something fast and unintelligible.

"Voilà. There is your Roquefort. And with that?"

For an answer, he dug into the baggy front pocket of his wool pants and extracted a leather coin purse, from which he tremblingly extracted three coins and snapped them onto the counter one after the other.

I had a vague idea of easing the kids into things with some pale and versatile protein, maybe ham, along with some cheese, a baguette, more Orangina perhaps.

But Marie's deli case was not there, it appeared, to ease American schoolkids into French gastronomy. It was an obstacle course of imposing culinary hurdles, which I surveyed with the idea gradually dawning on me that these were our new kitchen staples. These stacked coils of Toulouse sausage. These scimitars of *merguez*. These dark bladders of blood sausage. This row of salamis hanging from a wooden dowel. These meaty loaves of *magret de canard*. These rabbit legs. This wild boar pâté. This mold-speckled, collapsed, and runny wedge of Saint-Nectaire. This vacuum-sealed package of precooked tripe.

I looked around the store at bins of onions, shallots, and garlic, stacks of leeks and endive, carrots with dirt clinging to them, sacks of lentils and dried chickpeas, a crock of green olives in cloudy brine, and I felt both the eater's instinct to work my way through the entire store item by item and a simultaneous shock of recognition that I could think of almost nothing interesting to do with all of those ingredients that would not require a library of recipes and hours of devoted study.

"I owe you thirty centimes, Monsieur Castel. *Et voilà.* Good continuation, and give the bonjour to Mme Castel. How does it go, the leg? Better, I hear. *Allez. Au revoir!*"

And with that, Marie turned a sparkling smile on Eva, Joseph, and me.

I decided to start small.

"*Une baguette, s'il vous plaît.*"

There were no more baguettes, she informed me, and when I pointed to the two baguettes standing on end in the rack behind her, she explained that those had been reserved by Madame Cassagne. No, this late in the day, she rarely had baguettes. It was better to arrive right at five p.m., when she opened for the evening.

The kids had migrated to a tall rack of Lucite boxes filled with a tutti-frutti rainbow of gummy candies.

"Dad," said Eva, pointing.

"You take a basket from the top and use the tongs," called Marie. "You tell me how much of each one."

And the kids, whether understanding everything, or just enough, began filling wicker platters with tongfuls of radioactive-colored candy.

"You are Canadian?" asked Marie.

"American," I said.

"*Vous parlez très bien français.*"

"*Merci*," I said, and wondered if the bakery across the street might perhaps have a baguette, and Marie pouted and shrugged and did not think it likely, which upset my plans considerably, what there were of them, given that the one thing you can count on anywhere in France is some butter, sliced French ham, and hard cheese on a baguette.

"You are here until when?" asked Marie.

I was so startled at this first cracking open of the door of conversation that I blurted, practically shouting, "We are here until after Christmas!" And by the time I was done, Marie had been notified that our kids would be going to school here. Joseph would be at the elementary school in town, and Eva, his sister, would be going to the middle school in Murviel-lès-Béziers.

Marie absorbed my verbal assault calmly, and said that her nephew, Baptiste, was the same age as my *petit bonhomme* (little man), so they would be in class together.

"Could you assemble a small aperitif for us?" I asked, and, as she went to work, I informed her that we were renting a house on Avenue de la Liberté, that I had learned my French in Paris, and that the children had attended a French immersion school.

A collection of wrapped items accumulated on the counter. A wedge of semi-liquid Brie. A sliver of the same Roquefort that Monsieur Castel would share that evening with his hobbled wife. A length of dried sausage. A slice of country pâté. A tub of green olives—Lucques, Marie told me, a local variety. Delicious. And at each question, "Does this interest you?" I replied immediately and gratefully, "Yes! Yes! Very much!"

Did I know *Pélardon*? A goat cheese of the region. She grabbed one of several canvas-colored pucks, featuring a cartoon ram on the label chewing a green sprig. She excised a triangle from one of them and offered it to me on the flat of her knife, glancing briefly at the clock as, I assumed, her closing time approached.

"For you?" she asked the kids, who shook their heads.

As she wrapped the remainder of the round in white paper, I crushed the grainy cheese with my tongue, releasing into my mouth, my throat, my sinuses such a powerful musk of unapologetic goatiness and fermented reek that my reaction did not even take place in the realm of taste. I felt not just startled, but—I want to say—offended. Not because I was in any way physically repulsed by the flavor and smell, but simply shocked into an entirely new domain of awareness.

Whatever this was, it didn't seem, somehow, to be playing by the rules. It was like reaching out for a polite handshake and receiving a punch in the face. Culture and the rules of civility were meant to round off the edges of that kind of behavior. And when it came to goat cheese—in my experience up to that moment anyway—the idea was, similarly, to soften and refine the barnyard raunch of the base materials so that what was originally wild and glandular and animal became, in the final product, a suggestively earthy accent, like the anal secretions of a civet hiding deep inside a great perfume.

But this cheese had taken the frankness of goat scent—body and hair and full, dangling bags of hot milk—and seemingly isolated that universe of tastes and smells in order, not to refine them, but to exaggerate them. To revel in them. And then to ferment them so they were reduced and intensified and compressed into an edible essence of the rank and ill-tempered original animal and whatever it had consumed.

Mary Jo rejoined us. She stood next to Eva and quietly stole one of her candies. She was popping it in her mouth, with widened "Who, me?" eyes, when Eva caught her.

"How many?" Marie asked, sliding Joe's wicker tray toward herself.

The kids looked at me, and I gave them the silent stink eye. They pointed to one pile after another, and I had the pleasure, at last, of watching them, shyly but competently, call out the number of rubbery Day-Glo candies in each collection.

"*Et . . .*" said Mary Jo, pointing to her mouth.

"*C'est offert,*" said Marie. It's on the house.

I felt a finger below my ribs. Mary Jo was holding out her thrush.

"*Ask her,*" she whispered.

"OK, that's just . . ." said Eva.

"She's closing," I said.

"*Excusez-moi,*" said Mary Jo, and held the thrush out over the counter, a gesture that, in an American grocery store, might get you arrested.

"*Ah, une grive,*" said Marie, unfazed.

"*Euh,*" I said as the kids grabbed their baggies of candy and Mary Jo stood there like a cat who has just dropped a wet vole proudly on your pillow. "We passed a man on the street. I think he said these are good to eat? That did not sound correct, but we are Americans . . ."

"*Les grives?*" she said. "Yes, they are very good to eat, but now is not the season. In autumn, one hunts them in the hills behind the village. They are fatter then."

I translated for Mary Jo, who appeared satisfied, having not only an image, but a story ready for tomorrow's post.

As she rang me up, Marie said, "Higher, in the same hills, one may find the farm that makes the Pélardon. You can visit them. You go to Gabian, and follow the signs for Mas Rolland."

I said that it was very, very kind of her to mention this and that we would, without a single doubt, go visit the goat farm, and I handed her a crisp fifty-euro bill in exchange for our bag of groceries.

"Monsieur," she said thoughtfully to the note in her hand. "You don't by chance have change."

"I'm sorry," I said. "We have just arrived."

And with a weary exhalation, she left the store, ran across the street through a double swinging gate, and returned with change.

"If ever you desire rabbit," she said, as if this were likely, "I can order beautiful rabbits from the slaughterhouse in town." And this appeared to explain the mysterious noises I had been hearing in the quiet of the night.

"Bon appétit," she called, and the door slapped shut behind us.

The gate across the street was still ajar, and through it I glimpsed an orderly and appealing courtyard, with plants and chairs and a kind of banquet table set in the middle.

The bakery did not have baguettes.

They did have two undercooked *gros pains,* larger, breadier baguettes, like pale, inflated dachshunds, which I bought from a sullen young man in a wispy goatee whose interrupted cigarette lay smoking on the ground outside the delivery door. Every store in town stocked wine, I had noticed, and from the baker I bought a bottle of shockingly affordable red wine.

I gave the young man behind the counter a twenty-euro note, which he looked at as if I had slid across an entire gold brick. He opened the till and sort of waved his hand over it as if to say, "Where in here do you imagine I am going to find change like that?"

"You don't have a smaller bill, Monsieur?"

Not many minutes later, I was back with my family, thoughtfully chewing a bread butt as we walked down the street.

The low sun left the corridor of Avenue de la Liberté in a lavender sort of shade, beneath a bright lane of just-purpling sky.

"What did you get for dinner?"

"Pretty much what she told me to get."

"This is it?" asked Mary Jo when I had unwrapped all of my packages and arranged them on a cutting board.

"This is it," I said, and with it laid out like that, it was much more obvious to me than while enveloped in the persuasive whirlwind of Marie's advice that I had made, and acquiesced to, any number of what the French might call exaggerations.

"This is dinner?"

"I mean . . ."

"For a nine-year-old? Hon, they're starving. Pâté? Red wine? Roquefort?"

"It's not like they've never had Brie and a baguette before."

"Yes, but have you *smelled* that Brie? Have you looked at it?"

I had been looking at it, and it was one of the most delicious-looking things I had ever been so close to.

"Guys, I'm sorry," I said. "I just took the grocer's advice. And here's what we're going to do about that. We're going to make the best of it."

Joe tried a bite of coarse, heavily larded sausage. Eva's jaw muscles bunched as she worked grimly through her candy.

Mary Jo and I pecked at the cheese and pâté in silence, with sconce lighting casting romantic shadows on the stone wall.

Joe offered me one of his candies, and I gnawed for a while on something that tasted like watermelon-flavored whale blubber.

Then Eva, in a gesture meant, I assumed, to sum up her thoughts about dinner so far, and possibly the trip as a whole, broke a *gros pain* in half, dug elbow deep into each half in turn, excavated all of the soft white middle, set the crusts aside, and popped fluffy balls of bread into her mouth, one by one.

The approximately seven-dollar wine from the bakery, a wine called Domaine Balliccioni, which did not even sound French, was, however, remarkably good.

13

According to Marie, one arrived at the farm of Mas Rolland by traversing the village next door, named Laurens, and continuing eastward toward Gabian. In my gratitude at the time for her willingness to act as any kind of guide whatsoever, I had not thought what I was now thinking—that there are parts of France in which, for instance, one drives through Villefranche-sur-Mer on one's way to a seaside lunch in Nice, and that instead, we had chosen to live in a place where one drove through Laurens and Gabian, on one's way to a goat farm.

The route led generally eastward, and the same berm of dark hills that we had seen on our first village walk loomed low on the horizon, with an air, if not of menace, then of a sort of brooding disapproval. The kids were quiet in the back seat, and I was relieved to be doing anything that might appeal to them, and, frankly, to be away from Autignac for a few hours, where defeat seemed to hang in the air around me.

At the main square in Gabian, we stopped driving parallel to the hills and plunged north, straight into them.

We climbed through a strangely bipolar landscape. On one hand, the engineered precision of perfectly spaced vines imposing their striped geometry on plots of uneven ground; on the other hand a pervasive messiness and neglect.

"What's that?" asked Mary Jo.

To our left was a vacant lot, completely colonized by a tall-stemmed flower growing so densely that from a distance the field appeared covered in a low yellow mist. Mary Jo and I got out of the car, the heat baking a suggestive odor into the air.

The field was covered with green stalks, head high, sprouting lacy foliage and dill-like yellow flower heads. Mary Jo bent a stalk near its base and twisted it free with an "Oh my God, this smell." I took a few steps into the meadow, and ran my hand up one of the stems, against the resistance of the branchlets and over the soft grains of its flowers. I cupped my hand around my mouth and nose. A penetrating smell like anise and caraway filled my sinuses, along with something stronger and almost disinfectant. Camphor maybe.

"Wild fennel," said Mary Jo, and as she stacked one after another in my held-out arms, I felt woozy with their liquor.

Loading my double armful into the back of the car, I pinched off two of the flower heads and offered them to Eva and Joe to smell. They snuffed tentatively, and then, in slow graceful arcs, both flowers were summarily ejected from the vehicle.

Back on the road, we saw it everywhere, growing spindly and tall, and if I hugged the edge of the asphalt road, Mary Jo's hand could sweep over the lacy yellow umbrellas, adding to the already powerful scent from the cuttings in back. Joe covered his nose and said he would literally murder us.

The road climbed through switchbacks and blind curves. Each hairpin turn offered an incrementally longer view, until at one gravel turn-out, we all got out of the car. In the far distance, a thin blue band and a flat southern horizon told us we were looking at the Mediterranean.

The vegetation around us was mostly low bushes, with no two like species seeming ever to grow adjacent to each other, so that the color and texture of each plant varied from its neighbors, and gave a mottled, patched, and mended air to the fabric of branches and leaves. Some of the taller plants must certainly have been considered trees, although they didn't resemble trees so much as inflated and engorged bushes. In places the land might have been the work of a mad gardener who had tried to plant as many green and bristly plants as the limits of soil and botany would allow. Endless variations on dusty green. Cactus greens, and mossy greens, and asparagus greens, and fern greens, and greens between those greens, and more greens between them. From a distance, the landscape looked rounded and coarse, like a high-pile Berber car-pet, but now, up close, it felt chaotic, and dense, and thorny, and, despite the riot of growth, somehow desolate. This? This was the France of Pag-nol and Cézanne? Of Bardot and Grace Kelly?

Mary Jo bent to a thistle and, gingerly, from several angles and posi-tions, attempted to pinch its stem and break it off. Her fingers were bare, and in the end, she couldn't even reach the stem, much less apply enough force to break it. The stem bristled with thorns, and nestled between the longer thorns were nearly invisible glasslike needles. I tried myself, and earned a couple of pinpricks in the meat of my finger and thumb, well-ing with blood.

The air smelled like oregano and sage and scorched rock and dust, and there was a teasing chemical suspicion now and then of some sort of resin that was like someone snapping a branch of rosemary nearby and yet also like someone somewhere in the house soaking a paintbrush in turpentine.

The word "Ow" floated insistently in the air as Mary Jo bent now and then to negotiate with a thistle, or as one of the kids dragged a calf against the knife blade of a leaf.

"What even is this place?" asked Eva, standing off on her own, tak-ing pictures of the valley in the distance.

"It's incredible!" said Mary Jo.

She was a lover not only of things that, for her purposes, she considered beautiful. But also, as a scientist, a lover of nature's structures and extremities, of thistles, skeletons, stones, and surf-battered feathers. A lover of the murderous hooks along the canes of roses as much as the velvety buds ornamenting their tips. I could hear the excitement in her voice, and was reminded how the world came alive in the presence of her embracing enthusiasm.

Eva sent a look her way, assessing, if I had to guess, whether her mom's vital first plunge into this landscape was something she should piggyback on or not.

"Dad," Joe said, and rose slowly from behind a juniper bush. He raised his right arm, staring at it to make sure he didn't jostle the long-bodied brown mantis that sat alertly on four high-kneed rear legs on the back of his hand.

"Dad, how do I get it back to the car?"

"Joe, we don't have anything to put it in."

There was a quiet stubbornness about Joe. He tended to do things the way he wanted them, and if he anticipated that we might object, he would do them anyway, quietly, without saying anything.

He maneuvered out of the brush, holding his hand high, keeping his eyes on the mantis. He had reached open ground, with nothing but gravel between him and the car, when the mantis suddenly lifted the armored shields from its back and exploded in a rustle of crepe-paper wings, following a dipping path into the impenetrable scrub.

Joe watched it, his hand still raised. I could guess at least some of the visions that had run through his head for those few seconds—the joys of having a roommate in Autignac, one who prowled the walls of a bedside terrarium and ate insects foraged by his American zookeeper and best friend.

He gazed once more in the direction of the escaped, Durrellian treasure, and then turned back, his face reddened with grief, which his blank mask failed, as always, to hide.

Mary Jo emerged holding two plants upside down by one leaf each. Their stems were toothy with quills and they swayed, bouncing off her wrists and forearms as she walked toward me, her eyes wide with a combination of pain and self-mocking laughter, as she repeated a one-note mantra: "Ow. Ow. Ow. Ow. Ow."

Beside a wooden sign next to the road, featuring a goggle-eyed cartoon ram, smiling with a sprig in his mouth, we walked through the mixed smells of the wild mint that our tires had crushed as we parked, the scorched oil from the engine's exertions up the steep hillside, and the pleasantly rank odor of goat.

When we got to the glass side door of the house, we shaded our eyes and saw an empty salesroom, with a cash register and a display case against the far wall. We double-checked the posted hours, which reassured us that the farm of Mas Rolland was open for business at this very moment.

Around the corner of the house, a long, narrow sidewalk led to an open barn door. A heavy animal musk hung in the air.

A young man of about thirty stepped out of the doorway in front of us, dressed in overalls and knee-high rubber boots. He said, "Bonjour" in passing, as if we all saw each other every day in the hallway. He told us we were welcome to visit the goats, which needed to be milked, if we would excuse him.

In the dusty light of the barn, brown and black goats with broad rounded flanks and fat dangling udders milled around in fenced pens, their rear legs jostling the distended teats, or bedded in the hay, staring at nothing, with their lower jaws working in an elliptical rhythm.

The kids gingerly gripped the ridged horns of a line of goats that had thrust their heads through the fence to eat from a trough. They rubbed the groove in the goats' foreheads between their yellow eyes, which had slitted black pupils—projecting the same impersonal menace as the eyes of an insect.

A doe was sequestered with an agitated ram, who moved against her provokingly, like a bully trying to pick a fight, his tongue flicking over his wet nose.

In the milking room, a pump droned, and milk sprayed into a large glass cauldron.

"Ring the bell if you are buying cheese," the young man said, and roughly squeezed the udder of the nearest goat, which was plump but deflating visibly.

So we returned to the salesroom door and pushed a button that said "*Sonnez.*" (Ring.) The lights turned on inside, and a short, trim woman in a lab coat appeared behind the counter.

Her name was Laurence. How could she serve us?

We were an American family making an extended sojourn in the area and had eaten her cheese in Autignac, and had greatly appreciated it.

I was bracing for it, and it came. "But you speak French very well," said Laurence, and Mary Jo, with a maliciously playful expression mouthed the words "*Mais vous parlez TRRRÈS bien . . .*"

Eva was, not very discreetly, pinching her nose at the smell in the room, which was a distillation of the air in the barn translated into the idiom of dairy.

I stepped briefly between her and the counter.

"Eva, that's rude," I said.

"I can't," she said with a fearful look in her eyes.

"You like the smell of animals," I said.

"The goats were fine, but this cheese," she said and opened her eyes wider, pleading, until I gave her permission to wait outside with Joe.

With the rhythmic sound of the milking machines chunk-chunking in the room behind her, Laurence told us what qualified a cheese to be called a Pélardon, starting with a requirement that the goats spend at least 250 days each year browsing the spiky offerings of their corner of the local *garrigue,* so the flavors of the region find their way into the milk—raw milk only, *s'il vous plaît.* Then the cheese must be aged for at least eleven days to allow the flavors to develop.

"How," I wondered out loud, "did the goats forage in the *garrigue?* We just tried to walk in the *garrigue,* and after three meters . . ." I held my arms out in defeat.

"And the . . . the . . ." I stammered, searching for the word for "thorn" and stabbing the back of my hand with my index finger.

"Oh, the goats," she said, "there are some who even prefer the thorns. They have very hard mouths."

She set out five cheeses—a squat wheel covered in gray ash, an aged, caramel-colored *tomme*, and three fresh, white cylinders that decreased in size from youngest to oldest, evaporation having shrunken them.

"*Ce petit garçon-là*" (This little boy here), she said, slicing a thin wedge from the first cheese, a wet, loose round that still wept onto its white wrapping paper, "is one day old."

The cheese was tart, tender, a little grainy, and unmistakably goaty, with an astringency that made my mouth water and lightly chalked my tongue.

"Soon it will be fig season," Laurence announced. "You should return and have this one with figs."

We stood like pins on a map, on the first slopes of small mountains, eating cheese that couldn't be one day old anywhere else. It felt disorientingly as if our passage through the *garrigue* had somehow turned us into different people from who we had been when we climbed into the car.

"Someday if you would like to see Eric bring the goats home," said Laurence as she packaged our three chosen cheeses, "call me ahead of time, and I will tell you where to go."

On the way home, we all watched hilly, inhospitable goat country give way to flat coastal plain, and *garrigue* give way to vineyard.

Eva hated the smell of the cheese and covered her mouth and nose, and Joe hated the smell of the fennel and expounded on this at some length. Between downshifts and upshifts, I placed my thorn-scarred hand in Mary Jo's as she gazed out the window and made gentle stroking motions with her thumb. The taste of goat, and of what the goats had eaten, coated my mouth, lingering as if it still had something to tell me.

14

The *mairie,* or city hall, occupied the highest point in Murviel-lès-Béziers. The *lès* in this case (with a grave accent over the "e") meant "near," identifying the village as that particular Murviel located near the city of Béziers, as opposed to any other Murviel.

I left the *mairie* feeling that, despite some hiccups, which were to be expected, we had more or less won the day. Eva was registered for school. She had her schedule. She had had a chance to watch her dad do some of what he did best, which had me feeling, if not smug, then quietly centered in a way I had not felt often since our arrival.

Our vehicle had GPS, and I had chosen the voice of a Frenchwoman as our digital navigator, over the haughty-sounding Brit, who made me feel as if I had just spilled something a little bit revolting down the front of my shirt. On our twisting descent from the *mairie,* I carried out each command, which led us deeper and deeper into an ancient warren of streets built for donkeys and mules. The soothing French voice announced that in fifty meters, then in thirty, we should *tournez à gauche,* or turn left, and as we spiraled downward, I was thinking what a nightmare it would be to have to back up the way we had come. We turned a final corner and found ourselves pinched in a stone archway, with no more than an inch to spare on either side of our front hood.

As we sat still in the archway, with the diesel engine clattering, the GPS voice calmly instructed, *"Tournez à gauche."*

To our left, there appeared to be a sort of paved goat path, but being asked to turn left onto it was like having a well-modulated voice instruct, "In fifty meters, please lift off, and bear upwards, toward the moon."

"Evie, you need to get out," I said.

"What?"

"You need to get out and help me back up. There's no way we can go forward."

"I can't even open my door," she said.

"I'll pop the hatch."

"No way."

"Well, your other option is to take the wheel and back a diesel mini-van uphill using a stick shift."

"*Tournez à gauche*," said the voice.

In reverse we went, with Eva holding index fingers apart and slowly bringing them together as the corner of our rear bumper came closer and closer to crumpling against a series of stone doorways. Our brand-new tires shrieked as I turned them hard one way, then hard the other way, engine gunning.

"*A trente mètres, tournez à gauche.*"

Because Eva couldn't fit between the car and the walls to consult with me, she had to shout her instructions, and I had to shout back, and so here we were, on a quiet residential street, directly under people's bedroom and kitchen windows, our vehicle temporarily blocking every single one of their front doorways in succession, shouting in American English, while our diesel engine revved and reverberated off the stucco walls of their homes. We might as well have lit fireworks and held a little Fourth of July celebration for the good people of Murviel-lès-Béziers.

"*A cinquante mètres, tournez à gauche.*"

At this point, a woman who, as any sane person would, had walked from the *mairie* instead of driving, arrived behind us and, unable to get around, began helping Eva guide my wide rear end up the street, also shouting instructions in the local French that I couldn't have deciphered if I had been standing across from her, reading her lips.

With her help, such as it was, we reached a wide enough point in the road that Eva could rejoin me, our volunteer guide could slide past us, and I could back the rest of the way to the next intersection, just before which, the GPS told me to go straight ahead for one hundred meters, and turn left.

Back on the D16, Eva stared out her open window, watching, or possibly not watching, the countryside slide by. I could imagine her wishing she could take the wheel and not only get us home intact, but set this whole enterprise back on course.

"What you thinking about, honey?" I asked.

"Nothing," she said.

"I'm sorry you had to do that," I said.

"When are we going do something I want to do?" she asked.

"Whenever you want. Tell me what."

And as the electronic voice, designed to sound both authoritative and reassuring, guided us serenely home, Eva brooded, her thoughts a mystery.

15

The Abbaye de Sénanque is a ninth-century Cistercian abbey snugged into a valley of Provence's Vaucluse Mountains.

The monks of Sénanque grow lavender to fund their community, and this is why, when Eva delivered to us a handwritten list of destinations she had planned for us to visit, the Abbey of Sénanque occupied first place. The online photos she showed us were of lush furrows of lavender in bloom, their rows converging in the distance on a low stone church. A scene so iconically Provençal, it looked faked.

"Eva is not the boss of this trip," announced Mary Jo that evening as we sat on the terrace watching Joe fish dead and dying insects from the pool.

"Try telling her that," I said.

The autoroute called La Languedocienne sped us eastward along the Mediterranean coast, past vineyards and olive groves, past top-heavy parasol pines and low industrial warehouses, and, at one point, past a sign pointing out over what looked like a vast inland lake with grids of shellfish beds scattered across its surface. The sign said "Étang de Thau."

"Hey, that's where our oysters come from," I said.

"Dad," said Joe, looking up from an open book in his lap.

"Joe," I said.

"Can I have a pet hedgehog?"

"Of course."

"Hedgehogs and mantids both eat crickets, so I could feed them the same diet."

"Brilliant."

The sun winked off the surface of the Étang de Thau, and I was so pleased to be a part of the harmony both inside and outside the car—to be making Eva happy, to be in Joe's presence during one of his episodes of peak Joe-ness, to be holding hands with Mary Jo while her bare feet rested on the dashboard—that we were well past the Rhône River, deep into Provence, before I recognized a completely contradictory feeling that had crept up on me the farther east we had driven. It was a kind of gloom.

Provence was, simply, breathtaking. The villages we passed were intact, harmonious, crisply painted, and in bloom. The low rolling hills of the Bas-Languedoc were replaced here by dramatic, craggy mountains and those chalky vertical bluffs rising out of forested slopes. This was like the deluxe version of southern France. This was the Ritz, and our home was a Marriott.

We came out around a rocky cliff-side shoulder, where Mont Ventoux brooded in the heat haze to our north, while ahead, lines of mauve-colored mountains faded majestically, one behind the other, to the far horizon.

"We could have lived here," I said. "How bad could this have been?"

Mary Jo removed my right hand from the gearshift, where my thumb had been drawing determined curlicues, and placed it in her lap.

"Here we go, guys," I said. "Let's go look at some lavender." We turned left and there was the church, with its gray turret.

The furrows we had seen in every online photo ran in mounded stripes from just beside our car all the way to the far church wall. The car was silent.

"Where's the lavender?" asked Joe.

There was no lavender. Anywhere. The plants were all there, attractive in their way. Sort of a silvery olive-green.

We parked and approached the field. A sign informed us that it was forbidden to walk between the rows. In the gift shop, a preoccupied clerk let us know that they had harvested the last of the lavender yesterday.

"We should have called," said Mary Jo.

"Is there lavender anywhere else around here?" asked Eva, in English.

"I don't know," said the clerk, and dropped two lavender sachets into a gift bag for her customer.

We ambled around the grounds. Eva held her camera as if there were weights hanging from her elbows. She stopped to take photos, but they were hurried. Snapshots. She was going through the motions, but there was nothing she wanted here.

Mary Jo ignored the No Trespassing signs and took a few steps into the field to crouch before one of the shorn hedges, aiming her camera down the rows at the abbey. Something about this irked Eva further.

"Mom! My God," she said, and Mary Jo laughed with no sign of discomfort.

"Eva, everybody goes through this," said Mary Jo as we hummed along a back road, taking the longer, and we hoped more scenic, northern route home through the Vaucluse.

"You get the Eiffel Tower out of your system the first time you go to Paris, and then you can start to travel for yourself."

"That's super advice, Mom. Super."

"I know you're disappointed, honey."

Eva did not seem to think this warranted a response.

"Taking photos of something a million other people have photographed is just postcards of where you've been," said Mary Jo. "It's not a body of work."

"Lavender!" I said. And we turned off onto a dusty gravel road beside what may have been the last lavender field in bloom in the Vaucluse.

Back in the car, Mary Jo scrolled through the photos on her digital display, commenting on the variations of aperture and depth of field she had been playing with.

I could feel the air in the car crackle.

"Ooh, Eva, check this one out," she said, and held her camera over her shoulder.

"Mom, I don't want to see your photos," said Eva, who stared stone-faced out the window for fifty miles or so, before she joined Joseph in fitful sleep, and we drove back to our Languedoc Marriott.

16

I had spent several mornings now seated on a chaise on the terrace with an iPad in my lap, swiping through a blog called La Marmite de Gaston, or Gaston's Kettle.

Gaston had just the other evening held my hand through a pan-roasted *magret de canard*—the thickly fat-capped breasts produced specifically by ducks raised to make foie gras. He advised me to crosshatch the fatty side with cuts that sliced to the meat, but not into it, then render the duck fat on that side of the breast, before browning the opposite side in the clear fat. His *astuce du chef,* or chef's tip, suggested testing for doneness, not by stabbing the poor *magret* with a thermometer and spilling its tasty blood, but by prodding the breast with an index finger and comparing its consistency with the meat of my thumb in various positions.

Touch tip of thumb to index finger, and feel, in the muscle where the thumb joins the palm, the mushy elasticity of a rare steak. Touch thumb to pinky, on the other hand, and feel the flexed muscle of well done. I had aimed for *rosé*, or medium rare, by gently touching thumb to middle finger and testing the *magret* as it tightened to a similar pneumatic firmness. Ten minutes later, after the meat had rested, a dozen perfectly medium-rare slices fell onto the cutting board, like medallions of seared venison. We almost wept.

I liked to cook, and I liked the way that knowing how to cook sorted me into that subset of men I particularly admired—those whose masculinity tended to express itself as a by-product of gentleness and assurance.

This morning Gaston was proposing mackerel fillets served on a tomato *concassé*. Which was fortunate because at nine o'clock sharp, the town loudspeaker belted out another "*Allô? Allô!*" before announcing that the fisherman of Valras was installed in the promenade.

Mary Jo and I arrived to a softly buzzing congregation of villagers, and the pleasant sea smell of extremely fresh seafood. The fisherman had improvised a market stall, and trays full of ice and fish dripped in the rising heat of the morning. Ahead of us in line, a diminutive matron in a housecoat leaned toward her neighbor and said, in a voice loud enough for the fishmonger to hear, "Again, his prices have climbed. It is not possible."

This prompted the fishmonger to retreat to the back of his van, return with a pack of laminated price tags, and silently deal them onto the top of each tray of fish with a wrist flick and a bit of Vegas spin.

"Voilà, today's official prices, which you will see are more than I am charging you. When it is your turn, you can thank me."

He glanced a little grimly in our direction, appearing to pick us out as strangers in town, before returning his attention to a birdlike elderly customer who was lecturing him about the size of the squid she wanted.

"I said medium!" the woman scolded, slapping the back of his hand. "Not *énorme!*"

He let more catcalls and abuse bounce off his stout form while he made change from a black leather fanny pack tucked under the medicine ball of his belly.

I had done a lot of fishing at one point, and eaten a lot of fish, but I could make almost nothing of what I was seeing. Little red fish the size of goldfish, called *rougets,* appeared to be a great favorite, as did a tray of fleshy, headless tails shaped like drumsticks called *queues de lotte,* or monkfish tails. There was a pile of pinkish, cartilaginous triangles labeled *ailes de raie,* or skate wings. There were tiny chromium minnows—*jols*—no bigger than the size of my pinky. I couldn't imagine what one might do with a minnow that was not swimming in a bait bucket.

Other than some handsome silver-gray sea bass, the other trays contained such a collection of spiny, ugly, and bulbous creatures—sole, turbot, *merlu* (hake), *capelan* (called "poor cod" in English), squid, cuttlefish, eel, anchovy, sardine, a spotted shark labeled *roussette*—that I could have believed a joke was being played on me, and that soon enough, Monsieur Sauzet would disappear again into his van, and bring out the attractive pillows of fish he actually intended to sell.

It was my turn. "I'd like four mackerel," I told him.

"They are very good, the mackerel," he said, sorting the teal and silver missiles by size with his blunt fingers. "How big?"

"Rather small," I said.

Mary Jo had been photographing the trays of fish, and when she tried to sneak a photo of Monsieur Sauzet, he caught her, folded his arms, and posed in three-quarter profile, looking not a little Napoleonic.

"Ask him how to cook them," Mary Jo said.

"I already have a recipe," I said.

"Ask him anyway."

Feeling as if I could not refuse her even one more time, yet also feeling as if I were about to ask a cattleman out on the open range how one went about preparing a beefsteak, I said, "Do you have a favorite way to prepare them?"

A gesticulating crowd of villagers instantly surrounded me, everyone simultaneously either giving advice or contradicting the advice that had just been given.

Individual words—lemon, skin, grill—leaped out from the general confusion, then fell back into the roaring linguistic rapids, from which I could discern few other meaningful syllables of my supposed second language.

Monsieur Sauzet, apparently charmed at being considered worthy of a portrait, lifted a handful of the *jols* and dropped them in a second bag, instructing us to flour and fry them.

"One eats them how?" I asked. M. Sauzet tilted his head back and imitated eating a French fry.

"*Entiers,*" he said. Whole.

I fried them in flour and olive oil. They did, indeed, come out of the oil crisped like French fries. I salted them and brought them to the table, where Mary Jo and the kids sat peacefully together, journals open, borrowing and returning markers and colored pencils from the communal pile. Joe was inventing fanciful new species of insects, giving them names, and describing their defenses—an old form of self-soothing, dating back to toddlerhood, when he would bring us plastic dinosaurs and debate with us exactly what weapons each dinosaur possessed, and what each "did for danger."

"This one uses his tail like a baseball bat and knocks other dinos way up into the sky," we would say. And he would correct us, pointing out the creature's massive armored cranium, and arguing that he actually used his head like a hammer and crushed his enemies flat.

I set the fried *jols* on the table, and it was as if I had blown my nose onto the plate.

"Dad!" said Eva. "No!"

I tried one, popping it in my mouth and chewing. It tasted just like a fried fish, and crunched like a potato chip.

I was accused of belonging to that outcast tribe of humanity who eat fish brains and poop, and was asked to return to the kitchen and take my minnows with me.

As I prepared the mackerel, I divided my attention between my new friend Gaston and the scene across the room. Mary Jo was so good at this. Less than a week ago, I had watched her stir up Eva's wrath, and while I would have spent the intervening days trying somehow to atone, Mary Jo had simply gotten on with things, and never let it appear that her criticism was in any way related to her fundamental love and respect for Eva. And now here they were, giggling about Dad, consulting about color, sharing the progress of their improvised artwork.

I gutted and filleted the mackerel, sautéed the onions and garlic, peeled and diced the tomatoes, and boiled them down with a bay leaf and some dried thyme.

On each plate, comparing my composition carefully with Gaston's, I leaned a glistening mackerel fillet against a short berm of tomato *concassé*, and the iridescent mackerel against the red tomato sauce, flecked with specks of thyme, was quite beautiful, and . . . well . . .

Mackerel has a strong sea flavor. Not fishy in the way old salmon is fishy, but strong and dark. Despite the complaints of our neighbors in line at the promenade, it was some of the least expensive fish we could remember buying. But it was strong fish, from a strongly flavored region. In the end, nearly half of Monsieur Sauzet's beautiful fish lay in vivid waste on our plates. I ate more than my share in a sort of guilty penance, popping minnows into my mouth until I couldn't anymore.

We were a long way from the slate-gray waves of Minnesota lakes, and the mild, white-fleshed walleyes that hover deep below them. We were a long way from the reserved exchange of Nordic platitudes at Minnesota grocery checkouts. What we had taken on here, what I had agreed to, was taking shape. Bullet-shaped, and beautiful, and tasting like mackerel.

17

Late that night, I sat once again in an isolated bubble of laptop light.

My parents had replied to my earlier email. I hesitated. Leaned back and put my hands behind my head. I suspected what was in the email, and was debating whether it was entirely healthy for me to receive that kind of affirmation from that source on this specific night.

I poured a glass of wine. Opened my parents' email and read it through. A sort of agog communiqué as my mom was capable of writing, full of almost fawning incredulity at what we were managing to do here, full of further questions, and updates from their end. She passed on compliments from their friends, with whom they had shared my email, on our ambition, our parenting, and my letter writing.

"Keep the updates coming!"

I replied, recounting our trip to the goat farm, the roadside meadow of wild fennel, the day-old goat cheese, the contents of Marie's deli case, the spectacular drive through the Luberon, the comical scene at the Abbey of Sénanque.

I reread the email, edited a few turns of phrase, added a short bit about Eva's school, and sent it. It felt queasily good—after such a persistent series of failures to measure up on so many fronts—to be reminded that we were doing something a little bit extraordinary.

I opened the email again and read it through. Then I copied it, and sent the same message to my sister. Had a sip of wine and sent another copy to Mary Jo's sister. And another to her parents. And one to some Francophile friends of ours.

I heard the bed creak, and Mary Jo shuffled out into the hallway.

"What you up to?" she asked in a froggy murmur.

"I sent some emails home. Updates."

"Oh, nice. Did you copy me?"

"No. I didn't. I'll forward them."

"Who?"

"My folks. Your folks. Dee-Dee. The Sweeneys."

"The Sweeneys?"

"Yeah, I thought they—"

"Why the Sweeneys?"

"Well, we have a France thing with them and I thought . . ."

She padded toward me, emerging from the hallway's gloom into the faint computer glow. Squinting beneath a messy blond tousle.

"That's sort of weird."

"I don't know. I suppose it is."

"You're up at midnight emailing the Sweeneys?"

"It seemed like—"

"What did you say?"

"I'll show you the email in the morning. Just breezy kind of . . . you know . . ."

She stood leaning on the table next to me, puffy-eyed, with a frown of concentration that had the disorientation of interrupted sleep in it, but also a troubled air of trying to decode something mysterious.

"You have that look," she said.

"What look?"

"The look when you're hiding something."

"Is that what we're doing right now? In the middle of the—"

"Tell me you're not."

I leaned back into the creaky iron chair and folded my arms.

"How do you have energy for this, five minutes out of a sound sleep?" I asked.

"Stevie, there isn't even anything to report. Maybe . . . *maybe* . . . to the grandparents. But to the Sweeneys?"

"OK, I got an email from my folks and it was very nice, and it felt good. And maybe I needed a little affirmation."

"OK. So why are your cheeks flushed and why do you have that bad-dog look?"

"Because it's embarrassing. Because I made things seem better than they . . . I'll show you in the morning. Can we go to bed?"

"I don't get what's embarrassing."

"Hon, I don't know what I'm doing here. This isn't the trip I expected. It isn't the trip I wanted it to be. It's not the village I wanted it to be. It's not the climate I wanted it to be. It's not even the French food I wanted it to be. We're just here. For six months. And you're asking me to commit to all of this in some big way, and it feels like the wrong place to do that."

She pulled out a chair that clanged on the tile and sat. She looked very tired.

"Stevie, this is France. We're here. This is what you've wanted."

"It isn't *my* France. My France is Paris. It's bookstores and cafés and diesel fumes and Camus and dog shit on the sidewalks. It's me being the best me, in the place where that's the easiest. Nothing like that is happening here."

Her elbows were resting on the table. She made a tent of interlaced fingers and rested her forehead on it.

"I can't just walk up to people and say, 'Let's be friends,'" I said. "It's not in me."

My computer ka-bleeped softly. Quick glance. An email reply from my parents.

"Remember that trip to Greece I took before I came home from Paris?" I asked. "Did I ever tell you about the train?"

"I don't remember," she said. "I don't think so."

"I'm on the train between Patras and Athens. At least I think I am. I've got enough drachmas to buy a pack of cigarettes but not dinner. If I'm headed to Athens, I'm fine. If not, then I'm probably about to circle the Peloponnesian peninsula, and there's nowhere for me to get money.

It's getting dark. I'm starting to panic. All I have to do is ask someone around me if this is the train to Athens.

"I have a dictionary with me. Not English-Greek. It's French-Greek, because, I don't know. Because that's who I am. At the library before I left Paris, I taught myself a little modern Greek. So I approach one of the railway workers and I ask him, in Greek, whether he speaks French."

Mary Jo snorted the way she usually did when confronted with one of my "-isms," as she called them.

"The porter, or whatever he is, doesn't speak French. He asks everyone around us if any of them speak French. No one does. Probably half of them speak English, but that's not an option I'm willing to consider. I am completely willing to be outed as a lost French tourist, willing to sleep on benches, scrounging half-smoked cigarettes from train station platforms—all of that, rather than ask for help in American English."

"This should have been disclosed before we got married," said Mary Jo.

"My point is, I'm twenty-five years older than that kid, but I'm still that kid. That's how much I don't want to be seen as a tourist. Paris showed me what it meant to be . . . to be *naturalized* to another place and it ruined me. It ruined me for any kind of happy bumbling abroad."

She took a deep breath before lifting her head and facing me squarely.

"I don't know how to say this any other way, hon," she said. "But you have to sort of man up."

I stopped looking at my computer and stared at her. She stared back.

"Man up, huh?"

"Yup."

We kept staring each other down. Then, if I remember right, I giggled.

"God, I love you sometimes," I said.

"Sometimes?"

"All the time, except when you are extremely sure of yourself in the middle of the fucking night."

"First of all, I'm not asking you to happy bumble. I'm asking you to do Paris again. With us. Be a part of here. Even just for six months. Maybe this isn't your France. But this is going to be the kids' France.

This is what they're going to remember. If you want them to remember France as the place where Dad was in a pissy mood the whole time because he wasn't in Paris . . ."

"OK," I said. "OK. I'll double-check my balls and make sure they're still there."

"I could check them for you."

"That would be even better."

"But not tonight."

With a gasp, she took in a lungful of air, and let it out in a great, creaking yawn.

"Hon?" I asked.

"Mmm?"

A shuffling in my inbox. The Sweeneys had also replied.

"What . . . What do you want?" I asked.

"Me?" she asked.

"I know what I think you want me to want. What do you want?"

"What do you mean . . . Here?"

"Sure, I guess, but . . . You don't ever just think tactically. Strategically— third act of our lives—where are we headed, according to Mary Jo Hoffman? You don't have to commit to anything . . ."

"You haven't asked me that in a while," she said.

She sat back with her hands folded on the table. Seemed to think about it, but not for long.

"It hasn't really changed," she said. "I want the house with two wings."

18

There was an orchard outside of town. A simple grid of neatly pruned trees, evenly spaced, with the practical beauty of a worn but well-maintained old hand tool.

I took deliberate detours to drive past it, and, each time, I would slow to watch the compact, chalice shapes flicker past the passenger window.

I was driving Mary Jo past it one day, on our way home from a home and garden store called Monsieur Bricolage (roughly translated as "Mr. Putterer"), when I noticed Jean-Luc and Nicole's ancient Renault 4 squatting beside the orchard, and as we approached, there were Jean-Luc and Nicole themselves, puttering, appropriately enough, among the fruit trees.

"Let's stop and say hi," said Mary Jo.

I lifted off the accelerator instinctively, and then coasted through a brief personal purgatory as the turnoff into the orchard approached.

I could sense Mary Jo next to me. Curious, in her faintly mischievous way, about how this would turn out. Comfortable, certainly, in her role as benevolent provocatrice.

"Wait, I've got an idea," I said. "Let's stop and say hi."

Out my window, I could see Jean-Luc and Nicole pause in their work. Jean-Luc looked over his left shoulder, under a tree shaped like a red wineglass, with a two-handled lopper held just above his head. Nicole raised a hand to her forehead to peer in our direction.

The dusty tire arcs of several prior entrances and exits led me across a distressingly narrow concrete bridge spanning the roadside irrigation ditch. I eased onto a dirt trail, scraping and pinging through ten yards or so of brittle vegetation before parking our brand-new Renault behind our neighbor's very old Renault, which straddled the median on tall narrow tires, its tailgate lifted high.

"Bonjour!" I called, squinting into light that seemed to come from everywhere. Mary Jo edged around the car to join me, and when we had brushed through the snarl of weeds next to the trail and begun to wallow through the soft soil of the orchard, a tantalizing summer smell enveloped both of us, something musky, almost skunky, wrapped up in a breath of cool, high-pitched, menthol chill, which is to say that the weeds we had walked through were not exactly weeds, or anyway not exclusively weeds.

As Jean-Luc approached, I fanned my hands toward my face a few times and, with a bit too much enthusiasm, pointed at the tufts of pink flowered stalks I had just walked through.

"*Menthe!*" I said, as if trying to sell him on the delights of his own garden, and he pouted and rocked his hand back and forth in front of him.

"A variety," he said, "of wild mint," and he said it in a way that implied it was not a variety he thought much of, then held out the hand that was not holding his clippers and pumped my hand once and then Mary Jo's, asking, "*Ça va?*" each time, and then Nicole pulled past him and did the same and we all smiled at each other.

Jean-Luc commented on the fine weather, and I marveled at the blue of the cloudless sky, and he said that was because we were enjoying a north wind just now, blowing dry air down from the middle of the country.

In the French you learn in school, the word for bread, *pain,* is impossible to transliterate into English, but a close approximation would be to start saying the English word "pan" and then stop before pronouncing the "n." The word *vin,* for wine, is like saying the word "van" without the "n." It's a breathy nasal sound that you cut off not with a consonant but with your throat and sinuses clamping down and stopping the flow of air. In Midi French those words are pronounced "pang" and "vang." The word Jean-Luc had just pronounced, *vent* (wind), came out sounding like "vong." Which sounds impossibly comical and arbitrary, and, in some ways, it is. For whatever reason, the accent only exists here, fully formed and constantly employed—its own weird indefinable thing, as unlike Parisian French as a West Virginia twang is unlike my own flat Upper Midwest English.

In one of our very first conversations with Jean-Luc, it came out that we were both hunters. I asked him what species he hunted here, and he ticked them off on his fingers: "*La pang, la perdrix, le chevreuil, le lièvre, parfois le sanglier...*"

I was still puzzling over *la pang* several minutes later.

"Was that French?" asked Mary Jo as we climbed the stairs toward a very late breakfast.

"What's *la pang*?" asked Joseph.

And then it came to me that Jean-Luc had not been referring to some new species of exotic Asian waterfowl called "*la pang.*" In his dialect, he had been referring to "*lapang,*" more commonly known in French as *lapin,* or rabbit.

Jean-Luc said Minneapolis was where the big car race was, no? And I said no that was Indianapolis, and he frowned and asked where exactly we lived again, and I gave him my standard explanation, repeated so often that it was like a salesman's patter—that Minneapolis (mee-nay-ah-poh-LEESE) found itself in Minnesota (mee-nay-zoh-TAH) north of Chicago (shee-kah-GO), and shared a border with Canada, and he said, ah so very cold, and I laid my Minnesota trump card, which involved the mention of minus-thirty-degree Celsius winter temperatures.

Nicole said, "Oh!" with something like fright, and Jean-Luc flicked his hand as if shaking it dry and asked, "*Moins trente?*" (minus thirty) and I said yes and therefore here we were, and we all laughed as a car passed on the road, and Jean-Luc and Nicole followed its progress for a short time, still laughing, and then looked back at us.

"Is it yours?" I asked, gesturing toward the rows of trees that were casting cloud-shaped shadows on the rocky, furrowed moonscape.

And as Jean-Luc explained how he had inherited the land some fifteen years ago, and how his sister Suzette had taken the back half of the plot with the cistern for her garden and he and Nicole had taken the front half to plant an orchard, the four of us became one of those impromptu conversational groups that I had seen gathered around town—in front of the church, on benches beside deserted roads, in courtyards and doorways, and in the middle of the street.

I had intended a quick, polite get-to-know-you before we went home to replace light bulbs.

But Jean-Luc's arms were crossed over the pruning shears he held to his chest, and Nicole was leaning on her rake, one ankle propped in front of the other, specks of leaf clinging to the light sheen of sweat on her shins and muscular calves. Jean-Luc did most of the holding forth, with Nicole interjecting wry commentary in bursts of the fastest French we had heard yet.

Jean-Luc was talking about a fig tree his brother had once owned in the hills behind town that made the sweetest, most perfumed figs he had ever eaten, and he had tried to *bouturer* the tree, and when I asked what *bouturer* meant, he said it was when you took a *bouture* from an existing tree, and when I asked what a *bouture* was, he said, "Ah," and described what we would call a "cutting" in English, and he was off onto which trees could be transplanted by cuttings, and which couldn't, and which trees were cloned and which weren't, and which trees grew better grafted onto the rootstock of still other trees, as for example, almond trees, which were grafted onto a species of peach for non-limestone soil, and onto a plum for limestone soil.

In the end, he lamented, the *bouture* of that fig tree never did produce the kind of fruit in his orchard that the original had produced. He and Nicole went back and forth for a while about whether that had to do with the nature of the cutting itself, or, more likely, to do with the setting—the original tree growing in the rocks up in the hills and the transplanted tree growing in the soil of the plain. And as they talked, I would wedge my way into the brief and infrequent pauses in their conversation to translate for Mary Jo.

The soil of the orchard was the same color as the walls of our house, with stones and dried clods scattered among the hillocks. Below some of the trees lay fallen fruit, some fresh and plump, some bruised and misshapen, others burst and pulpy or half-eaten and browning.

I glanced back at our vehicles—ours looking brand-new and almost offensively shiny beside the dull putty color of theirs—and prepared my exit lines so we could leave these people, who couldn't possibly care about how cold it was in Minneapolis, in peace.

Except that Jean-Luc now announced that it was the end of apricot season, and there were a few left, and before I had time to take our leave, he was leading us on a short diagonal field trip across several rows, wading through the loose soil like beach sand, ducking under branches, edging around fallen fruit, where wasps fed at neat boreholes, their abdomens pulsing.

We arrived at a short-trunked tree with bark like wrinkled loose skin, and I don't know what Jean-Luc imagined were "a few apricots left," but inside the crown of leaves were half a dozen branches encrusted with skeins of marigold-colored fruit the size of hen's eggs.

They were so bright and frank that it was a peculiar shock to catch sight of them, as if a tree had been secretly strung with yellow-orange lights, and as I peered into the branches, someone suddenly flipped the switch.

"What will you do with them all?" I asked.

And Nicole, in French so fast that I succeeded only in pulling fragments of it into coherence, looked up at me through her thick-framed rectangular glasses, and talked, as far as I could tell, about preserves in a syrup, and jam, and apricot tarts.

But mostly, she said, apricots were to be eaten *comme ça*. As is.

Jean-Luc twisted two free for Mary Jo and me, and another two for Nicole and himself. The fruit was warm and small, with a shallow lengthwise suture in its velvet skin. I watched Jean-Luc take a bite and make a tea-sipping sound, and then I sank my teeth into the first apricot of my life not bought in a grocery store. It gave the insides of my lips a drying feeling of astringency before the melting softness of the flesh registered in my brain, and as I was processing that softness, there was a violent wringing at the hinge of my jaw as my salivary glands tried to keep up with sweet, tartly floral juice running down the sides of my tongue. My teeth scraped against the pit, and I had to wipe my wet lips on the sleeve of my shirt.

Something of the effect that the experience was having on me must have registered in my expression because Jean-Luc, eating merely one of a lifetime of apricots, smiled with juice-wet lips beneath his neat mustache and leaned toward Nicole, pointing at me with the hand that held his apricot.

"He is regaling himself," he said.

And Nicole said, "*Ça se voit*," which is a French expression I happen to love because it can't be said the same way in a language that doesn't make such extensive use of reflexive verbs. It means something like "evidently," or "clearly," but the direct translation is "That sees itself," as in, "That is so obvious it doesn't take eyes to see it."

I turned to Mary Jo, who was cupping a free hand under her dripping chin.

I had had good fruit before. We make good apples in Minnesota, and the sun still warms strawberries there, and I have eaten pears in my life that wept syrup onto my forearm.

But I had come to think of apricots as something I would have to take everybody's word for. They were either hard-meated little nuts, or they disintegrated into overripe palmfuls of mash, or they were mealy with an off-putting bitterness. I thought of them as a virtuous gesture— a collection of nutrients and fiber that I probably ought to eat more of, as part of a balanced diet.

Whatever was in my hand just now, though, was the color of a sunrise, and had a living gleam to its skin.

It was, simply, ripe. In the story of humankind, this was an unremarkable event. Fruit was supposed to do this. It was simply a matter—made incomprehensibly circuitous and difficult by contemporary life—of being nearby when it happened.

Whatever Jean-Luc read in my face or my body language, he appeared to switch gears at this point, and we were no longer just passing the time of day.

He now took us on a tour of the orchard, introducing the trees to us one by one, and we followed, still slurping at our apricots, not passing admiringly by at ninety kilometers per hour, but here inside the grid of trees, making footprints in the turned-over soil.

With the informal air that comes from talking while eating, Jean-

Luc gave us the name of each tree: peach, nectarine, apricot, cherry, plum, pear, apple, fig, persimmon, pomegranate, quince.

There were five rows, with six trees in each row.

Jean-Luc already knew the plot of the story he was telling us, but I was in the middle of my first reading, with surprises on every page. Plums like yellow tulip buds were clustered along branches in groups of ten or fifteen. An espaliered grapevine looked crucified, head hung, arms extended, black grapes hanging heavy and limp from thick stems. There was a shaggy snowball of a shrub, which I took to be decorative, until I got close enough to see that its interior was thick with the crab apple–sized swellings of immature pomegranates.

There is an expression in French, *faire rêver*, which means literally to "make one dream," but which carries with it a not entirely translatable baggage of other associations having to do with fantasy, enchantment, delight, and longing. To a Minnesota native, raised on the idea that orchards mean apples, and if you want to get crazy, maybe pears and sour cherries, the fruit trees on Jean-Luc's half acre made one dream.

As we wandered back and forth, Jean-Luc evoked, without ever putting it into explicit words, an entire unfolding fruit season that was several calendar seasons long. He pointed to the cherry that was now bare, and the apricot that was giving its last, and the peaches and nectarines that were reaching prime, and the figs that were on the cusp of it, and the apples and pears that would follow, and the quince that would follow that, and, sometime as late possibly as December, the persimmons that would still be on the tree, like round orange Christmas ornaments, when all the rest of the leaves of the orchard had fallen.

He talked about his trees like relatives, and like investments, and like a job. They were both work and pleasure. They took his time, and they gave back. It resembled a specific kind of integrated life that I had sometimes let myself imagine, where almost everything had at least two purposes and life folded in on itself in some satisfying and artful way. Where work was also exercise. Where an orchard was an annuity that paid off seasonally. Where trees were puzzles to be solved, and also sculptures that told of your skill, and givers of sensual gifts.

We had made the full circuit, plucking one nectarine each, and were standing back where we had begun what felt like a very long time ago. Nicole tossed her apricot pit, gnawed and glistening, onto the soil in front of us. I bit into my nectarine, and sucked at the bite I had taken, though it was not enough, and juice spilled down the ladder of my fingers and dripped on the ground.

I made an effort to wrap my French around what I thought about his orchard, and Jean-Luc nodded.

"*On aime les fruits,*" he said. (We like fruit.) Simple enough, but something about the statement made me want to give him a hug as he stood, slurping a nectarine pit clean, there in his orchard, planted not as a status object or a lifestyle signifier, but because he and his wife liked fruit.

When he was done, he took one final tour, peering into half a dozen trees, feeling the fruit, and gradually picking us a mixed armload before sending us on our way, a little dazed, with the feeling that we had just been given a brief tour of Eden and then been politely expelled because the owner had some pruning to do.

"Your daughter's foot," said Jean-Luc as we were loading the car. "It goes better?"

Eva had not lost her limp, and I tilted my open hand in front of me. "The same," I said.

He looked pensive for a moment, and then appeared to let go of whatever thought had occurred to him.

We left in possession of a couple pounds of yellow nectarines, white peaches, and purple plums, and with the beginnings of an idea of how one part of a year went by here. I backed out of the orchard onto the Rue de l'Égalité feeling that I had found a holder of some important keys— a concierge of sorts, whose services could be had for time spent in conversation.

19

The following Sunday morning, there was a knock on our door—the first time anyone had knocked on our door since we had arrived—and there were Jean-Luc and Nicole, smiling like the couple who bring new neighbors a plate of cookies, except that the foil-wrapped package in Nicole's hands was not a plate of cookies, but a tart—an apricot tart to be exact, because "Steve had the air of liking them."

It was Sunday, which meant that nothing would be open past about noon, and it seemed a kind of sin to accompany a homemade apricot tart, fresh from the orchard down the road, with a dinner of—based on the ingredients in our pantry and refrigerator—lowfat milk, Roquefort with no bread, spaghetti, butter, Spanish peanuts, and gummy candies.

I made it to Marie's just before she closed, and began looking around, and it was suddenly clear that without a recipe from Gaston waiting for me at home, I didn't have whatever it took to do whatever one did with dried chickpeas or leeks or eggplants, before cooking them in whatever way one cooked them.

I held out a monstrous, ivory-stemmed Swiss chard, asking, "This is what, in French?" It was the size of one of those palm fronds Cleopatra's eunuchs used to fan her with.

"*Une blette,*" Marie informed me.

She went on to describe how to prepare it so unhesitatingly that it was as if the method of cooking were an undifferentiated part of the name itself. One separated the leaf from the stem, chopping the stem into morsels and slicing the leaves *en chiffonade,* before blanching. She recommended finishing the dish, a little airily I thought, with *une petite béchamel.*

The kid with the spiked hair in the produce aisle at Cub Foods has never once recommended a béchamel with the Swiss chard he's stacking under the misting machines, and I assume that is because his béchamel never turns out that well, either.

In optimistic America, we like to talk about all the ways a food might be prepared. We don't like the idea of depriving any food of its right to self-actualization. "Of course you can grow up to be a dessert someday," we tell our baby beets.

In France, they're like, "Listen, we've done this. Just blanch your Swiss chard with the rib cut into sections and serve it with a nice bécha-mel. No, listen. It's for the best. We've tried all the other ways."

I placed my *blette* back, not willing to concede that I didn't know what went into a béchamel sauce.

Aware that she was closing, I hurried around the store—passing most of the basic elements of French home cooking laid out like an invi-tation I was unable to accept.

Marie followed my meandering through her store, wondering, I'm sure, when Monsieur was going to stop walking in circles.

In the end, I set a few tomatoes, a head of garlic, some fresh basil, and a box of penne on her countertop—about as French as Luciano Pavarotti—requested some Brie, and fumbled through the bills in my wallet for something less than a fifty-euro note.

I explained that I would be making dinner tonight to commemorate a beautiful *tarte aux abricots* from our neighbors, and asked Marie what she would be doing after she closed.

She and her family had lunch together every Sunday, across the street at her parents' home, where she also lived with her husband and sons.

"Every Sunday?"

"*Eh oui,*" she said, counting my change into my palm. "Four genera-tions."

There was a package of sorts, something cylindrical wrapped in white paper, sitting on the counter behind her. I asked what it was.

"From the abattoir," she said. "Papa adores rabbit."

She glanced out the window to her right, and I had to overcome my sense that she would prefer anything in the world just now to more of my dawdling.

"Is it still possible to order a rabbit?" I asked.

"Of course," she said. "When would you like it?"

"Whenever it would be convenient," I said. Marie wrote my order on a scrap of paper, and said it would be next week sometime.

Halfway home, I discovered that in my scatterbrained haste, I had forgotten to buy a baguette for our Brie. I turned around and ran back to Marie's, which was closed and locked, with all the lights extinguished.

I stood, breathing hard, fogging the glass door as I peered in, wondering without much hope whether she might still be somewhere inside. Behind me, I heard a soft hubbub of voices, and saw that the tall, arched, plank door in front of her parents' house had been left ajar. I walked over, and peeked through.

Behind the door was a walled courtyard, shaded by trees, and arranged with an elegant carelessness. In the center of the courtyard, a long banquet-style table was surrounded by, I guessed, twelve or fifteen smartly but informally dressed members of Marie's extended family, though I couldn't see all of them through my narrow peephole.

The table was set, with baguettes laid at intervals, several pitchers of water, glasses more or less full of a golden white wine, and more uncorked bottles at the ready.

Marie's mother crossed into view with a tureen, which moved from place to place around the table as adults and children all dipped the ladle and served themselves soup in wide, low bowls, while the conversation, or rather conversations, lapped in fluent waves along the table's shores.

This would be the first course of several, which, based on the few times I had been invited into someone's home for a proper French meal, would extend through much of the rest of the afternoon, in the tremulous light below the moving trees.

I stepped back from the door for fear of catching someone's eye, and took in the empty Sunday streets and the mute, mismatched, sun-faded façades, which were the measures I had thus far used to arrive at my judgment about what Autignac had to offer.

I had been outside, just as Mary Jo had said—walking or driving past the exterior of everything, with the single exception of Jean-Luc and Nicole's orchard.

Here was another glimpse of the inside. And this inside—in the vineyards and fields around town, and behind the walls that lined the village streets—appeared to me to have everything to do with the culture, the preparation, and the sharing of food and wine.

20

I was paging through a new book, in the middle of a hot and lazy afternoon, as Mary Jo arranged some of Jean-Luc and Nicole's fruit on a sheet of white tagboard below her camera and tripod, and the kids alternately cooled off in the pool, then dried off on lounge chairs in the sun.

I had found my book, called *Je Sais Cuisiner,* in the magazine section of our local Intermarché. It was the French equivalent of America's *Joy of Cooking.* The title translates as "I Know How to Cook."

Ginette Mathiot wrote the book at age twenty-five as a response to the domination of French cuisine by male chefs in restaurants, rather than by home cooks in kitchens. The latter, in reliably sexist France, were primarily wives and mothers, whose cumulative body of work could be said to match or exceed, in scope and magnificence, the glory work of haute cuisine. The author of *Je Sais Cuisiner* intended her book, and its hundreds of foundational recipes, used daily throughout France, as a self-evident argument to this effect.

The squat, yellow and purple hardcover was fat enough to stand on its own, and I was finding both its comprehensiveness and its impersonal style disconcerting. Some recipes included two or three subreferences to other building-block preparations that one was expected either to know already, or to look up, not by page number, but by referring to the recipe number, of which there were just over two thousand.

I was paging back and forth, trying to put together some idea of how to make *Pommes Dauphine,* when the most surprising noise suddenly filled the main floor of our house.

Our phone was ringing.

The woman on the other end spoke with a reassuring northern accent, and asked me whether we were "the Americans."

I said I believed so, and she said that she loved Americans and didn't get to see many around here, and would we interest ourselves in coming to visit her at her château the next afternoon. Château Grézan, it was called, just across the highway. The children would love to see a castle, would they not?

I pulled the phone away from my ear to ask Mary Jo what she thought, and decided I could not possibly summarize with sufficient brevity what had happened over the previous two minutes.

I put the phone back to my ear. "What time?" I asked.

We were all sitting in the kitchen of Château Grézan while its proprietress and chatelaine, Marie-France, sliced some beautifully marbled salami onto a very old-looking cutting board with a very old-looking knife.

We had just spent two hours as her guests and her audience. The conversation had not just been constant but relentless—a torrent of mixed French and English, interrupted by some minimal translation, as we toured the château itself, learned that the site had been a Roman villa occupied by a centurion before becoming a commandery of the Knights Templar somewhere around the year 1300, and was later refurbished in a neo-medieval style, using Carcassonne as a model, with turrets and crenellated battlements enclosing the central manor house, along with feudal outbuildings and a very non-medieval, Louis XIV garden of high Renaissance formality, now showing signs of neglect.

Marie-France was a Lanson, of the Lanson Champagne House. She had arrived here by marriage, and stayed after her divorce, which left her ex-husband with the vineyards and her with the château. She loved sacred and classical music, loved the history of the site, loved the artwork she had collected, and loved, or had loved, her mazelike garden, and her rectangular pool, now half-filled with greenish water.

Her circumstances might have come across as irresistibly romantic, had not an air of sadness hung over most of the day. Beyond our first impression of being welcomed, with an ecstatic sort of hospitality, by minor royalty; beyond Joseph's initial stupefaction at finding himself inside the stone parapets of a quite convincingly real castle; beyond the feast of photogenic vistas and details offering themselves up for photographs (which Mary Jo consumed hungrily; Eva, perfunctorily)—beyond all of this, what lingered was our hostess's talkativeness, which expressed itself more and more, as the afternoon wore on, as something resembling neediness. A desperation for company—and not just company, but company who appreciated her artwork, and could talk about classical music, and knew the names Viollet-le-Duc and Le Nôtre. She was lonely. She said as much. She had loved her big townhouse in Autignac, where she crossed paths with people on the street on her way to the bakery and the grocery store.

She was a northerner, like us. Regally tall, she had to dip her head, as did we, to fit through some of her doorways, which had been built with low-slung Mediterranean bodies in mind, not Vikings or Normans descending from the polar regions. The five of us fit snugly in a kitchen designed to accommodate a staff.

We nibbled salami, and sipped red wine. The salami, she said, came from Monsieur Congnard's in Laurens, the best butcher in the area. We would have to visit him.

She asked what had prompted us to settle here, of all places, and we explained the somewhat intentional randomness and lack of planning behind the initial vision. We said we nevertheless hoped to become a little part of the village before we left.

And here she smiled at us, with a smile so sad that I wished, despite my exhaustion at absorbing and translating her patter all afternoon, that I could somehow console her. She leaned against the counter of her dimly lit stone kitchen, holding a glass of wine made, no doubt, by her ex-husband.

She said that she had been here most of her adult life, had made wine here, had made friends, had put down roots, and yet, she would never really belong. She might mimic royalty in her castle surrounded by grapevines, but around here, the true royalty had peasant pedigrees that could be traced back to the Middle Ages. As far as her neighbors were concerned, she was, and always would be, from somewhere else.

"*Je suis une estrangère,*" she said, using the older, Occitan word for *étrangère,* meaning "foreigner," or "someone who doesn't live in the same village." It was a desolate-sounding word, coming from her just then.

"No," she said, without judgment, but with heavy resignation, "you will never be accepted here."

PART II

21

I got my first glimpse of Jean-Luc's garage one evening after a family walk in the vineyards behind the village. One of the village exits was a slender country highway leading north, past a twenty-foot iron crucifix that watched over the town, and eventually into the hills that formed the northern horizon.

We had been gathering, as we did on most family walks, and were returning with handfuls—and in my case armfuls—of the natural world to be posed and arranged in front of Mary Jo's camera. Joe had discovered a small treasure fixed to the trunk of a vine—the amber husk of an insect that had molted—about which he was theorizing to a plainly uninterested Eva, halting beside him.

We were not a family who simply went for a walk and came home. We stopped at piles of feathers, gathered interesting leaves, grasses, seed heads, insects, tufts of fur, and occasionally skeletons, and brought them home with us, and although we had made peace with where this placed us on the bell curve of normal family behavior, not everyone seeing us walking toward them, carrying dead animals, messy bundles of random stems, or a turtle skull, would feel entirely at ease.

Jean-Luc proved one exception.

We turned the corner onto Avenue de la Liberté, and there he was beside his tractor.

"Jean-Luc!" called Mary Jo.

"Oh! Marie-zho!" he called back.

Mary Jo had snipped a lethally thorned branch from a roadside shrub, laden with blue fruits like swollen blueberries, which she now held gingerly out to him.

"*Qu'est-ce que c'est?*" (What's this?), she asked, and Jean-Luc, with barely a glance, pronounced them *prunelles*.

"You found them where?" he asked.

We pointed.

"Past the Christ?" he asked, and we said no, on the village side of the Christ, and then, as if this were the usual way one greeted neighbors in the middle of the street, he tipped his head back, looking over my arm-load through his bifocals, and began naming the plants I was cradling, ending by pointing to several heads of Queen Anne's lace, and referring to them as *carottes sauvages*. Wild carrots.

Then he paused and made a strange gesture. He held his hands out below his face as if propping a sun reflector under his chin, closed his eyes, and raised his face to the sky. How was it, he wondered, that we were not at the beach with all the English, working on our *bronzage* (tan), but were instead on the street in Autignac asking Jean-Luc about *prunelles*?

We tried to convey to him, in French, the gist of Mary Jo's STILL project, the heart of which was something called a blog.

He absorbed this, and then recommended that I try one of the *prunelles*. I bit one in half and gave it a chew before its potent astringency essentially shut down the workings of my mouth and I winced and spit the morsel out.

Jean-Luc was already laughing at his little joke. "Eeh-hee!" he sang through his neat mustache as I tried, like the guy who has taken a fastball to the lower midsection, to smile it off.

Late in the fall, he told us, when the fruits had sweetened as much as they ever would, they could be harvested and made into a liqueur. And that liqueur "would make you forget, Steve, that you hadn't wanted to eat them all summer!"

"Joe-Joe, show Jean-Luc your bug," said Mary Jo, and Joseph, master of his particular brand of passive resistance, did not answer, and did not open his hand, until Jean-Luc crouched to his level and asked what he had found.

Joseph, shyly, hesitantly, held out the translucent exoskeleton, and

Jean-Luc made much of it, in a way that implied familiarity with young boys and their tough-tender needs. All of the cicadas (*cigales*) singing around us—did Joseph hear them? Joseph nodded, and Jean-Luc said that they all climbed out of the ground like this one had, and waited on vines or trees before they broke free and flew away as adults.

"Unless," he said, "the partridges eat them first. Then we eat the cicadas when we eat the partridges in the fall!" And here he showed himself, once again, to be perhaps the biggest living fan of his own jokes.

We trundled up the stairs with our burdens. I was carefully piling my sheaf of thorny stems in a far corner when Jean-Luc called from our open front door, asking me to redescend, if I had a little minute.

He led me next door, through the galvanized doorway into his garage.

It was dim and a little dusty inside. Agricultural hand tools ranging from well used to ancient hung from the walls, and there was an empty tractor-sized space in front of us. Beyond that, a fiberglass roof sheltered piles of woven sacks, full, I guessed, of fertilizer and chemicals. There was a faint whiff of diesel fuel, and phosphorous, and the vaguely chemical smell that hovers in garden and landscape shops.

This, he explained, was where they kept the goat, the cow, the horse, the chickens, and the ducks, here in the house where he had been born.

Which meant that this had been the *basse-cour*, the family barn, barnyard, and manger that is such a part of French rural, and to some extent French culinary, mythology. I felt an unexpected wave of rising hairs at the back of my neck.

As he led me toward a wooden door set into one of the walls, he described one legendary flood that brought water into the garage up to the belly of the mare standing under that courtyard roof, who waited, bewildered, for the tide to ebb as manure floated on the surface around her, and Jean-Luc's father stood with her, holding her bridle through the entire night, so the horse wouldn't panic and do herself harm.

He opened a low door in the wall to our left and tugged a pull-chain, which threw yellowish shadows around the interior of a combination root cellar and wine *cave*.

"*Jean-Luc, L'Apothicaire*," he said with a flourish, and a little self-mockery.

The shelves of his apothecary were lined with glass jars and pots, each with a handwritten label affixed to its side. Canned tomatoes, cherries, and peaches. Confitures of figs, strawberries, apricots, and watermelon, all in rows of Le Parfait canning jars with glass lids and oxidized wire hasps, and those unmistakable orange rubber gaskets. Jars like those I had bought back home, to store nuts, seeds, tea, and coffee, except that now those felt like make-believe. Like impersonations of these soldiers standing at attention in the dark, so usefully sober and real.

There were bottles of wine lying on their sides, and a gallon glass jug with the tantalizing label "Poire 2003" taped to its shoulder. There were other bottles full of colored liquids that might well belong in an apothecary—mint, verbena, walnut. Something called Quinquina. Something called Suze. He hunched, moving his hand over the necks, and tipping several backward to check their labels.

"Voilà," he said, and lifted a repurposed wine bottle labeled "Prunelle." He pulled the cork, and invited me to smell. There was an alcoholic rush from the neck of the bottle, followed by an explosion of earthy cherry.

"Liqueur de Prunelle," he said, and watched my face as if hoping to confirm something.

"How does one . . ." I began.

"There is not much left," he said. "We will have to make some more this fall," and I chewed on that word "we."

"Steve," he said as he closed the gate to his private playground. He hesitated. "I don't want to appear indiscreet."

"Not at all," I said.

"The foot of Eva," he said, and offered a single limping step in imitation of her gait. "You have tried everything . . . ?"

"Yes."

"I ask you because there is a place in the hills. In the Aveyron. I think that it could do no harm." He held up a hand: "Personally, I don't say I believe or don't believe. But it is said that the waters there . . . Eva, I recognize she does not have a malady . . . but the waters there are said to heal maladies of the skin, and I say to myself—"

"Waters," I said. "Like, holy water?"

"Who knows?" he said. "If it works, who is to say that it is the work of . . . Who is to say that there is not some mineral, something chemical that happens underground in this place? Nature, she contains more mysteries than we poor humans . . . Anyway, I ask myself—if it could do no harm, and could possibly do some good . . . ?"

"Yes, of course," I said. "Why not?"

"Nicole and I would drive with you. We could perhaps take with us a little *pique-nique.*"

And because the southern accent pronounces most vowels that are silent in other regions, the word came out not as I had been taught, "peek-neek," but, rather, as "peeka-neeka."

"That would give us pleasure," I said. "What is the name of the place?"

"Sang-meng," he said.

"Sang . . ."

"Meng. Sang-meng."

"Sang-Meng?"

He nodded. "Sang-Meng."

"One spells that how?" I asked.

And he spelled it for me: S-a-i-n-t. Hyphen. M-é-e-n. "Sang-Meng."

22

Marie was replenishing produce displays from boxes scattered on the floor.

She raised a fistful of red potatoes in greeting. "He arrived this morning!" she called, and thrust a chin toward the sales counter, where her mother, on cue, lifted a two-foot-long wrap of butcher paper, and set it between us.

"Maman knows everything on the rabbits," said Marie, and left me in Maman's delicate guiding hands. Maman unwrapped the rabbit from the butcher paper, and there he lay, next to the cash register.

"*Il est beau,*" I said. (He is handsome.)

"*Oh, oui, il est beau,*" said Maman, as if this were self-evident, although I could imagine those who might quibble with the morning-after, serial-murder-scene quality of the handsomeness of the rabbit. The entirely skinned body lay on its side, stretched to its full length, with a few spots of blood dappling the bright white butcher paper. One eye bulged up at us with an outraged expression I found understandable.

Maman lost no time, apparently believing, based on no evidence, that I would not only absorb an entire recipe and butchering lesson given in French, but retain both until dinnertime.

I was instructed to remove the liver and the kidneys, and then the lungs and the heart, which were there, yes there, in the chest.

"You take out the eyes, and pull out *le petit nerf là*" (the little nerve there—more likely the trachea, located in the pink gap made by the slit throat).

At this point I asked, "You keep the head?"

Oh, oui, you keep the head, and even Marie, distracted and moving about, chimed in that *oh, oui,* you keep the head because, among other things, "*les cervelles sont tres bonnes*" (the brains are very tasty).

Maman continued. What she had done just last night, because her husband adored rabbit, was to cut the rabbit in two, between the rib cage and the tenderloins, and . . .

"You have kitchen shears?"

She looked at me skeptically through thick lenses. I believed I had kitchen shears.

"*Bon,* you cut the rabbit in half, and . . . You have a *cocotte*?"

I did not have a *cocotte* nor was I entirely sure what one was. I mumbled an evasive "*Oui.*"

Bon, you cut the rabbit in two, and for a simple recipe like this, you use the back half because these are the best parts of the rabbit.

You put a little oil in the *cocotte,* and you brown—

"Olive oil?" I asked.

"Olive oil. Of course, olive oil."

She managed somehow to pair a wrenlike delicacy with absolute personal authority.

"You salt and pepper the rabbit and brown the back half until it is golden all over, and then set it aside." Quick glance to see if her student was paying attention.

"In the pan, you make sweat your shallots, and you deglaze with . . . You have white wine?"

I had white wine.

"You deglaze with . . . Is it dry?"

It was dry.

"You deglaze with *vin blanc sec,* you add your stock, you return the rabbit to the *cocotte* and, partially covered, you cook it slowly on the stovetop until it is done. Voilà."

And with no further explanation, including what "done" meant, she rewrapped the rabbit, and sent me on my way.

I bought a baguette and a supplemental bottle of white wine at the bakery—Domaine Balliccioni, as had become our custom. On my way home, I crossed paths with Nicole and introduced her to my *lapin.* "Ah—the wine of André," she said of the bottle I was carrying.

"We love it," I said.

She was on her way to the bakery herself, and wished me bon appétit as we parted, and *bon courage* with my *lapang.*

Late that afternoon, I took the rabbit back out of the refrigerator and unwrapped it. Beside me, Joe spent a brief but fun-packed time poking the bluish, tender tongue, which dangled out of the side of its mouth with an air of total defeat.

I felt a surge of comradely affinity with it, lying there on its white butcher paper, with nothing left to hide.

Among Maman's many unwarranted generosities that morning had been the presumption that across from her stood enough of a cook to make do with her simple preparation, one that required a certain authority at the stove—a feel for salting and seasoning, for doneness, for balancing a sauce with such meager tools as oil, wine, stock, and know-how.

I could still hear Maman's voice, imperative and unsentimental, pronouncing the word *cocotte* with two and a half syllables—cuh-CAUGHT-uh—as my gaze strayed across the room toward the iPad, which was humming some Paul Desmond, rather seductively, and which was, I knew, ripe with an entire internet's worth of romantically complicated recipes.

The recipe I found, and its reduction sauce, called for seven tablespoons of French mustard, among quite a number of other things, and this required a trip to the *tabac,* which had mustard but not capers, leading to a trip to Intermarché, and so it was already getting on toward dinnertime when I took kitchen shears in hand, and cut the rabbit in half.

"Hey," said Mary Jo at the dining room table.

"Hey yourself."

She looked up from her laptop. "Do you know what *prunelles* are in English?"

Eva and Joe were at the other end of the table, making a mostly contained mess with a set of watercolors.

"They're sloe berries. Like in sloe gin. I bet that drink Jean-Luc showed you was sloe gin."

"Around here we say Liqueur de Prunelles, thank you very much."

I was gradually creating a hybrid rabbit recipe, consisting of the instructions from this morning that I could remember, which were spotty, and the elaborate sauce from the recipe I'd found online. One thing was clear, however. We emphatically did not have a *cocotte* (a Dutch oven, per Google). We had two-handled pots of insubstantial steel, made for boiling pasta water, and I had already scorched my rabbit's backside.

"Jean-Luc was right," called Mary Jo. "Queen Anne's lace is in the carrot family. Who knew?"

"When's dinner?" asked Eva, breaking a baguette in half and reaching into the middle.

"Soon," I said.

"What does soon mean?"

"It means in a relatively short amount of time."

"Can I go check on my ant nests?" asked Joe.

"Eva, wait for dinner," I said.

I tried turning the rabbit, and a thready chunk of thigh pulled free and remained stuck to the pot.

"Can I?" asked Joe.

"I don't know, monkey. I guess so," said Mary Jo.

"Hey," I said. "Dinner will be ready soon."

"Soon," Eva said.

Joe bolted down the stairs and out the door.

I removed the rabbit, which had not turned "golden all over" but something more like "cigarettes stubbed out here and there."

The dry white wine exploded into droplets and steam at the first touch of the pan, and the stock was not stock because I couldn't find any stock, but was instead a powdered *fond de volailles* (chicken bouillon), dissolved in hot water, and I remembered as soon as I poured it in that I had not deglazed the pan. Instead I scraped a patch of blackened rabbit chips partially free from the bottom of the pan with a wooden spoon that appeared to have been gnawed by one or possibly several small dogs.

While the rabbit braised, I poured a glass of the remaining white wine for Mary Jo, who had lit candles on the table, as part of her nightly transition from the demands of the day to the pleasures of the evening. She had sliced the baguette with a dull, non-serrated knife that had deformed each slice into a little blond amoeba. "Are we getting close?" asked Mary Jo, buttering one of the amoebae.

"Yup," I said.

The sink had filled with pots by now, and I had to wash one to make the sauce. Then it occurred to me that in my apprehensive focus on the rabbit, I had not prepared anything to accompany it, and I said I would be right back, then literally ran to the *tabac* for a box of rice.

The sauce was reducing, and I had prodded the rabbit several times, not knowing how properly cooked rabbit should feel and wondering how it ought to compare to the flesh at the base of my thumb. I was sweating from the heat of the kitchen, from my sprint to and from the store, and from my enervated bustling around the kitchen.

Mary Jo had posted her photo for the day, and was writing in her journal in the candlelight, her wineglass empty. Beside her were two hollowed-out baguette halves. Eva had retired to the couch, from which location came the opening theme song to *Friends*.

"I'd feel better if Joe were home," said Mary Jo.

The rice was done. The sauce was done. The rabbit was, I had to believe, done.

"Do you mind checking on him?" she asked.

"Me?" I asked.

"I'd feel better," she said.

"You're concerned about his well-being?"

"Yes."

"Out there on the mean streets of Autignac?"

"Please?"

I found Joe sitting on his heels, staring at the ground, rapt.

"Joe, it's time for dinner."

He employed his fine-tuned passive-resistance technique by ignoring me completely.

"Alright, dude. Time to go."

As we walked home in the near-dark, I received a blow-by-blow reconstruction of the Great Ant Nest War he had provoked by repeatedly dropping ants from one nest onto the enemy from above, and watching them swarm as they sorted things out.

I set the table, refreshed the wine, scooped the rice into a bowl, and improvised a platter out of a rectangular Pyrex baking dish, in which the back half of the rabbit, which I had not pieced up as I now realized I should have, lay crookedly on one hip. It was still not golden all over, but a glazed and sickly brass color from the complicated sauce. I placed it on the table.

"That looks like a Chihuahua," Eva announced, and served herself some rice.

I pulled off the two legs with a crackling sound of hip sockets separating, and recognized that, from a certain perspective, I might appear to be dismembering the Chihuahua, after first cooking him in a mustard and caper sauce.

The meat had cooled during my rescue operation to the ant battlefield, and I hadn't wanted to reheat it for fear of overcooking what I now discovered was still slightly underdone rabbit. No one, with the exception of the chef, was willing to try more than a single tentative bite. Marie's handsome rabbit ended up as the neglected accompaniment to an extremely late, room-temperature dinner of white rice.

I felt, as I frequently do on such occasions, a stirring of resentment at the family's reception of a meal that had required so much effort. Afterward, at the sink, as I crashed my way through the endless dirty dishes my chosen recipe had created, I rehearsed a few short speeches for my ungrateful family, which I would never deliver.

Scraping rice into the wastebasket, I encountered the rabbit's supposedly tasty head, severed and staring up at me.

When I had finished, I took some consolation in blaming the precarious stack of secondhand kitchen tools drying on the counter for the evening's fiasco.

23

The next morning, I was still unpacking my grocery bag, which happened to contain a new frying pan, cutting board, knives, and spoon, when the doorbell rang.

I leaned out the front hallway window to see the salt-and-pepper helmet of Jean-Luc's hair below me. Mary Jo joined me for the conversation, as, inadvertently, did any number of our neighbors with open windows.

Jean-Luc was delivering some materials to the winery he was associated with. "It's the wine that you like," he said. "That they sell at the bakery." He asked, with a solicitousness that sounded as if he feared he might be imposing, whether we might join him.

Back inside, Eva and Joe, feeling that their worlds had been enlarged enough in recent days, chose a morning in the pool over a morning at a winery.

Mary Jo and I followed Jean-Luc's narrow tractor in a slow procession through town, Jean-Luc sitting erect in his seat, his two-wheeled trailer bouncing comically from one tire to the other like a kid who has to go to the bathroom.

"Why is he being so nice to us?" I asked Mary Jo.

"Maybe he likes us," she said.

"Impossible," I said.

Eventually, Jean-Luc reached out his window and patted the air with his left hand where a sign saying "Domaine Balliccioni" hung beside an iron gate.

Inside the gate, a curved flight of stone steps led to an elegant two-story house, above a street-level courtyard that was a very non-playful, non-residential working agricultural operation.

Jean-Luc, in his tidy blue laborer's jumpsuit, led us across the courtyard, through one of the twenty-foot-tall bay doors beneath the house, and down an aisle between rows of vats, where red, corrugated hoses snaked around and over each other, linked together by brass couplings. I remember feeling that here was one of the holy places in a country where wine was a religion, and I did not belong.

Out came a solidly built, sixty-something André Balliccioni, in a faded polo shirt, knee-high gum boots, and olive cargo pants, who strode up to us with a smile, shook Jean-Luc's hand then mine, kissed Mary Jo on each cheek, and led us immediately into the street, where he delivered a detailed sermon on the workings of a rumbling machine parked outside his gate, which was in the process of filtering most of his prior year's vintage of red wine.

"For a long time, we didn't filter our wines," he said with his hand on my shoulder, leading us back across the courtyard toward the roomful of vats. "But now we are no longer living like *hippies,* in the prehistory."

He collected four stubby wineglasses from above a porcelain sink, turned a faucet handle on a vat of wine, and half-filled each glass before handing them around.

"See?" he asked, swirling his glass and holding it to the light. "How clear?"

He took a sip, looked at the floor with a serious expression, swished, and swallowed.

"Mmf," he grunted with a nod that invited us to join him, and when it was clear that everyone present approved, he grinned under his short-banged Caesar haircut, showing off a boyish gap between his two front teeth.

"Other than afternoon and evening," he announced, "morning is the best time to drink wine."

Our tour of the rest of the winery doubled as a mini course in Wine-making 101. Despite the atmosphere of competence and relative calm surrounding us, André managed to convince us that each step in the winemaking process was teetering constantly on the edge of disaster. Hailstorms are a *catastrophe,* he explained. The fermentation process heats the wine, *c'est la catastrophe.* Too much volatile acidity starts turning wine into vinegar: *la catastrophe.* The yeast exhausts itself and stops fermenting: *une catastrophe*. Rain during the grape harvest? *Catastrophe nationale*. I had an image of André trotting gingerly though a minefield called "One Year's Worth of Good Wine." One false step, and whoops, *C'est la catastrophe*.

He introduced us to the vats, holding as much as fifty hectoliters (about 6,500 bottles) of wine. He showed us the powerful pump that moved all this liquid from one place to another. He led us into the back room, where about forty thousand bottles of finished wine were stacked head high against the walls, ready for shipping.

He also showed us the other half of his winery, which he rented to a longtime friend and colleague, a fellow named Thierry Rodriguez.

"Thierry, he makes a different kind of wine," André admitted with no sense either of rivalry or apology. "He has the means to take every little step."

There was a casualness about the entire morning that had me feeling off-balance. Surely this busy winemaker, on the cusp of his busiest season, surrounded by wine to filter, wine to sell, and wine to escort through a gauntlet of leering *catastrophes*—surely he had better things to do than stroll through his winery with a friend and two strangers, talking about malolactic fermentation, carbonic maceration, and the pleasures of a good leg of lamb.

We were his already. He had won us over with the Lauren Hutton smile, and the first taste of red from his vat of wine. He had no more winning over to do, and still the interactive tour continued, narrated in his soothing baritone, and punctuated by jokey asides, affectionate pats, and the occasional amplification from Jean-Luc of a finer point of viticultural how-to.

The wines surrounding us were all last year's, either aging in oak or waiting in vats for bottling. This year's harvest was still on the vine, and he and Jean-Luc talked about the results coming back from the laboratory, where samples of grapes were being tested for sugar content, concentration, and acidity. The grapes had not yet begun a process called *véraison*, a final metamorphosis into full maturity, during which they become sweeter. Their acidity drops. Their taste deepens. They put on their final color. They stop smelling like vegetation and begin smelling like fruit.

Jean-Luc managed to heighten the romance at this point by inviting us into the *chai,* or barrel room, where, in slanted light from the doorway, rows of stacked oak barrels sat in cool and solemn silence.

I said it had the air of a church.

André clapped his hands together. "Yes, but the wine, it is not to pray. It is to drink."

And with that, he opened the door to the adjacent tasting room.

I looked at Mary Jo, who shrugged.

"André," I said. "We should let you get back to work."

"This is work," said André, gesturing into the tasting room. "You will see." Then he tried out his English on us, which was the only true catastrophe of the day.

"Verr-RHEE Haahrd Wuhrrk," he said.

"We shouldn't overstay our welcome," I said to Mary Jo.

But she didn't have time to answer, because André gripped her left arm and my right, and led us through *La Porte du Bonheur* (the Door of Happiness) into the sixty-degree chill of the Balliccioni *caveau de dégustation.*

24

The Door of Happiness threw a sharp pyramid of light onto the pebbled floor of the tasting room. The effect was of stepping off a hot summer sidewalk into an air-conditioned theater. As the door handle clacked back into its hasp behind us, the commotion of machinery at work in the courtyard was instantly muted, replaced by the intimate beach-walk sound of our shoes clattering the stones.

The room was the size of a large living room. A squat table lamp with a single bulb sat on a bar to our right, bathing warmly in its own glow and throwing a grainy light around the room. We migrated naturally toward a circular wooden table and stood around it.

"Seat yourselves," said André, and gave me a shoulder pat in passing. He muttered to himself beside a stack of boxes, holding a series of bottles close to his face, then disappeared behind the bar and reappeared with a towel over his shoulder, holding two chiming wineglasses in each hand by their stems.

He leaned back in his rickety folding chair and, with casual ceremony, wiped each glass, held it out toward the candle-ish light of the lamp, and set it upright in front of him.

Jean-Luc sat forward with his elbows on the table, eager and alert.

I locked eyes with Mary Jo. She stuck out her lower lip, and her eyebrows lifted into a happy little interrogative.

"One begins with the white," announced André, and, with a slow angling of the wrist, he slipped the cork soundlessly from a green slope-shouldered bottle, and poured a finger of pale, glinting white wine into each of our four glasses.

I didn't know why one began with the white.

I didn't know to what extent we should consider this a transaction, with an invoice waiting at the end.

I didn't know what the relationship was between Jean-Luc and André, although it appeared that this was very much André's wine, but equally that Jean-Luc had had a hand in it somehow.

You could have filled one of André's fifty-hectoliter vats with all that Mary Jo and I did not know at that moment, and there would have been more of what we did not know left over.

The tasting, incredibly, would last through the afternoon, and the great volume of our ignorance would ebb steadily in André and Jean-Luc's company, as if it emptied into our glasses one chuckling pour at a time.

André said that his white was a Chardonnay, and went on to explain carefully, as if to people who might not be familiar with it, what a versatile grape it was, and how well it expressed itself in various soils and climates.

Mary Jo, who did not like Chardonnay in any of its manifestations—American, French, or anywhere else—and who was not afraid to tell anyone what she did and did not like, told André, in a French that spent much of its time in the present tense but that made itself perfectly clear, that she didn't like Chardonnay. Any Chardonnay.

André explained that Chardonnay was maybe the greatest white wine grape in France if not the world, and had Mary Jo ever tried this thing they had in France called Champagne, and Mary Jo picked up on the word "Champagne," and said, "OK maybe," and Jean-Luc laughed and told a story about how Champagne is such a cold region to grow grapes in that there are Champagne producers who arrive in the Languedoc each fall, in the middle of the night, with tanker trucks and cash, and ship perfectly sun-ripened Mediterranean Chardonnay grapes back north to be made into "Champagne."

André's Chardonnay was made and stored in stainless-steel vats only—no oak to turn it buttery and viscous as in California—and Mary Jo would find his wine refreshing as an aperitif on days like this one, and Mary Jo swirled her glass, and took a sip, and André leaned back and folded his hands behind his head, without apology, and she said with a rueful smile that made André sit back up with a triumphant "Ah-ha!" that she liked his Chardonnay.

I could see Mary Jo falling under the spell of his charming swagger, to which I myself was not immune.

André was already threading his corkscrew into a bottle of rosé, lightly frosted with condensation, when he appeared to recollect something and trotted back to the bar.

"You would like to spit?" he asked, setting a bucket in the middle of the table.

Mary Jo took a final sip of Chardonnay, swallowed, looked at André, and asked in mock confusion, "Why?"

André shrugged and turned to Jean-Luc. "*Pourquoi?*" he asked, and then, as if the spit bucket had been a tactlessly misguided idea from the start, he took it by the handle, threw it carelessly across the room, and leaned forward to pour shallow pools of rosé the color of a steelhead fillet into the glasses we held out to him in turn, and now we were talking about color.

André was particularly happy with the color of this rosé, which, in our different glasses at their various distances from the lamp, was not a single color but mixed of melon and salmon and copper and a rusty sort of tangerine.

A rosé should look happy to see you, he declared. It should not be shy, like some of these pale rosés from Provence that have bony legs and look as if they have seen a ghost.

I had a dawning sense that we were in the middle of something a little bit extraordinary, and yet I felt that it had come too quickly, that I needed to have lived my life differently in order to be ready for such an afternoon as this, and my instinct was to try to prove to André and Jean-Luc that they had not miscalculated in inviting these Americans—not just into this tasting room, but, it seemed, into their world.

I asked if I smelled a couple of different kinds of berries in the rosé, because that was how I had learned to talk about wine, and because I wanted to sound as if I knew what I was about, and André nodded distantly and said probably, and then talked about other things. Those other things all had to do with wine, and yet none of them had anything to do with what happened in the cubic foot of air above a half-full glass, and I found myself at a loss to discover the criteria they used to determine whether a glass of wine pleased them or not.

We learned we were in the Faugères wine appellation, a tiny subset of the Languedoc defined by its schist soil, which, according to André, had a sturdy and well-respected reputation for making high-quality wine in a part of France that had been disparaged, until recently, as the "lake of wine." The Languedoc was the largest vineyard in the world, but had made its name supplying mostly bad, inexpensive wines to the army.

Jean-Luc stepped in with a story about employers in his father's day, who paid their vineyard employees cash wages, plus a daily allowance of two liters of nine- or ten-degree wine, which was considered an important part of their nutrition, and it was expected that they would drink their daily allotment and come back the next day for more work, and more wine.

"Today, a Faugères is not worth making," André said, "if it's not thirteen or fourteen degrees." (Degrees, in French, meaning alcohol percentage.)

"There is," said André, shaking the final drops of rosé from his glass onto the floor and opening the first red of the day, "a pile of marketing [which he pronounced mark-eh-TEENG] around schist," but he felt there was a certain signature that schist left behind in the wines he made. A freshness. An elegance. Maybe a certain agreeable bitterness.

"An aroma of roasted stone," added Jean-Luc, and André nodded, and poured, and he was off on the story of the next wine.

It was named Jules, not after the region, or the appellation, or the grapes, but after André's grandfather.

Often winemakers would name particular wines after grandchildren, a tradition that André found sympathetic, but given that so far he had no grandchildren . . .

And we all clinked our glasses in the middle of the table, and, in various formulations, urged André's children on in their efforts to give him grandchildren.

Inside the tasting room, there was not a sense of time passing. I couldn't have said what time it had been when we had stepped in, nor what time it was now. Three bottles of wine stood near the edge of the table to André's left, in a conversational-looking group, with corks half stuck into their necks. They were markers of a series of moments that had once been ahead of us, and were now behind us, but whether those moments had occupied half an hour or two hours, I couldn't have said.

We tasted another wine named for Grandfather Léon, light-bodied and ruby-colored, which André said was better served a few degrees colder than this, and yet he still found it—and here he held his right hand in front of him, and rotated it as if turning a dial, and used a beautiful French word that doesn't quite translate into English—he found it *friand*, which comes from a variety of sweets and candies the French call *friandises*. He found his wine refreshingly candied, that is to say, which did not appear to mean sweet, because it was not a sweet wine, but something closer to lighthearted, or playful, or maybe he meant a fruitiness at the far, red end of fruit, where our mind tends to confound strawberries with candy.

The next bottle we recognized.

"Faugères Tradition, Rouge," announced André with a rascal's smile, and as he levered the cork out with a squeaking wiggle, I noticed it was the first cork of the day made of actual cork, not synthetic, and the first cork to be printed with the Balliccioni name, instead of a generic "*Mis en bouteille à la Proprieté*," and that it exactly matched the wine we had been buying at the bakery.

What was becoming clear was that, although the sense of chronological time was blurred inside the pool of light around the table, a momentum had been established. André's methodical opening and pouring and talking and setting aside was not a linear walk but a vertical climb.

The bottles didn't succeed each other so much as build on one another, and I was now aware of a kind of suspense, as the two unopened bottles sat in front of him, implying, by the fact of their being unopened, that both would somehow be more interesting than the five bottles we had already tried, and that each bottle in turn would be more interesting than the one before it, and that the last one would be the most interesting of all.

We tasted, and talked about the added fullness of this wine in our mouths, the wider palette of sensations and flavors it produced, the feeling of something we all managed to agree was "equilibrium," with different elements both contributing to the overall experience and simultaneously offsetting one another. And this was what a blended wine could do, said André, that a wine using a single grape variety—"like you Americans and your Cabernet Sauvignon"—often could not. Blending, in this part of the world, was the art that a winemaker brought to an otherwise agricultural craft.

"*Alors,*" said André, and spun the neck of the next bottle against the short knife blade attached to the corkscrew. The bottle was thicker at the base than the previous ones, and he handled it as if it were heavier. He leaned forward and poured something into our glasses that was immediately different, even to two Americans. "Orchis," he said simply.

It was purple-indigo, and it could be smelled across the table as it was poured.

"This is different," I said.

"I hope so very much," said André.

I sniffed my glass, and wanted to tell him why I thought it was different, to show him that I could keep up, but I did not have the vocabulary or the experience, and frankly wasn't sure I even grasped why it was different. And so, I let my guard down just a crack, because at this point in the afternoon, at this point in the story André was telling about his wines, I had begun to wish to understand.

"How is it different?" I asked, and understood on some level that I was asking perhaps the unanswerable question. "Why is it good?"

In the monologue that followed, I learned still more things I had not known before, and put other things together that had previously existed separately in my understanding.

There were any number of measurable and rational reasons that one bottle of wine might be better than another. It would come from a plot of ground that received closer to the optimal amount, and angle, of sunlight, while also absorbing the right amount of rainfall—enough but not too much. The grapes would be healthy and whole at harvest time, unmolested by drought, hail, fungus, or disease. The sugar and acidity inside the grapes would be testably in balance.

Then there were concrete steps that winemakers could take in order to bring the best out of what they had produced in a given year. They could prune in order to limit the number of bunches per vine, directing more energy and concentrated flavor into those that remained. They could harvest by hand instead of by machine. They could ferment the traditional way, in which the grapes were crushed, or could choose carbonic maceration, in which whole bunches went into the vat and fermentation happened inside each grape. They could age in barrels or in vats. They could age in larger barrels, like 500-liter oak casks, called *demi-muids*, or in smaller barrels, like the 225-liter *barriques* made famous in Bordeaux. Those barrels could be new oak, or oak that had held wine one or more times previously. The char on the inside of the barrel could be darker or lighter. The wine could be macerated with its skins and seeds a longer or shorter time, to generate more or less tannin.

Among other things.

I examined the wine in my glass.

"*C'est compliqué, un verre de vin*," said Jean-Luc. (It's complicated, a glass of wine.)

As my head swam with just how complicated it was, a glass of wine, he blinked both eyes at me in friendly commiseration.

"This one is mostly Mourvèdre," said André, "which is a difficult grape here because it matures so late, but it is muscular, very *charpenté* . . ." (very "carpentered").

"The dryness you feel in your mouth," interjected Jean-Luc. "Those are the tannins [which he pronounced *tanang*]. With Mourvèdre, the tannins are very, very fine. They will soften as the wine ages, but you can feel the structure of the wine in them already."

We all took a moment to assess the dusky wine in our glasses, and I thought of Homer's wine-dark sea, and the goblets of wine, described as "black," drunk at those feasts in the *Odyssey*, and felt more sensually connected to Homer's world here, of all places, in the daytime twilight of André's tasting room, than I ever had in my box-checking, small-spirited chasing around Mycenae and Athens as a younger man.

Jean-Luc sipped, and made little swishing sounds in his mouth. When he had processed the mouthful of wine, he did not try to be eloquent or descriptive. He just said, "*Eh, oui.*" As in, "Yes, that's it."

And I wanted to quiz him and ask him to explain all that was encompassed in that *Eh, oui*. What was he tasting? What was he experiencing? What chords of memory were being struck? What would the wine say to him if it could talk?

I had enjoyed wine in a particular way until now. Had tried to be educated about it. Had valued its connection to France. Had relished the parlor game of picking out scents. But this afternoon with André and Jean-Luc had given me a glimpse inside, and, in a way similar to my stolen glimpse through the gate at Marie's Sunday lunch, I was hungry for what I was seeing. I had been a member of the book club for years, and here I was sitting next to the authors, who for some reason were willing to talk to me.

It had become clear by now that if selling wine were what this was all about, we had just spent an afternoon with the worst couple of peddlers since Jack Lemmon tried to sell that old couple a lot in the Glen Ross development.

The afternoon was about something else. Education, maybe, but more than that. Our two hosts appeared to take it for granted that what was going on outside, in the world of filters and pumps and commerce, was not nearly as important as sitting in a rough circle, in a dimly lit room, talking with curious strangers for most of an afternoon, while bottles were uncorked and poured and talked about in their specific order.

Somewhere between Orchis and André's top-shelf Kallisté, made with Syrah and the blackest and most powerful of them all, I made a last, enfeebled gesture in the direction of letting these two working men get back to their work. But my northern sense of intrusion and trespass was already melting around the edges, and what, at home, we would consider a respectful social distance here already felt pinched and out of place. I couldn't even convince myself that we should leave, much less André, who cut me off with a "Pffff," and a lazy backhanded slap of the air between us, before explaining the origin of the name "Kallisté," Greek for "most beautiful," which was what the ancient Phocaeans had called the island of his birth: Corsica.

And still, in my fascination, I kept asking questions, trying to put the puzzle together of what I was feeling and why I was feeling that way, and what about these wines they could tell me—what elements of flavor and texture, what remnants of their origins in local plots of land, might be adding up to this whole that had kept me practically on the edge of my seat.

Jean-Luc looked mildly troubled as he listened to me try to take apart the afternoon, to pin the wines I had tasted to a board and try to tame, by analysis, the experience of sharing them in this company over this irreplaceable stretch of time.

He leaned forward now. "*Le vang, Steve,*" he said with professorial concern in his voice as André leaned and re-poured from a bottle we had all particularly liked. It seemed to bother Jean-Luc that I might fail to grasp what had really been happening while we had been together. "*Le vang, c'est le plaisir.*"

Wine, Steve. Wine is pleasure.

And even then, I could not quite accept that all this—this setting, these people, the makeup of these wines, this craft on display—didn't amount to something more than mere pleasure.

André sold us three cases that day, plus one "little surprise," a late-harvest dessert wine called Caprice de Femme—the only sweet wine Domaine Balliccioni made. He described the two enemies of this wine, made from grapes left on the vine until late in the fall. There is, first, wet November weather, which causes the grapes to rot. And there is, second, *les étourneaux,* the great swooping clouds of starlings that pass through each fall on their migration to Africa. They are capable of descending onto a field and, in one day, eating every remaining grape, and when that happens, of course, "*C'est la catastrophe.*"

"It commences when?" Jean-Luc asked André as we gathered at the gate, each toting a cardboard case full of Balliccioni wines.

"*La vendange?*" (The grape harvest?), asked André. "Oh, the whites in a couple of weeks, I imagine. Then all the rest, if the drought leaves us any grapes. You should convince this one to help." He looked at me and grinned.

I chuckled at the joke.

"Steve, he is made of beams," said Jean-Luc, lifting a hand over his head to represent my size. "In the vines, one should be made of twigs!" And he cackled at this latest knee-slapper.

I emerged from the winery as if from an altered state. It took a few minutes for the world to reassemble itself around me.

"What just happened?" asked Mary Jo.

"I have no clue," I said.

And we laughed for no reason, like two people who have just learned that a stranger left them all his money.

Even so, as the spell wore off in the car on the way home, I got that sinking feeling that comes when you awake with a hangover and your mind roams over the previous night, trying to remember what exactly you said and did, and whether you made a complete, or merely a partial, ass of yourself.

"Did we stay too long?" I asked.

"Why?" asked Mary Jo.

"I feel like we did."

"I don't," she said.

We were driving the same ring road we had walked on our first day in the village, but in the opposite direction.

"They liked us, Stevie. They wanted to like us, and then they did like us. It's pretty simple."

"I feel like we still owe them something for all that time. With all the shit they have going on? Three cases of wine is, like, a token."

She sighed.

"Stevie, I'm telling you, and if you couldn't see this then you are just going to have to take my word for it. They loved that. Yes, we loved it, too—*which is OK by the way!* You were interested in exactly what they wanted to talk about. And in their language! Jesus! Jean-Luc—I mean it's so clear—Jean-Luc wants a student as badly as you want a teacher."

"You think?"

"I swear to God. You are the smartest idiot I ever met."

"It's a gift," I said.

"By the way, you should absolutely go pick grapes with them," she said.

"They were just joking."

"No, they weren't, but even if . . ."

"Like they need a big . . . A middle-aged American trainee . . ."

"I'm just saying," she said.

25

It was Friday. The fishmonger had come and gone. Joe and I were walking across the main square toward the library. The café was just filling up for lunch, and a group of girls rattled across the cobbles, laughing and chasing each other on kick scooters.

"Want me to introduce you?" I asked.

"I will destroy you," said Joe, who'd been experimenting with this sort of pseudo tough-talk lately. He seemed to enjoy the grown-up feeling of flirting with vulgarity, and at the same time to recognize its absurdity—like the scratchy mewling of a lion cub.

I had my passport and Minnesota driver's license with me, ready for a bureaucratic tussle, but the librarian simply wrote my name and address in a ledger and said we were welcome to check out books as long as we were living here.

Joe worked his way thoughtfully around the perimeter of the diminutive library, while I parked myself in front of the literature section, scanning the spines of books that, as always, seemed to promise much of the beauty and most of the important secrets of life, if I could only read and understand them all, which, over the middle years of my life, I had so doggedly failed to do.

I worked alphabetically through the names of authors that were like distant friends I never got to see enough of—Balzac, Beauvoir, Camus, Duras, Flaubert, Hugo, Sand, Zola—and was wishing I could pick out a favorite childhood book from these shelves and share it with Joe. But my repertoire of French books came from college literature. I had studied them, and been influenced by them, but never loved them as you love something you have grown up with, something that pierces your childhood defenses and becomes a part of you.

The librarian snapped me out of my reverie, asking if I was searching for something in particular, and I asked her what she might recommend for someone of Joseph's age. Maybe a book set in the region.

She quickly established whether I knew Pagnol, which I did, and whether I had read his childhood autobiographical novels, *Souvenirs d'Enfance,* which I had not.

"Well, then, you must read *La Gloire de Mon Père* [*My Father's Glory*], and then *Le Château de Ma Mère* [*My Mother's Castle*]. We have the hardcover with the classic illustrations—"

"Dad!" cried Joe, holding a book out toward me. "Fabre!"

His soft fingers were wrapped around the spine of a book titled *Souvenirs Entomologiques,* the cover of which featured a green and black illustrated mantis, holding up its toothy front pincers like murderous lobster-shell crackers.

He was so transparently elated over such an odd and obscure private treasure that I felt . . . What did I feel? I felt almost bad for him, standing so slender and exposed on his side of the room, in his clunky sneakers that emphasized the skinniness of his calves. Or, rather, I felt an apprehensive fatherly premonition that such guilelessness could not long encounter the world without coming to emotional harm.

"You know Fabre?" asked the librarian. And the brightness of Joseph's face dimmed a few degrees as he sensed that he might have to explain to this adult authority his peculiar worship of a nineteenth-century French naturalist, entomologist, and autodidact.

He—we—had first encountered Fabre in the pages of Gerald Durrell. Young Gerry receives in the mail one day a thick brown package, and spends the rest of the afternoon under a tangerine tree beside their house in Corfu, plowing through the entirety of a book called *The Sacred Beetle and Others,* which is filled primarily with descriptions of the behavior and life cycles of dung beetles.

In his later life, Fabre more or less retired to his home and its surroundings, which he treated like a wild, open-air laboratory and which he studied into old age, with a dedicated and roving naturalist's eye. If Gerry Durrell had had the ideal boyhood, Fabre was Joseph's paradigm of an entire life lived just exactly right.

"He was born just north of here, in the Aveyron," said the librarian. "A great man, he." Her gaze lingered on Joe, not, it appeared, as one would condescend to a nerdy oddball, but with every indication of respect. "*Bravo, jeune homme,*" she said.

On the way home, I said, "Hey, Joe. Oysters for dinner? The shellfish truck comes tonight."

He did a hopping little dance around me, and then, settling back into his slapping, big-footed stride, he reached up absently, slipped his left hand into my right, and, holding hands, we walked the rest of the way home.

26

Joe was lounging on the couch with Fabre's *Souvenirs* in his lap. A shaft of sunlight through the open terrace door fell across him in a way that made his small piece of the living room appear to be generating its own light, emphasizing even more than usual his resemblance to Christopher Robin, living in his own world, apart from ours.

Eva and Mary Jo were sitting on the floor, bickering half-heartedly as they arranged a collection of plane-tree leaves on a white sheet of paper.

I had been thinking about the butcher Marie-France had recommended, and Gaston, as it happened, had just posted his take on the classic French veal stew, *blanquette de veau.*

"Who wants to go to the butcher shop?" I asked.

"Mom!" said Eva. "That looks terrible there."

"You boys go," said Mary Jo.

"Little-known fact," said Joe as we wound up the narrow streets of Laurens, past a beauty shop and the Café de la Paix, toward the center of town.

"Joseph Hoffman."

"Dung beetles make two different kinds of dung balls, depending on if they are laying an egg in it, or are just eating it themselves," he said. "The egg balls are purer, so the babies don't have to try to eat little stems and stuff."

"Just pure poop."

"Sort of cute," he said.

"Super cute."

"So, can I have a pet dung beetle?" he asked.

"Absolutely."

We walked into the iron smell of the tidy *boucherie traditionnelle,* where Monsieur Congnard was slicing something on his stainless-steel counter for the only other customer in the room.

M. Congnard was about five foot nine, fiftyish, with aggressive sideburns at odds with his mild features. He looked remarkably fit and trimwaisted for a butcher. He spoke softly with a regional accent, and gave the impression of friendly self-assurance, which is a good impression to give, I suppose, when you need to greet several dozen skeptical French citizens a day and sell them their dinner.

Joe wandered over to the display case, where a selection of precut portions were laid out without ceremony or decoration: a row of pork chops, a neatly trussed roast, a dark veal liver. There were lamb brains, veal sweetbreads, skewers of alternating kidneys and lard, and a plucked chicken with its feathered head tucked back along its body. Joe stared at the brains with his hands in his front pockets, rapt and a little unsure.

My recipe called for either veal shoulder or something called *tendron de veau,* and when I admitted I didn't know the difference, M. Congnard recommended the shoulder.

"Very good," I said. "I need one point two kilos."

What happened next was my first lesson in what it meant to be a *boucher traditionnel.*

In the grocery store meat department at home, I can browse among the prepackaged morsels in the refrigerator case, which give the impression of not ever having been animals, but, rather, wrapped in plastic by the Meat Fairy. Or I can proceed to the counter, where the butcher reduces an attractive large cut to several attractive smaller cuts before wrapping them demurely in bloodless white paper.

In Laurens, when I asked for a kilo-plus of veal shoulder, the butcher disappeared into the back room, and reappeared, tottering slightly, carrying the front quarter of a calf in his arms, including the ribs and the animal's left front leg. He hung this on a stainless-steel meat hook, and dragged his knife along his steel a few times.

"You are . . . Belgian?" he asked.

"American," I said.

He spun the rib cage away from me, and sliced into the armpit of what was once undeniably the former calf's shoulder. The shoulder and front leg fell away from the rib cage after about four deep cuts, and remained attached by one final ribbon of flesh.

Joe was beside me, agape.

"*Vous parlez très bien français,*" said M. Congnard, driving a meat hook into the leg. He cut it all the way free, and hung it next to the rib cage. It swung gently while he lifted the ribs from their hook, and then lurched back into the cooler.

He reappeared, and dropped the shoulder with the meat hook still in it onto a stainless-steel cutting surface.

As he resumed carving, he told a story about a tiny colossus of a man who used to deliver meat to him—shorter than himself—who would throw two hundred kilos of meat on his shoulder and dance around with it on the way to the meat locker.

His knife made sounds like tearing a cotton T-shirt as he cut through the seams between the muscles, and soon an ivory knob of scapula glistened among the rose-colored meat. More quickly than I could have imagined, a big, boneless shoulder muscle had been excised from the rest.

"I'm sorry," he said. "How much did you need? A kilo?"

It was as if I had just ordered a burger and the guy in the drive-through window had asked me to wait a moment while he went out back, shot the cow, then came back a few minutes later and asked, "I'm sorry, did you say hamburger or cheeseburger?"

I said a little more than that—twelve hundred grams. More or less.

He swiped a new knife against his steel with a *wee-shee wee-shee wee-shee* sound before cutting the veal shoulder into chunks and dropping them two by two onto a sheet of butcher paper draped over his digital scale. He dropped the last two chunks, and the scale read 1,237 grams.

"Perfect," I said.

"Almost perfect," he said. "You are here on vacation?"

"A little longer than that. We are here until early next year. Next door in Autignac."

He taped shut the bundle of veal and wrote a number in pencil in a notebook.

"And with that?" he asked.

"Joe?" I asked.

Joe beckoned me closer, refusing to look at the butcher, and whispered something.

"What's that?" I asked.

He jabbed his finger toward the display of white receptacles, like plastic ramekins, each containing exactly one pink and white brain.

"The brains," whispered Joe with his ferocious desire to possess such a specimen as the actual brain of a lamb warring with the acuteness of his self-consciousness before the godlike butcher whose work he had just witnessed.

"*Il veut des cervelles?*" asked the butcher, as if it were to be expected that a nine-year-old boy would covet lamb brains for dinner.

I held up two fingers. "Deux," I said.

"You do what in America," he asked, "that you can stay here so long?"

I attempted to explain to him what my profession was, without enough knowledge of the French tax system to know whether such a position as mine existed or was necessary in France, or even to use the specific vocabulary of the trade. I explained, at great and stammering length, that I helped people prepare the papers at the end of the year that reported to the government the taxes that they owed to . . . to the government . . . based on the salary, or rather the revenue, or rather . . . In any case, each American sent papers to the . . . to the government . . . each year that explained the taxes they owed, and then they paid their taxes based on those papers, and I helped them fill out those . . . those papers.

Even Joe was looking at me as if I should just stop talking now, and I ended my stem-winder feeling like a middle manager at a point-of-sale software company trying to explain my job to a lumberjack.

Monsieur Congnard did not help, at this point, by asking, "*C'est un métier, ça?*" Which translates as "That's really a job?" And I was able to verify that, indeed, that was a job, and because the job had a limited season, we could afford to be here for the fall semester, which no longer felt like anything to be particularly proud of, given the taint of what had made it possible.

About seven hours later, I was supposedly staring at a *blanquette de veau*.

"What's the meat?" asked Eva.

"Veal."

"You mean baby cow?"

"I mean veal."

"Don't they torture baby cows to make veal?"

"They used to. I don't think they do anymore."

"You don't think?" She poked through her stew in search of anything she could feel good about eating. "It's white. What is a stew doing being white?"

"Guys," I said. "Every French kid your age has grown up eating this. Begging for it. It's French spaghetti and meatballs."

"It's white torture stew," said Eva.

Joe was holding a spoon but not doing much with it, and I wondered if the rib cage, the shoulder bone, the ripping sounds, so enthralling as a spectacle across a counter, weren't coming back to visit him now as he worked to reimagine all of that flesh, blood, and bone as chunks of digestible food in the bowl before him—with the brains of baby sheep waiting in the fridge.

"Don't push," said Mary Jo.

"This is comfort food," I said. "This is as easy as it gets. This is what you gather around a table and eat with joy when you are a French family."

"We're not a French family."

"We are a family in France. And we're not here to hollow out baguettes and eat pasta. Not on my watch."

27

Imagine if you will, standing in one's French kitchen, reviewing step five of Ginette Mathiot's recipe for *crème Du Barry,* including its instruction to pass the cooked cream of cauliflower soup through a food mill. Well, then. What, one might ask, is one doing without a food mill?

This was the question I was asking myself.

With the possible exception of the copper saucepan, the food mill might be the most romantic French kitchen tool. It looks like a shallow colander with a big crank and a rubber ball–shaped handle. When you turn the crank, a sort of metal squeegee spins inside and sweeps cooked food through the strainer holes in the bottom of the mill. It is a tool, along with the ricer and the mortar and pestle, that food processors and blenders have largely replaced.

The great advantage of the food mill is not that it does anything better or faster than a Cuisinart. It does not. What a French food mill does is place the user, if they use their imagination, into the legendary line of descent of generations of French household cooks who have spent the centuries cranking French bourgeois cuisine through their *moulins à légumes*. No equivalent feeling of standing knee-deep in the great current of French culinary history can be produced by the electrified whir of metal blades. For my part, I bought a modest, mostly plastic Moulinex, at a very unromantic French discount store called Super U, and returned to my abandoned *crème Du Barry* recipe now that I could complete step five. And in an instant, I was no longer a pretender in a strange land. I was a French cook with a freaking Moulinex. That's who I was.

When I had finished cranking the last of the cauliflower florets through the fine sieve of my marvelously traditional French hand tool, then scrubbed the halo of spattered soup around the base of the pot, then disassembled the tool and rinsed the thickly *Du Barry*–encrusted components clean under a flow of hot water, I would say that at least half of the original volume of the recipe remained in the soup pot, blurping contentedly. At least half.

The Moulinex did wonders for the atmospherics of the kitchen, but I could tell that it was going to do more service as a sort of Certificate of Authenticity than as a culinary workhorse. There are only so many dishes, or only so many I felt I could convince my children to eat, that call for pureeing cooked vegetables.

On the other hand, the number of recipes in *Je Sais Cuisiner* that began with some variant of "Heat X grams of [choose your fat] in a *cocotte* . . ." reached into the hundreds.

What I had been heating X grams in was a pot that fit the minimum definition of a *cocotte*—a casserole with a lid and two handles. But it had hot spots where a crescent of chopped shallots would scorch, while the rest of the shallots in the pot had barely turned translucent. It wasn't ovenproof. It wasn't, to be quite specific, one of those enameled cast-iron works of high consumer art from Le Creuset or Staub.

Over the course of several family outings around this time, I slowed wistfully past kitchen displays in the specialty-shop windows of Béziers, and Sète, and Narbonne.

I would mope into a kitchen store to fondle the heavy thirty-centimeter round Staub *cocotte* with the matte black finish, like a cauldron that might have hung from a tripod to braise a haunch of venison while Charlemagne was alive. I would cup its buxom curves in my hands and imagine what we would be like together. And then I would place its twelve pounds of perfect engineering, its impossible beauty, and its three-hundred-euro price tag gingerly back on the display shelf.

So what to do about the fact that here was Ginette Mathiot proposing *potage bonne femme,* and *boeuf à la mode,* and here was Gaston proposing *fricassée de poulet au vinaigre,* each of which contained the instruction "Heat a *cocotte . . .*"?

What, moreover, to do about the instruction "*Enfournez la cocotte,*" or "Put the *cocotte* in the oven"? Was it simply time to learn to live within the limitations of a scratched stainless-steel pot with Bakelite handles?

One day, while closely supervising the sautéeing of a diced yellow onion, I googled the oven-safe properties of Bakelite and discovered that it was ovenproof (according to a website selling Bakelite-handled cookware that was very complimentary of Bakelite) "up to 350°F, for a maximum of one hour."

A day or two later, I lifted from my grocery bag a flame-colored *cocotte* that was neither Le Creuset nor Staub, but which I loved all the more for its two ovenproof enameled handles, and for the way that its discount-store price and somewhat awful color fit into life in this modest place where you didn't always get what you wanted.

"Well, would you look at this?" I exclaimed.

So began a love affair with the sturdy, sensible new helpmeet in our kitchen—which did not scorch shallots and which could remain in the oven both above 350°F and longer than one hour.

I was chopping tomatoes for a ratatouille to be made in our family's new *cocotte,* while beside me a browning pile of salted eggplant cubes dripped through a colander into the sink.

"Eva!" I said.

"What?"

"Come join me in the kitchen."

She approached just close enough to catch sight of the eggplant.

"Dad!" she said. "Make something I want to eat." And she walked out.

28

While I knew that Jean-Luc and Nicole intended our outing to the healing waters of Saint-Méen as a hospitable favor to us, I felt as if we were packing up that morning in order to, in some sense, humor them. As a pretext for spending some time together, taking a pleasant drive, perhaps learning a little more about life here, we would all pretend there was a possibility that the waters of *Sang-Meng* could heal Eva's foot, with its burden of Minnesota cedar driven somewhere deep inside it.

Eva did not like decisions being made for her.

"It's polite, Eva. You don't even have to do anything except get your feet wet."

"Do you really think there's going to be a miracle, Dad?"

"No. That's not really why we're doing it."

"You don't even like picnics."

"No, I don't."

"Then what are we doing this for?"

"You know why? You're going to like this one, I promise . . . Because Mom and Dad say so."

Jean-Luc wore white linen pants of a length somewhere between long shorts and short trousers and an ironed short-sleeved shirt. Nicole wore a calf-length blue sundress, and I wondered if Eva's tank top and shorts would get her banned from our sacred destination, but didn't have the energy to also make her change clothes.

Our hosts loaded several plastic jerry cans into the trunk of a gray Renault sedan, and we followed them straight north, into the dark hills that I had, until this day, thought of as possessing an ominous watchfulness, like a solemn line of dusky giants, keeping tabs on our puny comings and goings.

But it was a sunny day, as were more than three hundred days a year in this corner of the world, and the views kept getting longer and more dramatic as we wound our way upward. The last of the plain's vineyards and scrub gave way to dense, shrubby oak forest, and eventually to airy groves of pine and chestnut, and when we crested the shoulder of the hills visible from Autignac, those hills gave way to more and taller hills, with long vistas over folded green valleys and bald gray peaks, under the palest blue sky.

Jean-Luc pulled over at what he said was the highest point in these mountains—a range called the Caroux-Espinouse—foothills of the still grander Massif Central.

"Cah-ROOX. Es-pee-NOOZE," I pronounced to myself. A comical name, like so many of the place names that, I assumed, derived from Occitan. We saw signs for them all around: Fouzilhon, Pouzolles, Puissalicon, Espondeilhan. Southern names sounded pranksterish and jokey. Sounded un-French. Paris, Lyon, and Bordeaux were firstborns, trying to uphold the glory of the family name. Bouzigues and Fouzilhon were the screwball twins, stabbing each other with pencils.

Mary Jo went to pick some purple flowers with heads like clover, while Jean-Luc, in sunglasses, told the story of Caroux Mountain, referred to as *La Femme Allongée* for its resemblance to a reclining woman who, according to the myth, laid down for a nap one day and was turned to stone.

He examined the posy that Mary Jo had retrieved, and pronounced the flowers "*ciboulettes sauvages.*"

"Wild chives," I said, and Mary Jo, delighted, wet a napkin with Evian and wrapped it around their stems to keep them fresh. The car smelled like scallions by the time we saw the sign for "Saint-Méen."

While I had not expected Lourdes, with a Disney cathedral and hordes of pilgrims, I had nonetheless imagined we would be treated to the folksy glitz that seems to attach itself to religious shrines and other places where miracles have supposedly been documented.

Instead, Saint-Méen consisted of a small compound with a worn asphalt parking area. Inside the small chapel, a plain wooden table was covered, without explanation, by envelopes, cards, and letters—testimonials, prayers, and words of thanks from those who believed they had been healed. In a room nearby, the rear wall was tiled with marble and granite plaques, each anonymously thanking the patron saint of these waters with a humble, etched "*Merci, Saint-Méen.*"

My skepticism began to feel a little snarky here. If there were truly places on earth endowed with some sort of holiness, I thought, then the plainspoken austerity of Saint-Méen was as convincing a way of asking me to believe as I had encountered in a while.

Opposite the chapel, down a short flight of stairs, a dozen or so water spigots protruded from a stucco wall at just below knee height. We all removed our sandals and shoes and bathed our feet in the refreshing chill while Nicole filled jugs. I watched Eva for any sign of moral eye-rolling, but something about the place, or about Jean-Luc's kindness, seemed to have won her over. She let a stream of water run over both feet, and bent to massage it into her stricken right sole.

Jean-Luc told us the story of his own feet, which when he was a young man had smelled intolerably ("like a Camembert!")—which Nicole stoically confirmed—until he himself had washed them in these waters, and for whatever reason, the smell went away. He did not pretend to understand.

We had brought with us several pots filled with julienned vegetables, radishes, and one of Joseph's new favorites, hard-boiled quail eggs. I had bought some country pâté and sliced ham from the butcher of Laurens, a bottle of André's rosé, and, from Marie, a Pélardon goat cheese. We unpacked our spoils onto a shaded picnic table, and I was feeling that, as lunch partners, we had made a decent show of ourselves.

Jean-Luc and Nicole unpacked baguettes and two squat tins without labels, which they opened and set onto a cutting board.

Did we know *jambonneau*?

By the way they described it, I concluded it was pork hock, the meaty part of a pig's leg between the ham and the foot, and it looked like a coarse, loose pâté bound together by amber jelly.

The second tin was a pâté of wild boar, and here a bashful Jean-Luc admitted that, yes, the boar in question was one he himself had shot.

Then they lifted a plastic bag, fat with fruit, and unloaded it onto the table, narrating as they went.

"Some nectarines," said Nicole. "Some *pêches plates* [doughnut peaches]. Some white peaches . . ."

"From your orchard?" I asked.

"*Bien entendu.*" Of course.

"Do you know *reine claudes*?" asked Jean-Luc.

"You told us you grew them. A variety of plum?"

"The last of the year," he said.

The plums were a mottled, dusty green, looking underripe and undersized.

"*Vas-y. Mange!*" (Go ahead. Eat!), he said to Eva, seated closest to him. And, looking troubled, but succumbing either to the trust she had placed in him so far this afternoon, or simply to a sort of peer pressure, she lifted one of the green plums and examined it.

She bit into it, and I believe I witnessed in her face, and possibly even in her posture, something like what Jean-Luc had seen, watching me taste one of his ripe apricots.

Her eyes widened as she stared at the table and yet appeared, simultaneously, to be staring inward, assessing. She took another messy, slurping bite.

Keeping his eyes on me, Jean-Luc tilted his head in her direction.

It was late afternoon. Everybody was hungry, and the table got very busy. The fruits were warm and so ripe that some of their skins had torn by the mere action of piling some on top of others. Jean-Luc poured the cool rosé into water glasses, lifting the bottle toward each of the kids, who accepted, and we all washed it down with cold, iron-smooth Saint-Méen water frigid enough to give us headaches. We peeled quail eggs and salted them, and dipped radishes in butter and salted them, and folded ham onto torn pieces of baguette and smeared them with cheese. I dug out a spoonful of the *jambonneau,* wobbly with gelatin, and spread it chunky and high on a piece of bread.

"You like wild boar?" Jean-Luc asked Joseph. Joe was frankly fascinated by wild boar, or *sanglier,* as he had learned by reading the adventures of Asterix and his boar-mad brother in arms, Obelix. Jean-Luc carved a thin wedge of the *pâté de sanglier* and spread it onto a piece of bread for Joe, who, whether he really liked it or simply refused to dislike it, looked at Jean-Luc, chewing, and nodded his head, and Jean-Luc made him another.

The pâté had come from nearby Murat. It was best to make charcuterie here in the hills, where the humid sea air did not interfere with proper drying.

And they had another of those conversations, like the one about the grafted fig tree, in which they appeared to argue their way through the details of a story on which, in the end, they both agreed almost completely. Nicole had a blurting, zero-to-sixty speaking style, perfect for interjecting her points into the brief pauses in Jean-Luc's flowing oratory. But they agreed in the end that Autignac was fortunate in sitting close enough to the sea to have access to fresh seafood, yet close enough to the hills to have access to beef from Aubrac, and ducks and geese and their eggs, and lamb and pork, and pâtés and charcuterie, from the Tarn and the Aveyron.

"*Entre mer et montagne*," concluded Nicole, repeating a local expression that sloganized the specific joys of living where, for the time being, all of us happened to live: between sea and mountain.

Mary Jo drifted toward the brushy margins of the site, and Eva went her own way, to take photos of an Alpine meadow. Nicole asked Joseph about the upcoming school year, and Jean-Luc asked how he liked it here so far, and Joseph, while appearing to understand everything said to him, struggled to express himself, and I intervened here and there to translate in both directions.

I asked Jean-Luc about the thrush we had found in the street, and whether it was true they were still hunted and eaten here. I had spent long summer days in the North Woods listening, enchanted, to the ethereal piping of wood thrushes and hermit thrushes.

I did not receive the news I had hoped. Jean-Luc spent several minutes extolling the flavor of thrushes, and other songbirds, particularly the revered and now protected ortolan. He reminisced reverently over a morning many years ago, spent clearing brush on a neighbor's land, followed by a lunch of sumptuous *rouges-gorges* (European robins), grilled six to a spit, and eaten whole.

"Jean-Luc!" called Mary Jo, and he bustled over to serve as human field guide, visibly delighted by her lack of reserve, and her immersion in, and curiosity about, the natural world of his region, which he loved so transparently.

Then, "Joseph!" he called, and Joe and I joined him to pick some wild blackberries.

Then, "Jean-Luc!" called Eva, who was pointing to a bird hovering still in the air above the meadow, its body hanging, its wings ablur, and Jean-Luc told her that was the "Holy Spirit Bird." We all gathered to watch the bird hover and dip, then hover again—and Jean-Luc said its true name was *faucon crécerelle*. A kestrel.

We poured the last of the wine, and ate more fruit with our blackberry-stained fingers, and as the sun disappeared behind the hills to the west, we heard what sounded like dull bells in the distance, and then, one by one, a troop of brown cows emerged from the upper tree line and, with the bells around their necks tunking peacefully, ambled down the meadow in our direction.

There was one final "Jean-Luc!" from the direction of the black-berries, where Joe had returned to browse. He was standing still, peer-ing into the dense brush, and when we arrived, we could see the praying mantis, erect and still, clinging to a stem. Jean-Luc managed to coax the mantis onto the back of his sunspotted hand. Joe begged me with his eyes, and I explained to Jean-Luc that he would like very much to take it home with him, and together, the two of them transferred the priceless passenger safely onto a twig, which was angled carefully into a large glass Le Parfait jar with the lid cracked open so Joe's new pet mantis could breathe.

We drove home with several jugs of holy water in the back of our car, and instructions for Eva to soak her feet every day until the water ran out.

As we leveled out onto the plain again, with Autignac's water tower marking its location on the horizon, I was thinking about Jean-Luc and the ease with which he had inhabited the moments we had just lived through. He had, it seemed to me, simply lived the afternoon, and this was one of the things he had in common with Mary Jo.

I had spent the afternoon—an afternoon of leisure, ostensibly—not living, as they had, but striving. Jean-Luc and Mary Jo, and probably Nicole (though she had worked harder than anyone else, I had not failed to notice), would have described their afternoons as a pleasure, while I would have described mine as, more or less, a success.

29

Joe's mantis was large enough, according to Joe, to be a female. He named her April.

We had found a terrarium in Béziers. Joe had filled the bottom with sand and plastic boulders, under and around which a series of doomed crickets had done their best to take shelter from April's swift and accurate front legs.

Joe had scavenged a couple of twigs and some wild fennel stalks for her to perch on.

We were watching her now, hip to hip on the living room couch. Joe had just dropped breakfast into the terrarium, and her triangular head had rotated in an eerily mechanical way, like the gun turret of a tank.

"They have 3D vision," said Joe. "Their eyes can only see movement, so anything that sits still they can't detect."

She moved deliberately toward her oblivious victim, pausing when she got close enough, and swaying, with her comblike front pincers held below her chin like a begging dog, or, one might say, like a praying mantis.

"They only eat live prey," he said.

There was a lightning movement almost too fast to register, and the cricket was caught in the vise of the mantis's front legs, squirming, its antennae waving. April adjusted the cricket's position, pinning two legs, while the other four scrabbled at empty air or scraped ineffectually against the mantis's arms.

I turned to check on Joe, who was watching with a paralyzed kind of stillness.

"You OK, Joe-Joe?"

Soon a half-moon of the cricket's head was missing, like a bite taken out of a cookie, and still it flexed and writhed and waved its legs, and the mantis, with its unblinking wide-set eyes and black pinpricks for pupils, took bite after fleshy bite, chewing briefly, then bending its head for another bite as if eating a sandwich, until, after one spasmodically flexing leg had been pulled free and chewed, and the head had been completely consumed, and April had begun tucking into the thorax, the cricket was finally still, except for the movement given to it by its own methodical devouring.

It was the coming alive of so much that he had read about, and seen hinted at in children's nature shows, and now that it was happening in his very living room, I couldn't parse whether the slack-faced expression seen on his face was the fascination of a budding scientist, or the startled dismay of a not entirely prepared young boy.

"I love her," said Joe uncertainly. And it felt like another of his efforts to seem a little tougher and more grown-up than he felt.

I sat beside him, as unsettled as he. Wishing the world did not demand this of boys. This putting on the armor of pretending. This straightening of question marks into exclamation points.

30

Mary Jo and I were on the second leg of one of our daily round trips to the village square, with a baguette angled out from a bulging market bag, when a "*Ho! Les Américains!*" issued from Jean-Luc's open garage door.

He asked us to wait, and emerged with a delicate heart-leaved vine, which trailed clouds of airy white flowers. He explained that it was *salsepareille*, a variety of greenbrier or bindweed, and might Mary Jo like to photograph it?

"*Viens,*" said Mary Jo. (Come.) And we climbed to our living room, where sheaves of thorny stems and grasses, and collections of leaves and pods and insects and flowers, colonized most of the horizontal surfaces, except the dining room table, where her laptop sat.

She pulled up the STILL blog, thanked him for yesterday's post—an arrangement of wild chives—and then showed him how to scroll through her daily images.

"*Ça s'appelle encore . . . ?*" asked Jean-Luc. (What is it called again?)

"A blog," said Mary Jo.

"*Un blog,*" repeated Jean-Luc, who did not own a computer, but who stood at Mary Jo's shoulder, in work pants, making images scroll past, by the use of something called a touchpad.

Prior to our arrival in Autignac, the blog's twiggy, feathered, leaf-strewn heart had beaten very identifiably in the American Great Lakes bioregion. It would never have struck me as something to show a grape farmer in deep rural France.

But Mary Jo did not feel that there were parts of herself unworthy of sharing, and had intuited somehow that her very digital project would naturally appeal to Jean-Luc's very analog fascinations, and she was right. He got it. He nodded and spoke the names of the things he recognized. He asked questions about the things he didn't. He "oh-ho-ed" at striking compositions. At no point did he pointedly sigh, "*Eh, oui,*" or make any of the other small sounds that announce the coming end of a Frenchman's patience for a particular subject.

Ultimately, he saw the sense in sharing, in whatever form, the beloved and irreproducible specifics of one's region—whether through identifying a *prunelle,* or pouring a finger of local wine, or—why not—hurling digital files at the speed of light into the ether.

He caught sight of April on the living room table, and admired her and the austere kingdom Joe had fashioned for her. He asked Joe what she had been eating, and we showed him the carton of remaining gladiators who had not yet had the misfortune of entering the ring.

31

Two of my favorite French verbs, neither of which, by definition, could exist in English, are *vousvoyer* and *tutoyer*. They mean, respectively, "to address somebody as *vous*" (formal), and "to address somebody as *tu*" (informal). In other words, how formally or informally you address people in French is so important that words for it are embedded in the vocabulary. It would be as if English had two verbs: "to you" and "to thou." As in, "We've known each other a long time, Robert. I think we can stop youing each other and start thouing. Dost thou agree?"

There are stories of friends who, after decades of closeness, make a date to formalize the occasion on which they will cease to call each other *vous* and begin calling each other *tu*.

If you speak French well enough, at some point your ability to express yourself with some ease carries a sort of baggage, implying that you also know how to apply these kinds of rules correctly.

It made me wary of the term "fluent." I was comfortable in the language. Conversational, maybe. But not exactly fluent. There is, on one hand, holding up one end of most conversations competently, and there is, on the other, swimming in the language like a seal.

After just over a month in Autignac, my efforts to navigate the turbulent waters of *tu* and *vous* had me resembling a seal only in that we both have a layer of adorable subcutaneous fat.

It had only taken a few days of walking around to see that the default among adults in town (which was not at all the default in Paris) was to *tutoyer*, and that my greeting everyone as *vous*, though perfectly proper, subtly emphasized my status, and our family's, in every interaction we had, as visitors. Or as Marie-France would have said, as *estrangers*.

Our bell rang late one Saturday afternoon, and Jean-Luc stood below our window.

"Steve," he called up. "I might ask a small favor."

His old Renault 4 had gone under the knife for some minor surgery and was currently waiting at the shop in Laurens. As Nicole did not have a driver's license, would I come with him to retrieve the convalescent?

So it was that I found myself next to Jean-Luc in the front seat of his other work truck, a white *fourgonette,* one of the ubiquitous and massively useful trucklets that seemingly every French contractor and field-worker drives—part SUV, part covered subcompact pickup. I overflowed my passenger seat like some mythical giant. I ducked my head and it still fit tight against the ceiling. My knees were locked against the dashboard. My right elbow hung out the open window, adding to the impression that I was being squeezed out of the car like icing from a pastry bag.

Jean-Luc, comfortably seated, talked about the grape harvest, which was apparently approaching fast. Everyone was worried about the drought, he said. It hadn't rained enough all summer, and in the last few weeks it hadn't rained at all. I told him it sounded like one of André's *catastrophes,* and he chuckled and agreed.

I asked him about his last name, Vialles, assuming, with the double "l," that it had its origins somewhere across the Spanish border. But no, he was all French, and could trace his family back to Renaissance Provence.

"Ah, so you are royalty!" I said, reckoning suddenly with the fact that we had been sharing an adjoining wall with one of Marie-France's pedigreed *paysans.*

There was such a naturalness to our conversation, in such intimate confines, that it was possible to imagine there being some early form of friendship between us, which I wanted to be true, and maybe, as a result, I let myself dwell a little too self-indulgently, during the rest of our drive, on all that we had so improbably in common.

When we arrived, the Renault sat bulbous, dented, and wearily proud outside the shop.

During my days with the Little Brothers of the Poor, in Paris, I had been given access, on the weekends, to a dark blue Renault 4, which I had driven extensively enough that my Parisian coworkers took to asking me for directions.

Jean-Luc let me drive this one home, and I spent a nostalgic and thoughtful ten minutes behind the wheel of what looked like the cockpit of a World War II fighter plane, watching needles bob their way around dials, shoving the familiar dashboard-mounted gearshift forward, then yanking it back out as I whined up through the gears, a couple of decades older than the last time I had really felt a part of something in France.

By the time I eased up to the rear bumper of Jean-Luc's *fourgonette* in front of his house, I was bathed in a feeling of belonging that was so rare for me that I had trouble not reading significance into it, and when the stairwell light came on behind their front door, and Nicole stepped out into the golden afternoon sun, it seemed impossible that something new and important wasn't announcing itself through the events of the past hour.

I took a deep breath, leaning against the driver's-side door of the diminutive car, short enough that I could rest my elbow on the roof.

"*Dites-moi,*" I said. (Tell me.) "I've been noticing that most people in town tend to *tutoyer* each other, but I learned my French in Paris, where it is so much more formal than here in the Midi . . ." Jean-Luc nodded and widened his eyes invitingly.

I cleared my throat. "See, I tend to *vousvoyer* according to the rules I learned in Paris, but what has occurred to me is that, perhaps, I am giving offense in the other direction, by, possibly, employing *vous* too long, when it would be more friendly and better received if I switched to *tu* at this point."

The answer, from both, was definitive and immediate. They did not commiserate or hesitate.

"Nooooooo," they said in perfect unison.

"No offense at all," said Jean-Luc, holding his palm out toward me.

"*Pas du tout,*" seconded Nicole.

"No, in fact," said Jean-Luc, pointing across the street at the family mansion standing behind an extensive iron gate, "in that family there, the children even used to *vousvoyer* their parents! No, don't unquiet yourself, Steve."

I stood, a casual giant with his arm propped on the roof of their car, a gesture that had seemed an easygoing prelude to our new terms, but that now felt uncomfortably proprietary.

My question, of course, had been just indirect enough to leave me still uncertain about what I truly wanted to know. If I was Mary Jo, I would have simply started saying *tu* to them, and never looked back. But I was not Mary Jo.

Their tone had been so reassuring that I wanted to believe they were simply anxious to ease my mind on a point of etiquette. On the other hand, it had been such an immediate and vehement reaction that I wasn't willing to risk the follow-up question, "Yeah, but how about just between us?"

And so I adopted the resolution, which may not have been true, that it was not yet time. That *vous* was, for now, perhaps forever, the proper and fitting way to address each other.

I thanked them for their advice, as always. They were all smiles. I removed my arm from the car roof to shake their hands and turned back to the front door of our place.

"*Merci, Steve*," called Jean-Luc.

"Steve!" he called. There was a village fête coming up in the promenade next to the school. There would be music and local wine and possibly a spit-roasted cow from the hills where we had driven. My family and I might enjoy it.

"Thank you very much," I said, and turned to go.

"Bon appétit," called Nicole.

"*A vous aussi*," I replied.

32

April the mantis was acting strange. She spent a lot of time hanging from the mesh of the terrarium cover. Joe, concerned that she wasn't eating enough, offered more crickets. He researched possible remedies, but the literature on pet mantises was scant.

Her right forelimb turned brown and then black, and she stoically chewed it off.

Joe grew more frantic. Her abdomen was bloated. She struggled to hold it off the ground. Spots like freckles appeared on her wings. We left her hanging from her ceiling one night, and found her the next morning in approximately the same position, but on the floor of the terrarium, on her back, legs in the air, unresponsive.

Joe returned her to the *garrigue,* holding a short but respectful service before burying her. For the next two nights, the crickets' chirping provided such a painful reminder that he let them go, too. But he kept April's cage clean and furnished, just in case.

33

Joe is maybe three or four. We have just moved into our house.

He pads on bare feet to a large plastic tote, almost waist-high to him, then leans over to pull out a plastic dinosaur, his fat hand clamped across its broad back. The dinosaur's neck and tiny head extend almost as far forward from its shoulders as its long whip tail extends rearward from its haunches.

Joe calls this "yine-up." Sometimes he asks to "yine up" toy cars and trucks and construction vehicles, and we haul that tote from the basement, but mostly it is dinosaurs, always in straight lines, always with a preternatural seriousness, as if the materials at hand are not ever quite sufficient to execute the perfection of the vision in his head.

His back-and-forth resembles pacing more than play. He looks driven, not drawn, to this slow, necessary task of imposing order. He still has a lisp. He says, "Tee-wreckth." And "Thteg-uh-THOR-uth."

The four-legged diplodocus does not fit naturally against the upright stance of the T. rex, and Joe wrestles methodically with the two of them. He has started to blink his long, curved black lashes in the way that sometimes results in a slow crawl of frustrated tears down his smooth cheeks, past the bubble of mucus that is always threatening to drip from his nose, as if his immune system were just a little too weak to defend him from the assaults of his biome.

There is something about the world that makes him afraid, something chaotic that has designs on him, and that he needs powers to fend off. One of those powers is the ability to place dinosaurs in a perfect row, in the right order, all touching.

Earlier that week, I had watched a mother duck lead ten ducklings across a county highway. The ducklings had the gawky elongated bodies and thick beaks of juveniles, but were still spotted yellow and brown. They followed their mother in a weaving single file into my lane, where I had braked for them. The ducks crossed the solid white line in front of my bumper into the lane to my right, and suddenly a black Dodge Charger was in my side mirror, coming up behind me, too fast. The mother duck began to run, her mouth opening and closing, and the ducklings tried to catch up. The car flew past, rocking me with a thump of compressed air, and I watched it float through the intersection, just as the light turned red.

Eva has always been the strong one. At Joe's age, barely post-toddler, she was already stage-directing her life, demanding what she wanted, and arranging her world with self-assurance and something that might even be called vision.

Joe is different. Something ethereal attached to him early. Something delicate and almost dangerously exposed. He has that kind of gentleness that makes a parent want to invent a better world so that he can live there in peace.

Since seeing the ducklings on the highway, I have spent the week quietly agonizing about him—feeling that the world is a Dodge Charger trying to make a yellow light, and Joe is always about to step into the street.

I'm sure it's a feeling most parents endure during those spasms of protectiveness we are all subject to, when we are shaken from our routines long enough to notice our children's frailty.

But, for me, Joe has a shadow identity, in addition to his own. He is himself—serious, anxious, sweet-tempered, openhearted. And he is also me. Or at least, he is the only route by which I ever get to visit those qualities in the boy I once was. Like something seen in peripheral vision that vanishes when you look directly at it, I cannot look straight at my boyhood self and feel love for him.

But every once in a while, when I look at Joe—at the dimples over the knuckles of his soft hands, at his concentration, his carefulness as he introduces a brachiosaurus into his somber parade, and then looks at it to make sure it is in the right position to cast its crucial spell—every once in a while, my protectiveness is so wide and strong that it feels as if there is room inside it for both of us.

Joe runs out of dinosaurs before he reaches the front door, but yine-up appears to have done its work by the time he is done. He is cheerful and content.

That night I crawl into bed with him, where he has stacked the evening's books at the foot of the bed and will crawl down to retrieve each one in its turn. He puts his head on my shoulder and, a couple books in, falls softly, limply asleep, his mouth open, breathing hot against my neck. I pull his loose body tight against mine, and leave a guarding arm along his back, with love like a great sadness welling in my chest.

34

Jean-Luc and Nicole took their dogs out for a walk every evening, murmuring patois endearments to them in the twilight.

The breed was called Fauve de Bretagne, bred to hunt the thorny and impenetrable *garrigue,* impossible to run through but just possible to run beneath, which explained their unheroic proportions. They had wiry ginger fur, hanging ears, bodies shaped like braunschweiger, turned-out basset hound front paws, and eyebrows like ears of rye.

Jean-Luc asked us to join him one evening. There was a flower Mahree ZHO ought to see.

We threaded our way through the streets and down a country road with views of the quilted hills in the distance. Jean-Luc's dogs—Dolly, Daisy, and Gitane—were mostly allowed off leash except Daisy, who, he said, was a *machine à chasser* (a hunting machine). If he let her go, he might find her over the horizon sometime in the next few days.

The trail, when we reached it, was a brushy two-track, running through a patch of scrub between vineyards.

Mary Jo stopped here and there, exclaiming over some new discovery. Jean-Luc, far from acting put out by the halting pace, would stand beside her, and, with an *"Alors ça"* (Now this one . . .), would identify each plant she was photographing, and, more often than not, expand on the plant's use—culinary, medicinal, or practical.

Joe discovered a translucent amber capsule of dried sap, now as hard and beautiful as an agate. *"A l'époque"* (Back in the day), it had been used to make a kind of glue. Joe held it out to Mary Jo for a photo, then pocketed it with the nervy casualness of a boy who has just stolen something.

This was the magic of Mary Jo's STILL project, and of her contagious receptiveness to the natural world. What had been just another dirt path through undistinguished country would offer itself up for observation, and suddenly we were in a heightened state of noticing all that was beautiful, ugly, rare, interestingly misshapen, exquisitely colored, perfect, or perfectly imperfect within a short radius of wherever we happened to be.

"There!" said Jean-Luc. "There!"

The flower was demure and inconspicuous. Five pale pink petals the size of a quarter, serrated on their outer edges, emerging from a green sheath, like an unemphatic firework. It stood far off the ground on a fragile stalk, with good posture, and an air of self-possession.

"It's too beautiful!" said Mary Jo.

Jean-Luc, appearing equally smitten, told her it was an *oeillet sauvage*. A wild carnation.

My mind immediately lit up with literary associations. Pagnol's two scoundrels, Papet and Galinette, growing their carnations with stolen spring water. And one of my favorite French poems, memorized in college and never forgotten, called *"D'Un Vanneur de Blé aux Vents."* It is a rhymed plea, almost a prayer, from a man who is winnowing his wheat to the winds, asking that they blow over the field, and over him, as he sweats at his labor. In exchange he offers the beauty of the flowers that surround him: these violets, these lilies, these roses, and these carnations, too.

I recited the passage aloud:

J'offre ces violettes,
Ces lis et ces fleurettes,
Et ces roses ici,

Ces vermeillettes roses,
Tout fraîchement écloses,
Et ces oeillets aussi.

"*C'est joli,*" said Jean-Luc.

"*C'est du Bellay,*" I said, and immediately wondered whether he knew the poem, or knew Joachim du Bellay, and if he didn't, whether he felt funny about not knowing the French poem or the French poet just quoted by his American companion, and if he did know them, whether it had struck him as condescending that I would think to quote a poem to him about a simple laborer toiling in the heat of the day.

I don't believe, in retrospect, that Jean-Luc thought twice about the exchange. But it occupied my mind for days.

35

A thin haze of woodsmoke drifting in through our open windows announced the morning of the village fête.

We all followed our noses to a crackling fire at the far end of the promenade, where a couple of men were working to affix two unwieldy animal legs, which might have belonged to a brontosaurus, onto a long, heavy, iron spit.

The spit would turn all morning and most of the afternoon, dripping onto the orange coals and white ash below it and sending shifting tendrils of carbonized beef fat curling through the streets.

We were not the complete strangers we had been, but our little group still felt self-contained as we moved through the growing crowd of villagers toward the line of tables where winemakers were pouring glasses of their wines.

Joe wore a striped Breton fishing shirt and a straw trilby with a black hatband purchased at the lively Sunday market in Pézenas. He had begun, more willingly than was his usual custom, to adopt what he saw as the French style of dress around him. Eva remained in jeans, a plain T-shirt, and Velcro-strapped Teva sandals.

André flicked the brim of Joe's hat, shook my hand with a squeeze of my other arm below the shoulder, and kissed Eva and Mary Jo, before serving us two glasses of rosé. We stood near him for a while, the way you might stand against the wall with the only other person you know at the high school party. The talk around André's wine display ran heavily toward the upcoming harvest, and the cursed drought, and I translated here and there for Mary Jo.

If, hypothetically, someone were hoping for an opportunity to ask about picking wine grapes, perhaps no more a conducive set of circumstances could be put in place than this very conversation, and although Mary Jo was not sending a single insinuating vibration my way, I knew my asking, right now, would be a gesture she would appreciate even if I were ultimately turned down.

I was painfully aware that my efforts to cook my way into the life of the village had stalled, and had possibly been misguided from the start. I had been struggling to cook my way into the life of my own family.

Meanwhile, there had been a detectible surge of tractor traffic in the street below our window lately. Cars and trucks were parked here and there at the corners of vineyards, where solitary figures walked the rows, taking samples and assessing. As these signs of the approaching harvest had proliferated, one obvious conclusion had made itself clear: when you live in a place that is mostly covered in vines, then vines are where you ought to go, if you want to be a part of that place.

But I was at an emotional low. I kept seeing myself quoting poetry to Jean-Luc, standing next to him, stilted and tone-deaf. I was still and somewhat painfully scattering the word "*vous*" all over town. April the mantis was dead. I had a kitchen full of tools that felt clumsy in my hands. And through all of this, Mary Jo had, quietly, under the radar, established connections with Jean-Luc, with André, with Eva and Joseph, with the natural world. She was pure participation without the advantage of language, while I was all language waiting fruitlessly for an invitation to participate.

And although it was small of me and I knew it, I refused the invitation that had practically been laid at my feet to ask, in front of her, whether there might be room for me among the grape pickers, once the grape picking began. It was as if I couldn't give her another victory, just then—a pettiness I would have liked to believe was beneath me, and one I would already regret by the end of the day. There had been no explicit exchange between us, verbal or visual, but I felt sure, from two-plus decades together, that my choice had registered with her, and my awareness of this existed invisibly between us for the rest of the afternoon, distancing us, like the aftermath of an argument we had never had.

Jean-Luc spotted us and led us to a folding banquet table on the other side of the square. He and Nicole were seated beside Jean-Luc's brother Georges and his wife. His brother was retired, but not really retired, because he spent much of his life tending his pack of hunting dogs up in the hills. Jean-Luc regularly lent a hand, driving up to his brother's kennel in the evening to water and feed the dogs.

Georges was lean and muscular with flinty good looks and a deep baritone voice that, all together, spoke of a powerful alpha energy contrasting with Jean-Luc's quick, eager lightness of manner.

Georges had recently lost a dog, impaled on the tusk of a boar. Jean-Luc told the story of one of their dogs who had gone missing on a hunt a few years before. He had driven up and down every back road and navigable trail, stopping and listening for her, only to find her body beside the highway several days later.

Nicole, whose rapid-fire speaking style could be taken as a kind of gruffness, had chimed in here and there as Jean-Luc told his story, but when the story got to the discovered animal, lifted from the shoulder of the road and placed in the back of Jean-Luc's truck, she grew quiet, and, I thought, a little wet-eyed.

The beef was smoky and tender, served with white beans and something called *pommes de terre sarladaises,* sliced potatoes cooked in garlic and the fat drippings from the haunch of beef.

The kids, as so often when not at my table, ate with evident relish and zero complaints.

"You were making a *grillade,* the other night," said Jean-Luc.

"It's true," I said.

"Around here we make our *grillades* with vine wood. It is another thing entirely from charcoal. I will bring you some."

I gestured toward the cookfire at the far end of the square. "But they did not use vines to cook all that beef?"

"Steve," said Nicole. "In what region are we?" and she laughed, a high giggle in total contrast to the forcefulness of her standard speaking voice.

"They would naturally have burned *ceps de vigne* [vine stumps] this morning," said Jean-Luc, "but for the grill at home, one can also use *sarments de vigne* [vine branches]. Truly, you will see. The wood of the vine gives more heat, and there is a . . ." He lifted his nose and moved it like a hound trying to catch a scent. "Do you not remark that aroma? The smoke is . . . Well, it is not charcoal, I'm telling you."

By the time the band took the stage, presided over by a schmoozy emcee with a too-loud microphone, Marie and her family had stopped by to say hi, and André and his wife, Véronique, had brought over extra bottles. There was that tipsy glow, in which, after a few glasses of wine, anyone you have been sharing the table with for the previous hour or two, stranger or friend, appears to possess hidden depths that it is a pleasure to plumb.

The band, at the request of the master of ceremonies, took up a waltz.

Jean-Luc's brother and his wife were instantly on their feet, holding hands, part of a general exodus that poured past the dinner tables and emptied onto the dance floor, where most of the village paired off on the asphalt of the playground, under twinkle lights strung between the trunks of the plane trees.

Couples of every age lifted and fell, turning with the waltz's understated oom-pah-pah, gliding around the rocking horse and the jungle gym. And of all the excellent dancers, Jean-Luc's brother was perhaps the most beautiful, somehow shedding what had looked to be a bound-up, muscular denseness of frame, and moving, instead, with the dramatic range of motion and the feline composure of a toreador.

"Your brother," I said.

"Yes, they dance almost every weekend," said Jean-Luc.

"*Allez*," said Nicole when the next song started. She slapped Jean-Luc's upper arm with the back of her hand, and the two of them joined the other dancers, competently, and unselfconsciously.

"They're so cute!" said Eva.

"They're adorable," said Mary Jo.

"You guys should go dance," said Eva.

We were nearly the only adult couple still sitting, aside from a scattering of octogenarians who, by the expressions on their faces, would gladly have been out there cutting a rug if their bodies could have supported it.

The kids started chanting. "Go. Dance. Go. Dance. Go. Dance."

Mary Jo held out a hand. I hesitated and then took hold of it.

"Yes!" said Eva.

"Go, Dad!" said Joe.

I wanted nothing more than to dance with her. To throw off my self-consciousness and declare my love. I wanted to dance as devotedly and awkwardly as a crane—throwing my head back, drumming my feet, flapping my arms, tossing sticks and clumps of grass in the air. She was still what she had been our first summer and would always be. She was the before and after of my life. I wanted nothing that did not include her and everything we had made together.

"Are you going to ask me to dance, Mr. Hoffman?" she asked.

And I couldn't. I couldn't make her happy, because I was unhappy just then, and when I was unhappy I did not possess the reserves necessary to go make a joyful fool of myself. I couldn't turn my brain off long enough simply to act. I had been stupid and stubborn in front of André and I didn't know how much it had gotten under her skin, and I was too craven, or too bound up, or too something, to say, "Forget that, my love, I was silly. Let's dance."

I bent over her hand, and gave it a kiss, and released it, and sat back in my chair.

"That's the last thing any of you wants to see," I said.

We all sat quiet, sort of smiling, sipping from our glasses, listening to the band, watching the dancers and the shadows of their moving bodies on the façade of Joe's new school, on the far side of the square.

36

I spent the following day on the terrace, in brilliant sunlight that gave me no joy, while, in pool water that Jean-Luc had warned us was now far too cold to swim in, my Minnesota kids happily took one of their final dips before school, jumping in, hauling themselves back out, dripping onto the warm tile in their swimsuits and shivering until the sun dried them off again.

I was sitting in the corner near the lemon tree, with the sun baking the oils of the rosemary plant beside me into suggestive volatility. My laptop was open and I was surrounded by cookbooks that included my own small collection, plus several others I had borrowed from the library, steeped in the thought that I was no more a cook for sitting among cookbooks than I was a Frenchman for speaking French. My refusal last night had betrayed something about myself that I hadn't wanted to believe.

Because, if nothing else, I had always had, on my side of the ledger, that I was a good husband and father. Whatever the world threw at me, however doubtful it made me, at times, about my own virtue and competence, I had a safe little room into which I could retreat, and in that room, I was always a good husband and father.

The doorbell rang, and Jean-Luc informed us that he had spent the early morning in his sister's *jardang* behind the orchard, where he had discovered an excess of mature lettuce, one head of which, sifting fine soil onto the street, he now held out to Mary Jo.

He disappeared into his garage, and tottered back out, holding the neck of a fertilizer sack in both fists. The sack was full of gnarled vine stumps.

In addition to lettuce, he warned, we were never to pay for parsley, which he had in quantities "until his neck."

He disappeared again, reemerging with a witch's broom of smaller-gauge twigs bundled with twine.

The stumps in the bag were my *ceps de vigne,* and the twigs were my *sarments,* which could be used as kindling, or by themselves when less heat was needed for less time.

Mary Jo took the lettuce upstairs, I hoisted the bag of stumps, and Jean-Luc carried the bundle on his shoulder through our garage and out into the back courtyard, where the grill stood, and where the kids were still splashing in the pool.

He looked at them as if watching someone walk intentionally into and out of a burning building, and said, "*Ils sont fous ces Américains*" (They are mad, these Americans), a phrase borrowed from the Asterix comics, which he, like all French boys, had read to the point of memorization.

I had not known I would have a chance this soon to ask him what I wanted to ask, and, of course, now that the opportunity had presented itself, I was as hesitant to proceed as if yesterday hadn't happened.

"*La vidange,*" I hazarded. "She has commenced?"

I sensed something was wrong by the expression on Jean-Luc's face. He corrected me, explaining that a *vidange* was an oil change, and while, no, there was no oil change currently in process, what he assumed I meant was *vendange,* and, no, the grape harvest was not yet in process.

A pout formed under his salt-and-pepper mustache and, rocking his open hand back and forth between us, he peered at the sky.

"In several days," he said. "Not more."

"Perhaps in several days," I suggested, "you will need some help."

He looked me up and down, and translated his misgivings into a kind of smile.

"Visitors adore the *vendange*," he said. "They love to pick the grapes."

Then he made the peace sign and held it out to me.

"For two days," he said. "Then they wake up, and they don't love the *vendange* anymore. They love a coffee with their morning brioche, and they love dinner at the café with a pitcher of rosé."

Not yet ready to take no for an answer, I turned sideways and patted my kidneys.

"Strong back," I said.

He waggled a finger at me to say that strong backs didn't enter into it. Then he rapped on his right temple as if knocking on a door.

"Weak head," he said. "That's what is essential!" And he laughed his way out of the garage and back home.

37

At dinner the night before school started, Joe had been full of bravado and silliness, but now, in bed, he had turned quiet.

"Is everybody going to talk to me tomorrow?" he asked.

"No, they'll be as shy about you as you are about them. You're the only American in school."

"How much am I going to have to talk?"

"I don't know, Joe-Joe. But you've already done this. You've gone to school in French. This will be another day like that."

He had stacked his books beside the bed, next to the empty terrarium. We tried reading Pagnol, but Joe had trouble concentrating. He decided he wasn't in the mood for Fabre. And so, we resumed *My Family and Other Animals,* in which a family goes on an adventure together that we already knew would turn out well.

At dawn the next morning, I drove Eva to Collège le Cèdre, into a sunrise that lit blankets of mist hovering over dark vines.

Eva sat next to me, staring at the black road ahead, while the morning deejays introduced the same Top 40 songs they played at home, with the same mix of silly and sarcastic juvenility.

She spoke only once, admitting concern that she had lost much of her spoken French.

She had played piano for most of her school years, reaching the more accessible echelons of Scarlatti, Mozart, and Beethoven before deciding that she could be a pretty good piano player by expending much time and great effort at the keyboard, or she could be a much better something else, to be determined, once she discovered what that something was. She walked away from piano without much in the way of second thoughts, and remained a free agent while she worked out, by trial and error, what she might want to make of herself.

The progressively harder pieces she learned drove her closer and closer to the ceiling of her abilities, and I remembered watching her final recitals, where she had played with a muscular rigidity that was like her whole body concentrating. Her lower jaw, offset from the upper, would clench and work as she played, as if she were chipping the notes out of a granite wall. She had that look now. The look of someone getting through by sheer will.

We met the gate attendant at seven thirty sharp. I introduced Eva as the new American girl, and the attendant told us with a glassy smile that she could go right "up there."

"Will she know where to go?" I asked.

"Oh, don't alarm yourself," he reassured us with a grin that looked as if invisible threads were pulling back the corners of his mouth.

I sensed Eva's efforts to beg me telepathically, "Please. Please don't go up there with me."

The smile had not moved. "She will know where to go. If you want to go with her, you are welcome. Or if she's a big girl, she can go by herself."

And not knowing what else to do, I wished her good luck, and she made her way "up there," where the French talent for clarity, planning, and organization would surely help her find her way.

For his part, Joe woke up puffy-eyed, tousled, and somber.

Outside his school, we waited for the gate to open, smiling around us at unsmiling parents and grandparents, gathered into intimate groups that did not give off any of the body language of welcome or invitation. Joe leaned in to us and avoided eye contact with anyone his age.

He only interrupted his silent thoughts once, to ask us what we would do if he didn't like going to school here.

When the time came, we each gave him a lingering forehead kiss, and Joe, looking very alone, walked up the steps and through the chain-link gate into *la cour,* the elevated courtyard that served as the school's playground.

We had met the principal, Monsieur Deconchy, once before when we had registered Joe for school. He had the gentle manner of an aging hippie, with a shy smile, sandals, wire-rimmed glasses, and an unkempt mane of dark hair.

Joe shook his hand and then, contrary to all my reassurances of the previous night, was quickly made the center of a circle of grade school boys, who appeared to have several weeks of pent-up questions ready for the new American among them. They pushed each other to get closer to Joe, who had the awkward A-shaped part in his bangs that appeared when he nervously ran his hand through his hair. He was smiling queasily and turning toward each of his inquisitors as they delivered their questions—my innocent boy gazelle, being dismantled by a pack of wild dogs.

They were still peppering him when the bell rang.

Everybody lined up by classroom, Joe's blue-striped mariner shirt disappeared through the front door of the school. The courtyard was empty, and the school year had begun.

Mary Jo had stifled a few half sobs during Joe's ordeal.

"What have we done to that little bunny?" she asked.

"He's done this before," I said. "He's stronger than he looks."

"We didn't have to do this. We chose this."

"He's smart. He's always made friends."

"Did you see the look on his face?" she asked, and took in a rattling snuffle.

"As long as he has a predictable home life, he can handle anything. We've watched it before."

"You always know how to say the right thing, but that's not helping right now. God, I hope they have a good day," she said.

For all my efforts in the kitchen, I had not introduced anything new into our family meal rotation that I could plausibly imagine would offer comfort to the kids, certainly not anything French. And I had not inherited that kind of tradition from my own family. There had not been a mamma, a nonna, a yaya, an abuela. There had not been souvlaki, eggplant parmigiana, tortilla Española, pozole. My earliest memories of food had been of restaurants, sandwiches, a particular three-bean casserole, and dinners that came from freezers or cans.

We did have a gammy, however. Mary Jo's mom had been a dedicated and frugal home cook, incorporating the dishes of her Romanian mother-in-law into her own repertoire of mid-century American classics, all of which had combined to create a cuisine of its own that her kids, and now her grandkids, thought of with nostalgia, and lustily craved.

As a result, I spent the afternoon playing sous-chef as Mary Jo made Gammy's Spaghetti and Meatballs, and her Apple Delight—a frosted double-crust apple-slab pie.

Joe looked a little dazed when we picked him up, and Eva was quiet on the drive home. As they twirled their spaghetti and ate big, messy squares of Apple Delight, we did our best to restrain the zillion questions we had. They agreed with each other about how fast everyone spoke, and that was about it, until Eva announced, "They made me sing."

"What do you mean, sing?" asked Mary Jo.

"In music class. We all had to sing."

"You can't sing. None of us can sing."

"Tell me about it."

"You mean in a group?"

"No. By myself. Everyone had to sing a solo in front of the class to place us in the choir."

"Oh my God," said Mary Jo. "In French?"

Eva gave her a look.

"Oh, honey. Were you scared?"

"Mom, I'm not a baby," she said.

Mary Jo looked at me pleadingly, as if there were some way to go back and undo this.

I sliced up a couple of Jean-Luc's nectarines and placed a plate in front of each kid as a sort of apology. Eva, without acknowledging the gesture, worked her way around the circle of slices.

"Anyway, we're going to learn the song for the holidays," she said.

And that was all we learned. The kids were so plainly wiped out that we joined them for a short *Friends* binge on the couch, during which they each fell asleep.

Mary Jo roused Eva, and I carried Joe upstairs.

He awoke as I laid him on the bed. I undressed him and slipped him into his striped jammies and lay down next to him.

"How was it, Joe, really?" I asked him.

"I miss April," he said blearily, and had just enough left in him to scooch tight to my side, throw a knee over me, and put his head on my shoulder before he fell back asleep.

In bed that night, an unnerved Mary Jo faced me on her pillow.

"What are we doing?" she asked.

"We're fucking up our kids, like all good parents."

"Not funny."

She sat up and pulled the sheet around her like a shawl.

"Stevie, this is why I need you. Why I need to be able to . . . Trust you isn't quite what I mean, but . . ."

"OK, come on, hon."

"I don't mean trust you like you'll remember to take out the garbage. Or like your intentions are good. Yes, your heart is always in the right place. I know that. I mean trust like . . . I don't know, I honestly don't know if we're piling too much on these two . . . these two supersensitive kids."

"Do you really think they can't handle this?"

"I think they probably can," she said. "But I don't know. I need to feel OK that we're making good decisions. And if Stevie, my sounding board, my teammate, is making decisions out of . . . I don't know, nostalgia, or ego, or magical thinking, or dreams of escape, then we're not making good decisions."

"We always make good decisions," I said.

"Together. Yes."

"We are together."

She sat there, looking uncharacteristically glum. Then she cocked her right leg and gave me a half-hearted donkey kick.

"You big dummy," she said.

In college, Mary Jo was diagnosed with an autoimmune disorder called Sjögren's syndrome, which expressed itself in her case primarily in the form of dry eyes and dry mouth, though it can also be associated with rheumatoid arthritis and lupus.

In practical terms, it meant she had to carry little plastic vials around with her, and put drops in her eyes every few hours, depending on conditions.

More fundamentally, it brought home to her, very early and concretely, the idea of her own finitude.

She was also an engineer—not just by occupation but by disposition. Whether structures, systems, bodies of work, or relationships, life was about building things. And life, as she had been forced to reckon with since her diagnosis as a teen, only moved in one direction. For all of my young man's enamored fooling about among the ideas of Nietzsche and Camus, it would take me years to understand that, in Mary Jo, I had married an actual, practicing existentialist.

This way of accepting the terms of the world—life is short, build things—came with two emotional corollaries. The first was a sort of code, the engineer's promise that one took responsibility for what one built, both by making it well in the first place, and by taking whatever blame fell your way if it failed.

There is a concept in spaceflight called "loss of craft, loss of crew." A friend of Mary Jo's from her undergrad internship at NASA worked most of his career on the space shuttle. He once counted off a partial list of the unfathomable number of contingencies that had to be engineered for on every single shuttle flight. The failure of any component of any of those systems—many operating at the outer edge of their structural and material limits—would result, without recourse, in "loss of craft, loss of crew."

This didn't mean Mary Jo spent her life catastrophizing, but rather that she was familiar with things that could not be salvaged or undone, and was used to taking responsibility for them, professionally and personally, whereas I was good at charming my way out of such things as limits, deadlines, and expectations, and convincing myself of their ultimate flexibility. Time was expandable. What had been lost could always be recovered. And it was difficult for Mary Jo at times to watch me fool myself—to quite literally waste time—in this way.

The second emotional consequence of Mary Jo's sense of responsibility was maybe as close as she had to an Achilles' heel, and that was her fear of regret. It was a latent fear, made up of her belief that almost everything could be anticipated and engineered for, and that bad outcomes were not primarily the result of bad luck but of bad planning.

Regret, in Mary Jo's world, was not a feeling of loss, but the recognition that someone else was going to get hurt because you, however unwittingly, had been careless.

This fear lay dormant beneath Mary Jo's habitual sunniness, and only came to life when she was under stress. At those times, though, it could send her spiraling into something like panic as she frantically rifled through the drawers of her memory looking for the key to why this had happened.

Part of what we were building here in Autignac, if we were doing this right, was a family. There was a way of doing that well, and a way of doing it less well. I don't think she was truly afraid that we were going to traumatize our two kids in some irreversible way. But she had been faced with consequences that afternoon, and was organizing herself to assess and take responsibility, and that had reduced the margin of error in her life just enough to warrant double-checking that every system was sound. I was one of those systems, and the stakes were high—our kids' well-being was in some sense on the line. And I think she wanted the emotional comfort of feeling unmixed about me just then.

But she had recently witnessed my unwillingness to, in her words, get over myself. To face up to the life that my own decisions had laid before me.

And when she asked herself if she could, at that moment, confidently hand the reins of her life to me, the answer would just recently have moved from a yes to a qualified yes.

And that threw other things into question. And raised other possibilities for regret.

38

The next evening, I stood outside Jean-Luc and Nicole's front door. I had just heard his tractor rumble up, and had watched him from my window, turned stiffly in his cockpit, as a trailer, and then the tractor itself, disappeared into his garage.

Now the sparrows were chirping in the vines growing up our neighbor's wall, and the light was softening along Avenue de la Liberté. I could hear faint voices upstairs chattering in a happy key. I held my hand up to their doorbell and stared at it for several seconds.

Then I pushed the doorbell before I could think too much more about it. A short electronic chime. The sparrows rocketed from the vines overhead with a low roar, and peeled off like coveys of quail.

A racket of barking dogs. A pause.

Slow footsteps down the stairs, and the door swung open.

"Ah, it's Steve," said Jean-Luc.

"Bonsoir, Jean-Luc," I said.

He stood there, not offering to see me in, but friendly.

"I don't know how to tell you," I said, "how much I would like to pick grapes. Perhaps I will have no talent, perhaps I will be too tall, perhaps you will tell me to go home and eat my brioche, but I would like to give it an effort. Very much. Do you think it is possible?"

His expression had shifted, from openly receptive to sober and a bit wary. He didn't say anything for several beats as I felt a flush climb my cheeks.

I rapped my head with the knuckles of my right hand. "*Vide*," I said. (Empty.)

He broke into a smile. "I will talk to our team," he said.

That night, we smelled cigarette smoke and heard animated Spanish spilling over the wall from Jean-Luc and Nicole's terrace.

Just before dark, I heard Jean-Luc call softly. There was a spot at the top of our stairway where the wall between us was low enough to see over. Jean-Luc was there, and another man I had never seen before stood against their railing, smoking.

"*Ça commence demaing,*" said Jean-Luc. (It starts tomorrow.)

PART III

39

I arrived at a dusty fork the next morning, and walked across the road in Carhartt work shorts and a pair of American hiking shoes, with no sense of what awaited me. In an elevated field beyond the truck, I could see Jean-Luc's tractor pulling a red steel trailer slowly down a row of vines.

In the end, what awaited me was Nicole, who handed me a blue bucket and a well-used pair of orange hand clippers, handles worn to gray. The clippers had just been sharpened, so attention to my fingers, warned Nicole, whose love language I was just beginning to understand. She expressed her affection with a kind of mothering that resembled the brisk, efficient caretaking of a busy floor nurse.

My bucket had once had a wooden grip on the wire handle, but the wood had cracked over the years and only half of it was left. It clunked as Nicole and I hauled ourselves up the brushy slope to the field, spraying little showers of grasshoppers ahead of us.

Jean-Luc had left his tractor parked twenty-five yards or so down one of the rows. He extended a stiff right arm to shake hands.

Behind him spread a slope of sprawling, waist-high vines, planted without trellises. Their branches burst out from their stumps and trailed toward the ground, like tightly held bouquets of ivy.

It was just after seven. A half-moon still hung in the pale sky to our west, and above the eastern horizon, a glowing white halo suggested, but did not yet include, the sun.

I reassured Jean-Luc and Nicole that they had nothing left to fear, because the American grape picker was now here. It was one of those not particularly funny dad jokes that Joe had just begun to call me on.

But Jean-Luc liked my dad jokes, and he put his left hand on my shoulder, and gestured with his right, while we had one of those rapid, escalating back-and-forths that happen when two guys find something funny.

As the laughter and gesturing subsided, there was the sound of crackling tires. A white SUV pulled in behind their truck, and behind it a boxy old burgundy-colored Renault sedan. Headlights blinked shut, doors swung open, and several more of this morning's crew folded themselves out of the vehicles, murmuring and stretching in the cool dawn air, calling to Jean-Luc about where to find buckets and shears, then helping themselves before making their way up the hill into the vineyard.

I had been part of this ragged early-morning assembly several hundred other times in my life, on jobsites as a handyman and subcontractor in my twenties and thirties. But what happened on the first day of the *vendange* was not like any other such event I'd ever witnessed.

The remaining crew arrived in successive waves of ones and twos, looking a little bit scraggly, mostly in shorts, T-shirts, and tennis shoes. They were an even mix of men and women. Gabi, from Romania, introduced herself and her two well-built nephews. The Frenchmen were short and stocky with sparse beards and black hair, looking for the most part like the ex-welterweight you wouldn't want to mess with at the bar.

They called to Jean-Luc and Nicole and to each other, and when they got close, they put their hands on each other's shoulders, and kissed each other almost tenderly on both cheeks. They exchanged brief family updates, and then patted each other and moved on to the next stubbly crewmate, maybe resting a palm behind his neck, and kissing him. And when the strength of the team had gathered their buckets and their clippers and arranged themselves on either side of the rows of vines, a final carful of pickers arrived, grabbed their gear, and before starting work, walked up each row to embrace their comrades, and then walked out of that row and up the next one, until they had kissed and greeted everyone present, in a spirit that, as far as I could tell, contained no trace of the glum workday resignation, or even the jokey bitching that had been a fixture of most of the lunch-bucket working teams I had ever been a part of.

Freestanding vines like the ones in this parcel are said to be pruned *en gobelet,* in goblet form, and they look like unruly shrubs.

My grape-picking career began across one of these shrubs from Jean-Luc, with Nicole working behind me on her row, and the rest of the crew spread out on either side of us.

I stood there with a bucket at my feet and a clipper in my right hand, wanting to be informed of all the mistakes I could possibly make so I could avoid them. I wanted to know how fast I should be expected to move, and what role the tractor played. I wanted to know which grapes we were picking and whether I should treat them in a certain way because they were that particular variety of grape and not another.

Instead, at some point, Jean-Luc unceremoniously pulled a series of branches aside, wrestling his way into the center of our first vine, until he found a dangling, bluish bunch of grapes. He leaned to the side to make sure I had a clear view.

"You hold the bunch from below, *là,*" he said.

"You clip from above, *là.*"

"You look at *la grappe* [the bunch of grapes] to see that there is not too much damage, and, *hop!* In the bucket it goes."

With this brief curriculum under my belt, I had graduated to grape picker, and was soon crouched in the draping embrace of a vine pruned *en gobelet,* attempting, as instructed, to hold from below and snip from above, before extricating myself from what felt like abrasive, clinging tentacles, to reengage with a different section of the vine.

I felt a quick flush of not-quite panic as, already a little out of breath, I finished my first vine of the day. I saw bent backs and heads popping up and disappearing in the rows around me, several of them already a stump or two ahead of us. I grabbed my bucket and followed Jean-Luc to the next vine.

Rosettes of dandelion and several spiny thistle flowers had staked various claims between the rows, as had more Queen Anne's lace, which,

I told Jean-Luc, we had confirmed was indeed a wild carrot. He broke off a stem and smelled it, and offered it to me, and of course it smelled just exactly like carrot, which appeared to delight him.

We were among Cinsault vines, he said. A classic southern grape, fatter and juicier than the small-berried Syrah and Mourvèdre, whose ratio of astringent skin to sweet juice was higher. Those other grapes formed the backbone of the tannic red wines of the region. Cinsault, for its part, was a dreamer—pale and floral and delicate, and in a dry year like this, it would add delicacy and finesse when blended into the local red wines, which otherwise risked being too concentrated and alcoholic, after pulling so little water from the soil to deliver to the thirsty clusters sucking at their branches.

Jean-Luc clipped a bunch of grapes and plucked one of the translucent blue marbles to hand to me. "Try it," he said. "This afternoon we will be in Syrah, and you will taste the difference."

I popped it in my mouth—the first wine grape I'd ever eaten rather than drunk.

The skin was so delicate that the grape detonated between my teeth, as if the juice had been held in place by a membrane of its own surface tension rather than anything as coarse as the crunchy, quasi-leathery hide on the pale green table grapes that had defined the word "grape" for my entire life. The seeds creaked between my teeth as I chewed them.

It was another revelation at the hands of professor Jean-Luc and I asked him how the grape in my mouth could possibly be this sweet. He blinked his eyes and gave a short nod. Wine grapes, of course, were always sweeter than table grapes, but the real story was not the variety but where it grew. The sun had time, here, to ripen grapes all the way to their natural maturity—a maturity that added up to the sweetness I was tasting in my mouth. This region—the Languedoc specifically, but more generally *le Midi*—was made to grow grapes, where long, hot summers coaxed all the sugar that the plant was capable of producing into the fruit before it was time to pick them. Other places could grow them, of course, but their natural home was here in the Mediterranean, and when one lived here as he did, one eventually came to consider this the natural state of things, and to consider regions north of here, from Bordeaux to Burgundy to the Loire to Champagne, to be engaged at some level with the problem of immature grapes.

"*Vous voyez?*" he asked. (You see?)

The sun was soon over the horizon, and the uniform green cast of the light inside the vines changed into patchy white flares. I moved to a new vine, and my long shadow scrabbled across the uneven ground.

The perfect bunches were easy. They were dense and dusty blue, with all the grapes intact, and my fingers left shiny black prints where they rubbed off the powdery bloom. The imperfect bunches were what slowed me. I walked regularly over to Jean-Luc or Nicole, asking the same question each time.

"Keep or toss?"

They would inspect my damaged goods. "*Oh, ce n'est pas méchant, ça.*" (Oh, that's not too naughty.) The saggy grapes on this bunch were "*un peu malade*" (feeling a little sick), but were OK. But this bunch had the kind of black mildewy rot that needed to be tossed, every time, *systématiquement.*

And back I would go, to get a little bit intimate with my vine, and perform my slow triage.

The bunches did not all dangle prettily, presenting themselves for snipping. They grew too close to each other and their sides burst. They flopped over stems and the process of pulling them free ripped the bunches in half. They hid behind greenery like the most wily raspberries. I would think I had picked a vine clean, then lift the canes to peer underneath, and three or four bunches would hang there, nonchalantly, like, "Dude, I've been here the whole time."

Nicole worked several stumps ahead of Jean-Luc and me, focused and efficient, but contributing to the general conversation in animated bursts of commentary.

The other pickers advanced unevenly in their lanes, gradually pulling away. I eyed the growing gap between our row and everyone else's, and the German ancestors in my blood instructed me to buckle down, work more efficiently, bend my legs more at the knees. Hoffman. Lane 6. *Schnell.*

But then Jean-Luc would stop me to point out a bird's nest in one of the vines. He would unearth a chalky boulder that turned out to be fossilized coral in this dry land that had once been seafloor. He would talk about how Ibrahimović had just gotten a contract to play soccer for fourteen million euros a year, and how was Ibrahimović, *le pauvre petit* (the poor little guy), going to get by on fourteen million a year?

Whether intentional or not, these unhurried asides served to remind me that we were not in Hong Kong, or Manhattan—or Paris for that matter—but were fifty minutes, give or take, from the Mediterranean. It was probably going to get hot this afternoon. Life in this part of the world was rewarding to talk about. The pleasant vistas surrounding us could not be enjoyed by peering into a hedge of vines. Grapes do not flee like children when unsupervised. Lunch was just around the corner.

Our buckets filled just as we drew up to the tractor, and we all leaned stiff-armed against our handles and heaved our bunches of grapes into the trailer before returning to our rows. The grapes fell softly to the bottom with a muted gong, and lay vividly purple against the red metal of the trailer.

Jean-Luc lifted his bucket awkwardly, without raising his right arm above his shoulder, and I asked him if he was in pain.

"All the time!" he said cheerfully. His back hurt constantly from years of bending over grapevines. But his arm was another story. A childhood afternoon spent hunting with friends. The old, loose-hinged shotgun. The fence that needed to be hurdled. The exploding gun, the shell's worth of bird shot tearing into his right chest and shoulder, the refusal to tell his mother until he saw the red trickle seeping onto the floor of the car from the blood-saturated car seat he was sitting on. The surgery, and the pellets that still littered his interior, including several lodged against the inside of his shoulder blade, which meant that he could raise his arm parallel to the ground but no higher.

"*Le Bon Dieu* [the Good Lord] has tried to kill Jean-Luc three times," he said, "but until now he has not succeeded."

And he sent a belch of diesel smoke skyward as the tractor rumbled forward just far enough that we would reach it when our buckets were full again.

As the tractor coughed itself quiet, the engine sounds were replaced by the sounds that would fill most of the rest of the morning. The windy rushing sound of leaves as they were pushed out of the way. The clicking of shears. The irregular thudding of grape clusters. The clanking of wire handles against the sides of buckets.

But mostly the sound was talk. Other than my faintly American-tinged Parisian French, and the soft rolled "r's" of the Romanians, all of the talk would be in the strange music of the region—the Midi accent that was uniquely of this place.

There was talk about oidium, and powdery mildew, and botrytis, and something called *le vers de la grappe,* which Jean-Luc introduced to me by pointing out several neat round holes the size of a ballpoint pen tip in a couple of grapes, then gently crushing the soft grapes and sifting through the pulp until a grub the color of motor oil could be seen squirming in the juice on his thumb.

There was also a lot of talk that I didn't understand.

But it was clear that this much talk, this sustained, was a muscle that had to be trained and developed, and that the people around me were athletes. I found that I enjoyed this sound—the sound of speech being used to ease time's passing.

At some point, I noticed that I could tell where the sun was, not because I was looking for it, or even looking where it cast its shadow, but because when I was facing away from it, I could feel it on my neck, and when I was facing toward it, I could feel it on my forehead. Now and then, my glasses would slip down my nose or a drop of sweat would land on the inside of the lens and blur everything.

I was finding it harder to lean forward into a vine without resting a hand on my knee, and finding it harder to crouch all the way onto my heels to find the bunches that sometimes hung as low as my shins. I was tiring from reaching in, off-balance, bent double or squatting, to cup the bunch of grapes from below, and clip them from above.

Instead of taking care to get my hand under the bunches as I snipped them, I started grabbing the top of the stems and then snipping right next to my fingers, which is like driving with your eyes closed, or smoking two packs a day. You can get away with it for a while.

Snip.

"*Merde!*"

I sucked my thumb, and showed the wide crescent-shaped incision to Nicole behind me. The slit wrapped itself halfway around the thumb, and Nicole announced impassively to the group, "*Steve s'est taillé*" (Steve pruned himself).

I had mostly been ignored so far by my fellow pickers, and could imagine any number of ways I might have preferred to draw their attention. But here they stopped ignoring me and offered general commiseration, as well as reassurances that I had passed an important and inevitable milestone.

Jean-Luc told the story of being dragged by his parents to pick grapes when he was a kid, and how he and his siblings would sometimes nick their fingers on purpose so they could display their wounds and ask to be excused. But his father would look at the cut, pronounce, "*Je ne vois pas de tripes*" (I don't see any intestines), and send them back to work.

Nicole did as much now, declaring that my bloody thumb was not *la fin du monde* (the end of the world) and returning to her abandoned vine stump, while I tore a piece of my T-shirt and wrapped it around my sweaty, stinging thumb.

As the buckets were filled and dumped and set back on the ground, and occasionally tipped or kicked over, every part of them—the insides, the outsides, the handles—got stickier and stickier with layers of grape juice that the sun baked into a kind of jam, and everyone's hands acquired a tacky coating that dirt and bits of vine leaf stuck to. Our clippers adhered to our fingers and palms, and eventually their handles built up the same coating of reddish syrupy glaze.

Jean-Luc's wiry hair, meanwhile, was still crisp and dry, and his plaid shirt looked ironed. Some pickers finished their rows before others and carried their buckets to a neighbor's row, working back until the two of them met.

One of the Romanian boys met Jean-Luc and me two or three stumps from our finish line, and as we walked toward the tractor with our buckets, he asked in French where I lived in the United States, and I answered him in French that I lived in Minnesota, not too far from Chicago, and he said, in English, "I go to Chicago one time, see uncle," and we smiled at each other, smitten with the success of our efforts to understand one another.

Nicole had already come back from the truck with a portable cooler full of water jugs, which we poured over our sticky hands and clippers, before tipping the bottles and splashing water into our mouths.

Jean-Luc pulled the trailer in a delicate arc, into the middle of our next set of lanes, and in the process he must have crushed some of the wild fennel growing next to the field, because we were all wrapped in an intensifying anise-scented fog, and it was back to work, among the rustling of feet, the snick of clipping shears, the faint tang of body odor, and the murmur of Latin languages floating in the late-summer air.

When lunchtime was announced, there were just a few rows left unpicked. My body felt heavy and sore. I was having trouble rising from a crouch. A fresh sunburn chafed my collar line. But the American in me couldn't help asking Jean-Luc, "Why not pick those last rows before we stop?"

"Because it is the lunch hour," said Jean-Luc.

40

I walked Joe home from school that evening with the gingerly gait of a middle-aged cubicle worker after a weekend laying patio pavers. As we approached our house, we saw a stranger sitting on his heels in Jean-Luc's garage doorway.

He was methodically filling sticky blue grape buckets with water, scrubbing them clean, and dumping the red-stained water into the gutter.

Jean-Luc hauled another stack of buckets out from the back of his truck, looking as if they had been dipped in grape jelly, and introduced us to José, which he pronounced Zho-SAY, not Ho-Say, because when you're in France, your name gets pronounced in French, even though, as I would learn, Jean-Luc speaks almost fluent Spanish.

José stood and shook our hands. He was a sad-eyed, chain-smoking Andalusian who had been coming to pick grapes every year since boyhood, spending a month and sometimes two as Jean-Luc and Nicole's autumn houseguest. Jean-Luc described him as a gunslinger—the fastest picker in the south—who moved among several professional picking crews in order to make enough money to get through the rest of the year in a region with the highest poverty rate in Spain.

He spoke a hybrid Franco-Andalou-Español, and once we had all caught up, he turned to Joseph and asked urgently, in a nasal minor key, "*Joseph! Real Madrid ou Barcelona?*"

Joseph, a committed Leo Messi disciple, answered hesitantly, "Barça."

"No no no no no," lamented José. He walked a grieving circle with his fingers laced into his hair, looked to the sky, and wiped his face with his palms. "Joseph," he said, attempting to regroup. He leaned over Joe and held one wrist for emphasis. "Real Madrid, Joseph. Real Madrid."

Then he pulled a small handful of nuts from his pants pocket.

"Eh-STEVE-eh," he said, and let a couple of them fall into my palm. He made an eating motion with his hand. "*Almendras. Les Amandes.*"

I popped the almonds in my mouth, feeling that a strange but beautiful moment was unfolding.

Then, after the second or third chew, I tasted a revolting, intolerable bitterness fill my mouth, and I spit almond shards onto the street, to the howling glee of Jean-Luc and José.

There are two kinds of almonds in the region, explained Jean-Luc. Sweet and bitter. The bitter almonds, though beautifully scented, contain awful tasting (and, in quantity, potentially toxic) traces of hydrogen cyanide. The only reliable way to know which you're picking is to taste a sample.

Even Joe was laughing.

"*¡Gracias!*" José said, and performed a hurried sign of the cross before tossing the rest of his almonds in the gutter, the mystery solved.

Then he lit a Chesterfield and, with a "*Bonne soirée, compañeros,*" resumed rinsing grape skins from buckets.

"I love José," said Joseph on the way upstairs.

"I gotta rinse my mouth out," I said, which Joseph found offensively hilarious.

41

I returned to the vines the next day, and the day after that, though by the third morning I could empathize with those visitors who, after two days of grape picking, tended to resume lives of late mornings with coffee and late evenings with wine.

Still, when I woke for day four of the *vendange,* I had, in theory, exceeded Jean-Luc's expectations of my commitment and durability. Whether in acknowledgment of this or not, he intercepted Mary Jo and me on our walk home from Joe's school (I walking much more carefully than she). He had something for us to see. Mary Jo should bring her camera.

Half an hour later, we stood side by side, looking down a row of Syrah vines. Other than the fact that grapes were being harvested, the scene couldn't have differed more from the pastoral calm of the days I had just spent picking grapes by hand, and part of me was having trouble adjusting.

Mary Jo stood upright with her camera held to her eye. Advancing on her with roaring diesel engine and a deafening clanking sound was a huge blue machine, on six-foot tires, with a vertical mouth that appeared to be swallowing the entire row of vines at a pace of five or six miles per hour, and excreting them, somewhat the worse for wear, out its back end.

Eventually, Mary Jo stepped out of the way. The towering machine ran over the spot where we'd been standing, executed a delicate one-eighty with a turning radius near zero, and hammered down the next row.

The machine was a grape harvester; this was our introduction to *vendange à la machine*.

The harvester was twelve or fifteen feet tall, a square, inverted U tall enough to straddle each row of vines. On the interior of the U were five or six rows of flexible bars that shimmied rapidly back and forth, with the general idea of shaking the hell out of the vines as the machine passed.

Maybe it was the purity of Jean-Luc's glee at the speed and power of the machine that was throwing me off. My days in the field had felt so ancient and satisfying that I was fighting the idea of this big, roaring machine, and its ugly efficacy. I didn't want all this noise and speed to profane the quiet vineyards I had been working in.

The driver finished a row and waved to Jean-Luc, who asked for a ride in improvised sign language. He motioned Mary Jo up first and climbed the ladder behind her to a steel-mesh platform looking over the churning guts of the machine, which performed its surprisingly elegant Dance of the Three-Point Turn, engaged the deafening blowers, and punished its way down a new row of vines.

In a scene that would give OSHA the vapors, Mary Jo stood balanced on a catwalk fifteen feet in the air on top of a machine moving at a fast walking pace over uneven ground. She held her camera with one hand above two toothed conveyor belts, while Jean-Luc cupped her left upper arm, allowing her to lean forward over the screaming maw below. He used his other hand to point to various aspects of the marvelous contraption, and to encourage her to lean farther over in order to photograph them better.

Two rows later, I got my turn. It was thrilling in the gee-whiz way that machines and automation can be thrilling. Faced with the problem of harvesting delicate, ripe-to-bursting pockets of juice hanging mostly hidden among tough, woody vines, whoever first proposed banging the bejeezus out of everything in sight to get the grapes to drop was surely laughed out of a number of early pitch sessions. But, yes, dammit. It was working—catching the grapes as they fell, carrying them upward on two parallel conveyor belts, blowing the leaves and chaff free, and depositing the grapes into two collection bins like saddlebags.

In a corner of one of the collection bins, struggling to make sense of things, crouched one big green lizard, who had probably been eyeing a juicy cicada when suddenly the apocalypse arrived with a roar. When you shake a whole row of vines, a lot of things fall other than grapes.

But there's another machine for that.

Later that day, Mary Jo and I stood in the courtyard of the Balliccioni winery next to a machine called a *grappoir* (de-stemmer).

André pushed a button, and we got to watch the second bit of mechanical magic of the day, like one of those cartoons where a line of pigs walks into one end of a pulsing machine, and a string of sausage links comes dancing out the other. A big trailer had backed into André's courtyard and was filling the hopper of the *grappoir* with falling grape bunches, leaves, branches, and, I'm sure, snails, lizards, wasps, and beetles. Out the bottom of the machine dropped grapes and juice, which were pumped into one of the big fermentation vats behind us. Out the back of the machine spat everything else, including, one would hope, most of the creatures whose day had begun so much more hopefully than it would end.

Mary Jo and I spent the rest of the afternoon in the winery. For the most part, the men were dressed in work clothes and rubber boots, except one, an elegant-looking man in his fifties, who wore dark blue jeans and a V-neck sweater over a collared shirt, and who moved deliberately around the winery with a formality that set him apart from the joking and playfulness of the rest of the crew, though he, too, appeared to be a participant in each step of the work being done.

I asked Jean-Luc as unobtrusively as I could who he was, and he told me that was Thierry Rodriguez, André's friend and fellow winemaker, who rented one of the bays of Domaine Balliccioni to make his own wine.

"And what wine," said Jean-Luc.

Thierry looked at us with a solemn and forbidding seriousness.

Meanwhile, I gimped around while sixty-two-year-old Jean-Luc moved like a teenager, pointing things out to us, watching our reactions, intent on our absorbing some kind of lesson from this day that had been so industrial, dirty, sticky, and loud. A day that had evoked downtown Chicago more than the French countryside.

He was like a teacher trying to pass on knowledge that he loved so much it had become who he was, and teaching it turned into a gift not only of knowledge but of himself.

No part of the day, converted to images, would manage to sell a single postcard. No part of it, recorded, would sell a single film about the timeless beauty of southern France.

"That," said Mary Jo, on our way to pick up Joe at school, "was . . . awesome."

42

Jean-Luc took a detour on the way home for lunch, after a morning picking Syrah with his sister, Suzette, and her husband, Bernard. Syrah was the next grape to ripen after the whites and the Cinsault, to be followed by Grenache, Carignan, and Mourvèdre. Syrah was earlier because it had originally been brought in from more northern latitudes.

That morning, he had held an ongoing, participatory seminar on the grapes of the region—the timing in spring of their budding and flowering, which insect-related diseases they were susceptible to and which fungal diseases. How Syrah did not do well in a drought, but Carignan and Cinsault did, in part because they were natives, and had been bred for this hot, dry climate.

"In a year like this, Syrah is like a tourist with a sun hat and a red face," said Jean-Luc. He clipped a bunch of grapes and brought them to me. On one side of the bunch, the grape skins looked leathery and black, against the healthy midnight blue of the rest of the bunch, which trailed—small, fruited, and slender—off the end of his palm.

The darkened side had faced outward toward the sun, and received a *coup de soleil.* The grapes were sunburned.

Red wine grapes turned slightly black like this when they were *grillés.* White grapes got spots of brownish pink on them.

"Like Anglo-Saxons," he had said.

Suzette had burst into laughter, and imagined out loud the poor, grilled Anglo-Saxons "who are driving home in their rental cars from the beach!"

"Do you have to go retrieve something?" I asked Jean-Luc as we bumped down a dusty side road.

"In a manner of speaking," he said.

It made sense that after living in the same place for almost sixty years—spending many of those years outdoors—Jean-Luc would have, even more than most casual hunters and foragers, his selection of secret spots.

On a family walk the other evening, I had watched his truck, distant but unmistakable, make its way toward his brother's kennel, presumably to feed the dogs. He had stopped here and there, whether on the side of the road or at a series of shallow turnouts, exiting the truck briefly each time, then continuing on his way.

My heart had sunk at what I was witnessing. This man I was coming so to appreciate and admire had not lost his taste, it seemed, for song-birds grilled on skewers, or for the ethically and, depending on species, legally dubious tradition of trapping them in the wild. For too many reasons to mention, I was not in a position to openly criticize such behavior, but, as a hunter myself, it lodged in my mind as a demerit that such an open and enlightened Frenchman would engage in something, however ancestrally important, that took place outside the established ethics of hunting and fair chase, and was, in this way and others, such an insult to the natural world he professed to love.

This morning, though, we were not checking traps. He parked at the corner of a vineyard, and told me to follow him. He took a shallow basket from the back of the truck, and climbed a rise of loose schist into another, higher vineyard, where our tracks in the powdery soil mingled with the tracks of several wild boar.

An indistinct vegetative mound appeared to be our destination, and as we approached, the mound resolved itself into a fig tree, smothered by a chaos of blackberry, the wild variety called *ronces,* an ugly word that matches the opinion in which it is held. All blackberries have thorns, but here their proportions approached the Triassic, with canes as thick as my thumb, two-inch thorns shaped like shark fins.

Out of the bulk of this treacherous embrace, the outer branches of the fig tree extended in every direction, looking like flailing arms as they swayed in the wind, their fingers ending in clusters of figs bulging out like underfilled water balloons.

These were called *figues blanches,* white figs, and were different from the black figs that would ripen soon after. The white figs that were ready to pick were so bloated with sweetness that they would leak syrup.

He pulled a branch down and pointed to one of the figs. Out of an opening in its plump bottom, a drop of honey-colored nectar had bulged and begun to seep. He twisted off this little palmful of lewdness and pulled the fig apart lengthwise. The skin burst with the pressure of being torn, and sent a jet of juice onto the ground. He tore the two halves apart and handed me one. The inside of the fig was the color of raspberry jam, with fine threads like vermicelli tipped with brown seeds.

The tenderly fibrous skin crunched a little between my teeth, but the interior was a syrupy jam as sweet and musky and wet as the center of a melon.

All of the figs on the tree could have been called ripe. They were all edible, and sun-plumped, and warm, and would taste good. But if this hillside was a microclimate in which this tree had reached maturity, the tree itself was also a microclimate, and each branch a micro-microclimate, with figs in every state of underripe, perfectly ripe, and overripe. And if you knew what you were looking for, you could capture something at a moment of perfect poise between the forces of growth and decay, and this fig, as alive as an oyster in my mouth, had been seized at that moment. The moment was what Jean-Luc had been trying to tell me about in his orchard, when he had declared, with what now appeared to have been a preposterous lack of pretense, that he and Nicole liked fruit.

This moment was happening all around us just now, with farmers and winemakers and picking crews all trying to read bunches of grapes, and then pick them when they were, as much as weather and pests and drought would allow, perfect.

Jean-Luc watched as I chewed and swallowed and then stood still for a moment. I tilted my face to the sky and walked an ecstatic circle.

"*Il se régale*," said Jean-Luc, and chuckled, and we resumed picking figs, eating perhaps every sixth fig, or maybe it was every fifth, as we covered the bottom of his ancient cane basket with *figues blanches,* all excreting nectar.

Jean-Luc sent me upstairs with a plateful of them, and I told Mary Jo she had to try one now—no, *right* now—and the next thing I did was to call the farm of Mas Rolland, to explain to Laurence that this was the American from Autignac, and I had a plateful of figs ready to accompany her cheese, and could we also please watch Eric bring the goats home.

I sliced several figs for dessert that night. Neither kid could quite get past the vaguely wormy appearance of the fruit's flesh.

"Dad," said Eva. "Cut me a nectarine."

43

The kids had Wednesdays free and had offered their opinion that of all the ways to spend a day off school, perhaps the worst was to travel with their parents back up the prickly hills into the land of "devil cheese."

But here we were, having hiked up a dusty path leading out of the hamlet of Montesquieu, between walls of brittle vegetation. The dwarf oaks, *chêne kermès* and *chêne vert,* had names now, as did the cistus flowers, the wild teasel, the juniper, the broom, the gorse.

Now that we had spent more time in it, and heard more talk of it, the *garrigue* had assumed a character in our minds that was much closer to our home territory. It held a place in the imagination here similar to our North Woods. It was the hardscrabble place of origin where ancestors eked out difficult, canny lives, close to the land. It was shorthand for wildness. It was where (mostly) men went to hunt, and where they secretly believed they could return, if it all went to hell someday, to live by their wits and ancestral skills, roasting partridge over tidy twilight fires.

But the reverence for the *garrigue,* unlike our love affair with the northland, also included an understanding that out in its stony aridity could be found the origins and the heart of the region's cuisine, which was at once world-renowned and explicitly local: thyme, sage, rosemary, lavender, savory, fennel, figs, olives, almonds, garlic, capers. The word "*garrigue*" was used, gastronomically, to describe a briary, herbaceous expression in local wines, and, applied to food, a certain rough-edged yet refined distillation of those woody-stemmed, resinous, musky herbs.

At the gravel turnout Laurence had described, we waited under the still piercing late-season sun. Eva carried her camera around her neck, though she had lost much of her fire for photography, as it had become clear how hard she would have to work to compete with Mary Jo's discipline and explosive imagination.

Joe spent this brief lull among the arthropods, and was observing something very small, very close to the ground, when the first faint tink of a bell reached our ears.

They approached from uphill, and then, as if they had been right there all the time, a dusty procession of brown goats with black stripes along their spines had filled the width of the road. They all wore collars and some wore bells, and they moved tranquilly on their splayed hooves. Laurence had asked us not to talk to them or try to touch them, so we just watched them pass, unhurried, down the hill, through the streets of Montesquieu, on the way to their evening milking. Eric, rangy and tan under a bucket hat, walked with slow, long strides, ignoring us completely, and talking to them in a wordless language of falsetto "lululu-lulu" sounds. He carried on his back a hard-sided case, perhaps a medical kit, perhaps his own lunch.

To their credit, the kids had not insisted on their right to remain unfazed by the spectacle. Their soft cries of "Mom, look!" and "I can't stand it" joined the cattle sounds of the moving herd. Something about the presence of a goatherd in our midst, something about the way he talked to his charges, something about the animal procession through the peopled streets, something primeval and fitting about the movement from pasture to shelter appeared to have lifted them out of their wry detachment and brought them to attention.

We bought our day-old goat cheese to accompany our white figs, and thanked Laurence for making this all happen. On the way back to the car, I noticed Eric walking back from the barn, and approached him.

"Can I ask what you carry on your back?"

He had the painfully shy air of a tall schoolboy who always receives more attention than he wants. He smiled bashfully and said he didn't really tell people about that.

I said I understood. I was just curious.

"Thank you," I said, and shook his hand. "That was beautiful to watch."

"It is a saxophone," he said, and sort of ducked his head. "To play for people, I am not good enough. I try to perfect myself among the goats. They don't pay attention to my lack of talent."

On the terrace that evening, before dinner was served, there was cheese from the goats we had just watched, and figs from a tree just up the hill, and the kids refused both, categorically.

But later, as we tucked into the duck breasts that they now allowed me to serve them, because they tasted acceptably enough like steak, Joe, who had been pensive, took advantage of a pause in the conversation to ask if we thought he could be a goatherd someday.

I had been half thinking the same thing. My recent time spent in vineyards, however preliminary, had reactivated a familiar itch, dating back at least to my days at Saint John's among monks in black tunics, to retreat from the noise of my time, and see if I couldn't find more clarity in the customs of an earlier and quieter one. Eric of Mas Rolland had retained a connection to something ancient and unbroken. Watching him, I had felt the charm of an occupation with an old and pastoral lineage, and recognized, in a fellow introvert, the pull of a romantic sort of loneliness. I could envy his morning commute along a rocky trail to spend the day in a pagan landscape, alone with his imperfection, serenading his animals.

". . . and coming home to his wife," said Mary Jo when I was done rhapsodizing on the rewards of such a life.

"Of course," I said. "I was just getting to that."

It turned out we had both been a little bit seduced that day.

"We could do that," she said, spreading goat cheese on a thin slice of baguette.

"What, keep goats?"

The baguette stopped halfway to her mouth. "What they have going on," she said. "We could have that. For half the year, anyway. We're practically doing it now."

We were talking again, if only metaphorically this time, about something we called the house with two wings.

The sketches, collages, doodles, and quotes in Mary Jo's art journals have been interrupted more or less annually by a single page that looks like the outline for a tenth-grade expository essay, and which expresses—in the nerdy syntax of Roman numerals, subheads, and bullets—our attempts to quantify what a good life looks like, in the form of five-year plans.

Very early in our marriage, a session like this had resulted in a sketch of what we decided would be our ideal house.

The house would be a simple U shape, with two wings connected at the base, and a garden in the center courtyard. One wing would serve as an art studio for Mary Jo, the other a writing studio for me. We would retreat into our separate studios each morning, meet for lunch, and then either resume our individual work or collaborate on a joint project in the afternoon. We would regather in the evening in the base of the U, to reconnect with each other and with kids, should there be any, in the living area and kitchen, over good food and wine: outside in the summer, or next to a fire in the winter. An image of a fully realized life, satisfying nearly all of our deepest needs.

What began as an exercise in daydreaming took on more and more weight, as we were unable ever to improve on the original prototype, and came to understand that it wasn't just a house we had designed, but a life. Or rather two semiautonomous lives connected by a hearth—by food, by family, by the warmth of a fire, by the heat of a desire that had never died.

Now when we talked about the house with two wings, we were talking less about a house we might build someday than about a time when the space had been cleared, and the elements put in place, to step across some future threshold into the third act of our lives.

With STILL, Mary Jo had begun to furnish her wing of that house. On my side, the space was cluttered with the debris left behind by each abandoned version of myself that I had embraced and then found unfulfilling, in my quest for some invulnerable Renaissance man completeness.

Mary Jo had told me once, "You think I want you to keep adding skills. I don't. I want you to start shedding illusions."

Because this was uncomfortable to talk about, and because the incessant presentness required to raise a family didn't easily lend itself to that kind of dreaming, the house with two wings, and the life it represented, had lain dormant for years, though we were both aware of it, and aware of not talking about it, and aware of falling short of its promise, despite how generally good our life together was in almost every conventional way.

44

Up to this point, the arched garage doors that lined the streets of Autignac had appeared to enclose merely the vehicles, the rear courtyards, and the private lives of our neighbors. But now, at the peak of the *vendange,* strange clankings, electric whining, raised voices, and the scouring sound of high-pressure hoses seeped out from under those doors, as did a musty sweet cloud that hung in the air, fumey with alcohol, part rotting apple, part snifter of cognac.

The smell was unmistakable and though sometimes it drifted a little elusively on a swirling current of air, mostly it hovered—concentrated and dense—outside specific doors behind which wine was being made.

On our way to the Balliccioni *cave* one morning, Mary Jo and I heard what sounded like the trickle of a leaky faucet. As we came around a bend of the otherwise deserted street, we saw a stubby iron pipe protruding from a stucco wall, splashing a thin stream of blood-red liquid into the gutter, and bouncing a haze of fine droplets in a pinkish wash against the wall. Pipes like this were bleeding all over town, sending rusty rivulets snaking down the edges of village streets as winemakers hosed out fermentation vats, or grape-stained trailers, or rows of sticky buckets.

Enough of the houses lining the streets were still, for now at least, worth more as wineries than as vacation homes that an industry dating back to the ancient Greeks landing at Massalia (Marseille) could provide the primary economic engine for a twenty-first-century French village. And as if in celebration of this, for much of the duration of the *vendange,* wine literally flowed in the streets of Autignac.

Mary Jo and I were reporting for duty chez Balliccioni on the orders of Véronique, André's wife and partner and our sometime crew boss, who had told us it might be more interesting today in the winery than in the fields.

We picked our way through the fallen fruit of a particularly prolific fig tree in the alley next to the winery, and tentatively let ourselves in through the front gate. I tried to get a glimpse of somebody I could wave to so I didn't show up at André's elbow like some creepy apparition.

We heard voices and made our way to the left-hand fermentation room, high-ceilinged but narrow, with a single concrete corridor running between a double row of vats. Thierry Rodriguez made his wine here, renting this space and paying an additional surcharge most months for André's labor, which André—according to both Thierry and Véronique—routinely underreported. It was a complicated small-village arrangement with a lot of overlap, but their two wines, Mas Gabinèle and Domaine Balliccioni, were grown, made, marketed, and sold under separate labels.

It was here that we happened upon our . . . Our what, exactly? Our hosts? Our guides? Our coworkers? Our bosses?

Whatever they were, there were three of them, pressed tightly together in the narrow passageway.

André, who didn't appear to know how to make a visitor feel uncomfortable, said, "Ah it's you," and stepped over a couple of hoses to come greet us, and then, with an arm around Mary Jo's shoulders, moving with a little buccaneer sashay in his tall boots, he led her back to the vat they were working on, where a shyly smiling Thierry shook our hands.

This left Yvan, whose bare torso was coated with sweat already, despite the morning chill. He was younger than the other two, maybe in his thirties, built like a voyageur, compact and muscular, with black hair and a jumpy energy. He was a carpenter in the village, I would later learn, and, like many of his fellow villagers, took time off every year to work the *vendange.*

He greeted us warily, with a nod and a quick handshake, but without saying hello. There had been a comfortable air of collegial purpose about the three of them when we arrived, and I wondered if he didn't like having this extra company around, messing with the vibe.

Yvan was the most purely a villager of the three of them. He didn't have anything to sell us, in the way that both Thierry and André, ambassadors of their own wine, could be seen to have a vested interest in our good opinion. The only people he had to please were André and Thierry.

We were gathered in front of one of the vats, towering over us like a windowless skyscraper. Its bottom half was painted butterscotch and its top half a sort of buttercream, and the fluorescent light on the ochre walls did not so much illuminate the space as spray a yellowish mist in the air around us.

On the ground in front of the vat sat a pump attached to a metal hopper.

Yvan stooped and loosened two thumbscrews on the vat's hatch door, while André and Thierry wrestled with a stiff, corrugated red tube like a fire hose that fought them with the stubbornness of a limp dog. Grunting softly, they manhandled it into position and attached it to the pump. Mary Jo circled and took photos, and I shuffled back and forth, trying to stay out of the way.

André wiped his temple against his shirtsleeve, then explained that the goal today was not to fill a vat with grapes but to empty one, in a process called a *décuvage.* The grapes and juice in the vat had been macerating for about two weeks and, based on the advice of Thierry's oenologist, were now ready to be *décuvés,* or de-vatted.

A rectangular whiteboard told us, in blue marker, that this was

"*Cuve 6, Syrah.*" There were three columns, with dates, temperatures, and a list of numbers that descended from 1095 to 995. André explained that this was a record of the liquid's specific gravity, measured daily, and correlating almost exactly with its sugar content. This number had progressively fallen—properly so—as the sugar in the original grape juice had gradually been eaten by live yeast and turned into alcohol. The numbers had fallen fast, and then, for the last four or five, had stabilized at around 995, meaning that effectively all the sugar available to the yeast had been transformed into alcohol and the former juice, now wine, was as dry as it would ever be.

To André, the winemaker, a dry wine was not something you assessed on your tongue. It was simply a wine with a specific gravity of 0.995. A fully fermented wine.

Because this particular Syrah had been fully fermented for several days already, what had been going on in the vat since then had no longer been fermentation but extraction, like leaves steeping in a cup of tea. The steeping adds flavor, but if you leave the liquid in contact with the solids for too long, you get tastes you don't want.

So today's task would be to separate the juice from the skins and seeds in a process not entirely unlike removing a tea bag from one cup and wringing it into a second. Ideally, the tea left in the original cup would be balanced and aromatic, and the tea squeezed into the second cup would be more intense, but not overpowering.

The riskier cup, of course, would be the second one. If you squeezed too hard or long, or if the bag had already spent too much time in the liquid, you might get an unpleasantly bitter or tannic flavor. But if the wrung-out tea in the second cup was still balanced and smooth, in theory you could add it back to the first cup for an especially rich, full-bodied drink.

The flavors in the grape juice would be different, but the principles were nearly identical.

Already this morning Yvan and André had pumped out about thirteen hundred gallons of the fermented juice, and sent that to "cup one," a vat to our right. What was left behind were the steeped grape skins, stems, and seeds, known as *marc*, or, in English, "pomace." These had settled to the bottom of the vat in a densely packed, waist-deep mat that would now need to be removed through a hatch door barely larger than a laundry chute.

As Yvan unscrewed the final bolt on the door, the dregs of reddish-purple juice in the vat seeped through the hatch's broken seal into the stainless-steel hopper. The door swung open with a clang and a gush. A lump of compressed *marc* cleaved from the rest and thudded wetly into the tub, looking the way grapes might look if they had made their way through a bear. They glistened and broke apart, and the smell that had swirled through the village for weeks now wrapped itself around us, full of black fruit and brandy and a bright autumn-leaf sourness.

With a white polypropylene pitchfork, Yvan scraped at the wall of macerated skins and seeds that were visible through the minuscule hatch door. What he managed to pry loose would plunk into the hopper, where a steel screw pushed the clumps of grapes into the pump, manned by Thierry, which began the rackety work of ka-chunking a solid mass of wet fruit uphill through thirty yards of corrugated tubing into the big metal *pressoir*, or grape press.

I had just called out the words "*Est-ce que . . .*" over the sounds of the machines, on my way toward asking if I could do anything to help, when Yvan, in a comically deep voice for his short frame, grunted something back to Thierry at the pump, thrust a white pitchfork at me, and then, astoundingly, disappeared into the vat.

It's difficult to convey just how small the door looked compared to the size of a grown human. It was noticeably smaller than a kitchen cabinet. But more than that, the gesture was so unexpected that it contained a splash of magic. As if the furnace repair guy had carefully removed the front panel, set it aside, and then simply stepped into the furnace and vanished. Yvan ducked, stuck one arm into the hatch door, and like a swimmer doing a sidestroke, smoothly slid inside. His right arm re-emerged, I handed him the pitchfork, and that disappeared, too.

We heard some muted bongings, and then big piles of *marc* started falling out of the vat, sometimes by the forkful, sometimes swept out by a green rubber boot. Even over the pump, I could hear echoing grunts and the strained vocalizations of intense work done in awkward quarters.

André ambled down from his work at the *pressoir* and poked his head into the vat.

"*Tu veux un café?*" (Want a coffee?), he shouted at the sweating Yvan, who cursed him.

Feeling something like the opposite of helpful, Mary Jo and I followed André back to the grape press.

He had climbed onto the frame of the machine, the heart of which was a ten-foot-long steel drum like a concrete mixer, pierced all over its exterior by narrow grooves where the juice would run out like pasta water through a colander. Next to his head, the business end of the pump hose was strapped to the top of the machine, and short, cylindrical lumps of compressed grape skins pushed rhythmically out the end and fell through a hatch door into the *pressoir* with damp slapping sounds. André was using a pitchfork to distribute the falling skins so the drum filled evenly. He said the bigger wineries have this process automated, with sensors and computers.

"Me, I still like to put my hands in the dough," he said.

He called to the others, and their replies—halfway there, three-quarters—drifted back.

As the *pressoir* filled, André's job got harder and harder, and he began visibly to strain.

We would eventually learn that there was an acknowledged segregation between the field-workers and the winery workers. André and Yvan would never once work in the vines, and almost none of the team of pickers would ever step foot in the winery. Only a select few—Véronique, Jean-Luc, and a tall friendly fellow named Richard—were accepted in both locations.

But we were Americans, and one of the perks of our status as foreigners would turn out to be our ignorance at first, and later our ability to straddle and ignore without offense, these strata of class and position that natives often couldn't escape.

So when I climbed up next to André, I didn't know that I was breaking a petty taboo. That I was a field-worker presuming to join the work in the winery. I just knew that André looked like he could use a hand. If I had known the rules, I probably would have stayed on the sidelines.

I was aware of Mary Jo as I worked, and happy that she was there.

André didn't thank me. He just started telling me what to do.

We worked together, Mary Jo taking photographs of my grape-stained forearms, and of the sweat falling rhythmically from the tip of André's nose into the wet, heavy *marc* of the Syrah. In the other room, the pump knocked and jumped as it pushed thousands of pounds of nearly solid material with an effort that must have seemed supernatural once to men who had spent years doing the same job with wheelbarrows and wooden carts.

Thierry and Yvan appeared from below. Yvan lit a cigarette, still shirtless and sweating, and watched us finish our work.

We closed the heavy hatches with a double clang and a screech of steel retainer bars sliding through metal eyes. André pushed a big red button, and the *pressoir* gave a sustained, one-note roar.

As the drum spun, two flat plates crushed steadily inward, and a viscous purple wash flowed out, staining the entire exterior surface, as the pressed juice rained into the catch basin, and traveled through yet one more tube and another pump, to fill an empty vat—cup two.

We stood in a loose circle on the concrete floor, and talked above the sound of the motor about how the morning had gone. About what needed to happen now. Mary Jo looked typically comfortable in this masculine environment—an athlete and tomboy used to playing with the boys. We watched the *pressoir* turn and the steel plates grind glacially toward each other along a screw, one of the oldest tools known to man. My skin looked painted with purple watercolor, and collapsed grape skins blistered my forearms and the backs of my hands like a pox. We washed our dirty hands and arms with hoses, taking turns spraying each other off.

Yvan had disappeared for a few minutes, I assumed for another cigarette, but then suddenly he was between Mary Jo and me, holding a double handful of soft, bluish fruit.

"*Tu veux une figue?*" he asked, in the offhand way you'd ask a sweaty coworker on a jobsite. "Sip of water?"

At home, figs were those rare and precious things that got quartered and placed in an exquisite mound on one end of the cheese plate. Here, ubiquitous and free, they were the blue-collar refreshment that Yvan the carpenter grabbed from the tree in the alley.

In a similar way, wine here was not a minor life enhancer in a glass. It was what got pumped from vats, and shoveled into machinery, and spilled into purple creeks running like veins through the streets.

Yvan popped a whole fig into his mouth, working it like a chaw of tobacco, and then, smiling for the first time that morning, slurred with his mouth full, "*C'est bon.*"

André confirmed, in English, that "eat eez verrhy goohd, zuh feegs."

And with a bell tower standing in for a factory steam whistle, Mary Jo and I finished out our shift with handshakes and kisses. As we were on our way through the square to get a baguette for lunch, the owner of the café stared at me, with my purpled arms and grape-stained work shorts, and did not appear to know what to make of the sight, while behind us, Yvan, Thierry, and André went back to work, with unhurried purpose, surrounded by sounds of the Industrial Age.

45

At parent pickup, Joe's classroom teacher, Marie-Pierre, motioned us up for a talk in the courtyard. I began practicing how to say "slow to join," "cautious," and "rule follower" in French so we could reassure her that whatever behavior she was observing in Joseph was perfectly normal.

She didn't want to talk about Joe's behavior, though. She wanted to talk about his penmanship. We joined her under the lush mulberry tree in the middle of the courtyard, and she pulled a notebook from a plastic folder to show us a recent page of Joseph's handwriting.

In fact, what she showed us couldn't be called handwriting. It was the rotund printing that American students are taught to cinch between those horizontal lines that run like two-way streets across their grade school worksheets. Avenues, really—broad enough that perhaps six of them fit into the confines of a letter-sized sheet. By American standards, and for his age, Joe's printing was quite good.

But French students learn to write controlled, flowing cursive. The traditional Séyès stationery pattern divides each page into eight-millimeter blue squares and then into fainter two-millimeter horizontal lines. Marie-Pierre was showing us the results of Joe's first attempts to steer his monstrous American SUV down the cramped French sidestreets of his *cahier de brouillons* (practice notebook).

"Do you see where his letters are supposed to fit, and how they are not fitting?" she asked.

We did see how they were not fitting.

"Is he . . . Is this . . ."

Her attempt at a reassuring smile turned into a wondering, searching look. It was the expression on your face just before you look hard at someone and ask, "Is everything OK?"

I think she was trying to discern, through a language barrier, a culture gap, and the inhibitions of discretion, whether this was truly the way Joe had been taught to write in his homeland, or whether our quiet, slow-to-join Joseph was damaged in some way she ought to know about.

"This," I said, nodding energetically and pointing to the notebook in her hand. "This is the fashion in which one teaches students to write in the United States."

While we talked, Joe had half joined the after-school game of soccer on the far side of the courtyard. He made a nice pass with the outside of his foot, and then, glancing sidelong in our direction, drifted behind the play.

"I brought Joe's American school notebooks with us," said Mary Jo. "Tell her we can show her, so she sees how he's been learning."

I explained this to Marie-Pierre, and it appeared to alleviate the worst of her fears, which no doubt included special-needs services for a nonresident, temporary American student who spoke French as a second language.

Still, she was a French elementary schoolteacher, and one does not take issues of penmanship lightly.

So, with a French schoolteacher's unconcern for the potential embarrassment of her students, she called to Joe across the playground, in the same voice she used, according to Joe, to call out publicly the grades of each student in class when she had corrected an assignment.

Joe separated himself from the sudden hush of what had been a soccer game, and made the long walk toward us, wearing the frozen expression of an introvert who knows he's the center of attention.

When he arrived, Marie-Pierre bent to him, and explained in musical French that he would need to work hard on his *orthographe*, his spelling and penmanship, so it grew straighter and stayed between the lines. She showed him the notebook, and underlined with her index finger.

Joe nodded seriously, looking at an example of some of his best work.

"We'll help him with this at home," I offered.

"Right, Joe?" asked Mary Jo, sensing the imminence of the blinking stare and the shaky voice.

Joe nodded again.

Mary Jo murmured into his sweaty hair, "OK?"

He nodded a final time.

We thanked Marie-Pierre, who shook each of our hands firmly with a single pump.

Eva worked that evening on her homework for *physique chimie* (physics and chemistry). Maybe it shouldn't have surprised us, given the nature of the region where we now lived, but her very first assignment was to understand the chemical process by which glucose and fructose molecules are broken down anaerobically into ethanol and carbon dioxide. Before anything else, in other words, what you learned in middle school chem at Collège le Cèdre was alcoholic fermentation.

Joe spent the evening in self-imposed exile at the dining room table, training the flabby American muscles in his right hand to imitate the precise, fluid curves of French cursive, and because he was a perfectionist, and because handwriting is not something that can be learned in an evening no matter how hard-fought, we heard the occasional snuffle from his corner of the table, and saw the occasional palm wiped up his face.

That night, in the cricketless quiet of Joe's bedroom, we read, for perhaps the tenth time, the story of the great war of attrition in Gerry Durrell's Corfu bedroom between the mantis and the gecko.

46

I was spending most mornings in the vines, and most afternoons in André's winery, though I had the luxury, unlike my teammates, of taking a morning, an afternoon, or an entire day off when the kids were home, or when I occasionally accepted Jean-Luc's frequent recommendation to "repose myself."

I was welcome, but not needed. I had family to attend to. "*C'est normal, Steve.*"

On those days, I would gravitate to the corner of the terrace, sitting with a book, or my laptop. The olive tree changed color all day. The faint smell of Jean-Luc's fertilizer and agricultural chemicals would sometimes rise on a swirling breeze from his *cave* next door, which I found as pleasant and evocative in its way as I had found diesel and black tobacco in Paris.

I didn't have to look anymore, or not often, toward whatever buzzing thing was swooping around the terrace. I learned to tell the keening of a gnat from the droning of a wasp from the revving of the enormous but completely harmless violet carpenter bees that occasionally careened up from the courtyard, clumsy and out of control, looking like shiny black Volkswagens held aloft on blue wings, and sounding like muffled dirt bikes. One day I heard a soft throbbing to my right, and saw a humming-bird moth stand still on blurred wings, and unfurl an enormous proboscis to sip what nectar was on offer by the geranium against the railing.

I had begun imagining an herb garden for the opposite corner of the terrace, which would welcome some of the spirit of the *garrigue,* and some of its tastes and smells, into the kitchen, but instead, this lunch hour, I found emails in my inbox.

Eva appeared, gnawing a *jambon beurre.* I patted the chaise next to me.

"Come sit with me," I said.

"Gotta study," she said.

One of the emails was from my mom, on the surface quite harmless and well-intentioned. News from home. How are the kidlets? Had I received the books they had sent? Please send more of your wonderful updates.

I took Eva back to school, then spent the bulk of the afternoon writing a description of Joe's handwriting struggles. Of the grape picking, both by hand and machine. Of the *décuvage.* I described how the kids had absorbed the blow of the early days of school and were, if a little wobbly, back on their feet. How Mary Jo was in the middle of a self-taught master class in Mediterranean flora. How I sometimes wondered what we had done to earn all that Jean-Luc had introduced us to. How we found ourselves knee-deep in vineyards and winemaking.

At some point I sort of shook myself awake and reread what I had written, and when I finished I couldn't imagine sending it out to be passed among my parents' friends. Not that I had anything in particular against any of them. They were good people. But Mary Jo. Joseph. Eva. Jean-Luc. Nicole. André. José. The Espinouse hills, Saint-Méen, Jean-Luc's orchard, and rows of Syrah vines. It all felt too—I didn't know what. Too intimate. Too full of delicious secrets. Too fragile and important to offer up as entertainment—or to use as a sneaky sort of entreaty for personal affirmation among childhood acquaintances and semi-strangers.

Instead, I titled the long document I had created "Languedoc Journal," and saved it to my laptop. Then, as an afterthought, I sent a copy to Mary Jo.

47

I listened to a lot of pop music, in both French and English, on the road between Autignac and Murviel-lès-Béziers, in my role as Eva's chauffeur.

I had spent the first four years of her life as her primary caregiver, changing diapers, thawing bags of frozen breast milk, serenading her into red-cheeked oblivion with naptime renditions of "The Fox" and "*La Chasse aux Papillons,*" and pushing her on rubber-seated Northeast Minneapolis playground swings while she refused, at any point, to try pumping her legs and swinging herself. I was a part-time real estate broker at the time, and I would sling her on my hip and take her to showings, where she would strut through 1930s bungalows and inform my clients, "Diss a nice pwayce." Afterward, we would debrief over coffee and hot chocolate and play napkin games of tic-tac-toe.

Every subsequent career would be a demotion from my first, when for four years I toiled in uninterrupted felicity as a servant in the court of my imperious and demanding daughter.

However much she might later insist on growing up, she would always be to some extent the bossy, bobbed preschooler in red Mary Janes, with a single dimple on her right cheek, who interrogated me endlessly from the back seat on the morning drive to Miniapple Montessori, where I would unbuckle her car seat, and send her through the gate with a pooch-lipped peck and a pat on her newly diaperless fanny.

Eleven years later, the morning drive to Murviel was as staringly mute as the drive to preschool had once been exhaustingly talkative. There were days when I would have relished any topic of engagement. Why bicycles only have two wheels or where the sun goes when it rains.

What we had, instead of talk, was pop music. If the soundtrack to our stay in France featured regular evening sessions with Stan Getz and Ahmad Jamal and Francis Cabrel, it equally included dance hits in the car with blandly suggestive lyrics and big bass beats. Eva and I listened to Taio Cruz, to Pitbull, to Flo Rida and Rihanna, who sang to us about clubs and booties and shorties and what tonight would bring. We listened endless times to Khaled's endlessly repetitive *"C'est la Vie."* The songs came from America and France and Spain and Algeria, and other places where young people went dancing, and tongue-tied fathers watched them grow up. The songs were mostly about love. For a while, they carried the conversation, and a little more emotional weight than they could bear, on sunrise drives to school, and on wordless stretches of homeward road.

48

Grape pickers can tell who's making good wine.

A short time working rows of weed-choked vines, bowing with crowded grape bunches, can tell you as much about the wine a vintner makes as a nose plunged into a glass of the finished product.

I crossed paths with José one afternoon on the way home from Marie's. He was sitting on Jean-Luc and Nicole's front step, smoking a cigarette after the nightly ritual of hosing out the buckets.

"*Zho-SAY,*" I called.

"*Oui, Chef.*"

"*Buenas tardes.*"

He looked up approvingly. "*Bien, bien, Eh-STEVE-eh! Buenas tardes.*"

"*Que tal?*" I asked.

"*EEM-pay-cobb-lay.*"

José, as always, was feeling impeccable.

I asked him how his day had gone.

He described in pidgin French his disaster of a morning—a whole field damaged by the *vers de la grappe.* He pantomimed how it had gone by flipping one imaginary bunch of grapes after another onto the ground at his feet.

"*Pas bon.*" Flip. "*Pas bon.*" Flip. "*Pas bon.*" Flip.

But then, in the afternoon, and here he kissed his fingers. Almost no triage. Every bunch went into the buckets. Perfectly pruned vines. Like statues. *EEM-pay-cobb-lay.*

I asked if he knew whose vines they were.

They were the vines of Thierry Rodriguez.

I was working next to Yvan one day, helping him wrestle a pump hose into place in Thierry's half of the winery. Thierry stopped in to check our progress. Asked a question of Yvan. Nodded and disappeared around the corner toward André's vat room.

"*C'est un homme sérieux,*" said Yvan, which technically translates as "He's a serious man," but in French means something more like "He is a man to be taken seriously." A man of consequence. A trustworthy man.

He asked me if I had tasted Thierry's wines, and I said that I had not.

He just shook his head as he clamped the hose into place.

Thierry consulted a clipboard regularly as he moved around the winery, appearing to check things off. He was clearly very close to André. They talked all day, confirming which vats would be empty to receive new grapes, and when the team would be ready for the next *décuvage.*

He managed to be friendly with everybody, but it was a respectful friendliness that was different from André's overflowing natural warmth.

Thierry had earned the esteem of all those who worked for André and him, and, as one of those workers, I thought of Thierry as something like the boss of my boss, with layers of management and supervision between me, on the factory floor, and him, in the corner office.

So when he approached Mary Jo and me one day before lunchtime, I assumed he would be asking us to hose off some tools, or help him disconnect or reconnect one of the heavy discharge tubes.

Instead, he asked Mary Jo, shyly, and in good English that had a little bit of French and a little bit of British in it, whether she was a photographer.

He had a parcel of grapes, Grenache Gris, which he considered the most beautiful variety in France. Before that vineyard was harvested, would we consider joining him for a visit, and perhaps Mary Jo would consent to take some photos. Perhaps he could use them for marketing.

The vineyard sprawled across a slope of land beside a capillary of country road. We pulled off next to a recently constructed outbuilding, which Thierry intended—for he did not appear to do anything without intention—as a visual nod to an old custom. It was a *gabinèle,* in Occitan a hut that historically sat at the corner of a vineyard, most often with a tall spire of cypress standing beside it, so its location could be seen from anywhere in the surrounding country. With a *gabinèle* on his land, a grape farmer could wait out the rain, or eat lunch out of reach of the penetrating sun, or store his tools, or shelter his donkey for the day, or, in a pinch, stay the night.

With that homage in mind, Thierry had chosen the name Mas Gabinèle for his wines, and his label was a stylized winemaker's hut flanked by a pair of cypress trees—all conjured by a few minimalist brushstrokes against a white background.

He had spent a year working with designers to get the label right.

A stone bench next to the hut looked across the narrow road over more of his vines, then a patchwork valley rising to meet the dark foothills of the Caroux-Espinouse.

Thierry explained that he was both a *vigneron* and a *négociant.* As a *vigneron,* or winemaker, he owned vines in the Faugères appellation, harvested those grapes, and turned them into Mas Gabinèle wine.

As a *négociant,* Thierry acted more like a broker. He could buy grapes, juice, or finished wine from multiple producers in multiple locations, and either blend them into wines he would sell himself, or fashion a wine to the specifications of a client, who might want to sell a wine containing particular characteristics or grape varietals.

As a winemaker, he was an artisan. As a *négociant,* he was something like a brand manager.

"And where does Jean-Luc find himself among all of this?" I asked.

Well, Jean-Luc had done a little of everything in his day, but for now, he was primarily a *viticulteur.* A grape farmer. A producer who owned and tended his own vines—his and Nicole's to be exact—and sold what he produced to other winemakers, without, at this point, making the wine himself. One of those winemakers was the local *cave cooperative* (like an American farmer selling corn and soybeans to the local co-op). The other winemaker was André Balliccioni, who bought Jean-Luc's grapes (specifically his Faugères grapes), and added them to his own, in order to make Domaine Balliccioni Faugères.

Thierry pointed to a plot across the road that he said he would like to own. It was adjacent to his land and buying it would repair a bit of the fractured heredity of the valley, but it was clear, too, that a part of him just liked looking at beautiful country, and it would help, in this case, to spiff up that corner of his vista, which was currently maintained by someone without the rigorous aesthetic standards of Thierry Rodriguez.

His vines spoke, in their spareness and their intentionally low yields, of ambition and a finicky attention to detail. They spoke of moderate wealth—a richer man might have staked his claim in the Rhône Valley or Bordeaux; a poorer man could not have maintained fourteen hectares to such standards.

The vines and their surroundings whispered, too, of an aesthete's urge to make things not just correct but beautiful. There was no profit in leaving the graceful old oak standing at the edge of the vineyard, where its roots stole precious water from his vines. No profit in planting, along-side the field of Grenache Gris, a row of Lucques olive trees, which were not numerous enough to turn a profit selling the olives or making oil, but which served as a striking graphic element in the breathtaking diorama surrounding us. Each of these had been the decision of a man with something on his mind other than the optimal conversion of square meters of fallen sunlight into euros' worth of wine, and I suspected that his invitation to Mary Jo had had far less to do with the stated pretense of "marketing" than with the tantalizing prospect of possessing several beautiful photos of particularly beautiful grapes at the peak of their ripeness.

We walked through the vines together, and he explained that Grenache Gris made his white wines. It was an expression of the Grenache grape between Grenache Noir and Grenache Blanc—similar to the relationship of Pinot Grigio (Pinot Gris in French) to Pinot Noir and Pinot Blanc.

Grenache Gris had been a popular grape years ago, because it retained its acidity—difficult in this hot climate that tended to bake out acid in white grapes and bake in sugar and alcohol. But too many winemakers had yanked it in order to plant Chardonnay for an international market, and, as a result, Grenache Gris was now rare. We passed bunch after dangling bunch of rose- and lilac-colored grapes, pale and round, hanging in asymmetrical bunches, and Thierry stopped here and there to cup one of them and share with us the translucent blush of their loveliness.

Mary Jo spent a strenuous quarter hour on her side, on tiptoes, on her back, and crouched on her heels as Thierry described what it took, over an average year, to make a wine like his crown jewel, Rarissime—a bottle that sold for fifty dollars in a region of five-dollar bottles of good local red.

It took, among other things, a weekly visit from a lab technician during the growing season to keep disease and pests under control. It took a spring "debudding" pass through every vineyard to head off excess branch growth. It took a second sweep, the *vendange verte*, or green harvest, to remove young grape clusters, leaving the remaining bunches uncrowded and well ventilated. It took harvesting by hand, not machine, to damage as few bunches as possible en route to the fermentation vat. And it took a visit every other day during the *vendange* from his oenologist, Jean Natoli, to taste from vats and barrels, to update the to-do list on Thierry's clipboard.

For a big man, he spoke in an unexpectedly soft tenor. Soon enough, there would be the *assemblage,* or blending of the fermented wines, and then the bottling, each with its attendant risks, costs, and headaches.

In the brief silence that fell while Mary Jo composed a photo of an almost platonically perfect grape bunch, Thierry gazed thoughtfully at his shoes—brown leather with treaded black soles. The kind that could be worn to the office, or to a casual restaurant, or on a short hike. They were dusted, in a way I would have found very gratifying, with the soil of his vineyards. He glanced up at me then, raising his eyes without lifting his head.

It was an oddly solicitous look that seemed to be asking whether it was still making sense to us, all of this effort and expense and life energy, put to an end that, seen a certain way, amounted to mere bottles of wine.

It made me wonder for the first time what he really thought of us— these Americans showing up for six months in the French equivalent of Des Moines, temporary laborers who agreed to work for no pay. Did he understand, even then, that he had, in Mary Jo and me, not just a better-than-average photographer and a slower-than-average grape picker, but, in fact, fellow admirers of gratuitous rows of olive trees, and of the kind of life that would prioritize such a thing?

His smile briefly turned down the corners of his mouth as Mary Jo rejoined us. The three of us proceeded toward the car, along an aisle of the most beautiful grapes in France. Stepping through the schist soil of Faugères together.

49

Joe and I had taken up Marcel Pagnol's *My Father's Glory,* and were engrossed in young Marcel's formative first summer in a family cabin north of Marseille, surrounded by hundreds of acres of *garrigue.*

We were once more serenaded by bedside crickets, who waited their turn to face September, the new bright green mantis Joe had found on one of the after-school walks he took to shake off the rigors of Marie-Pierre's classroom.

Tonight, the Pagnol family was hiking up the last hillsides between the train station and their new summer house:

Then my father showed us—with his left hand . . . a little house on the opposite hill, half hidden by a large fig tree.

"There," he said. "That's the Bastide-Neuve. Our holiday refuge. The garden on the left is ours, too!" . . . I could make out nothing but a small forest of olive and almond trees, which joined their tangled branches above the messy brush. But this virgin forest in miniature, I had seen it in all of my dreams, and, followed by my brother Paul, I rushed forward, shouting with joy.

Eva walked in, brushing her teeth. Said something through toothpaste foam and disappeared.

"What was that, Eva?"

She returned and stood in the doorway. "I want to take horse lessons," she said.

I looked at Joe, who shrugged.

"OK, have you asked your . . ." I began. But she was gone.

50

I held out a bullet-shaped endive to Maman, under the fluorescent lights of Le Jardin de Marie.

Maman and her husband were pulling an evening shift at the till, to free Marie for some unavoidable form of parenting.

It had finally gotten through to me what I had in Maman, this family cook who had spent fifty years or so placing variations on the French canon in front of her four-generation household. It was like wanting to get rich someday, and then discovering that the teller at your local bank was a talkative fellow, name of Buffett.

Today I was asking about endive, while Papa Casties stocked produce.

"One does what with this?" I asked.

"If one is French," she said, "one makes a salad."

I wondered aloud how one might make such a salad if, by some misfortune, one were not French.

She took the tight ivory-colored head from me, and as she talked, she gently sliced it, with the edge of her hand, into imaginary half-inch chevrons, which she scattered into an invisible bowl. She suggested tossing this with *une petite vinaigrette*.

And here she had me.

What might her recipe for vinaigrette be, I asked, in a way that I hoped did not convey my own fraught history with this supposedly straightforward mix of acid and oil.

"It's very simple. I take my vinegar and a little salt, and then I . . . You have mustard?"

"Yes."

"*De Dijon?*"

"Yes."

"So. A little mustard to emulsify, and then I whisk in the olive oil."

"How much olive oil?"

"Enough olive oil," she said, with a slightly wide-eyed playfulness, "until it tastes like vinaigrette."

"White wine vinegar or red wine vinegar?" I asked.

"Oh, red wine vinegar!" she said, and the first shadow of concern crossed her face.

After a thoughtful-looking hesitation, she asked, "You have what type of vinegar?"

"Well, we have red wine vinegar, because I have had trouble finding white wine vinegar."

"Finding?" she asked. "Finding where?"

"At the grocery store."

"*Oh là là*" was all she could manage in reply.

She was now truly alarmed. We were no longer amicably roofing the house of her vinaigrette recipe. We were shoveling furiously to shore up the foundation.

"You mean you don't have *du vrai vinaigre?*"

"*Du vrai vinaigre?*"

"Yes, of course. *Du vrai.* That you have made. At your house."

My attempt at an apologetic smile was all the answer she needed.

"*Chéri!*" she called, and ordered Papa across the street immediately to fetch this young man some real vinegar so he might make a proper vinaigrette for his *salade d'endives*.

Papa, appearing to recognize the acuteness of the emergency, dropped a double handful of shallots into their display and left the store at a slow trot, fists pulled to his chest.

"So, you make your own vinegar?" I asked.

"Monsieur, every family makes its own vinegar. You will see. It has nothing to do with vinegar from the store."

The Casties family vinegar resided in the basement of their house, across the street, in a ceramic crock, and was fed regularly with the un-drunk remains of bottles of good red wine. The "mother"—a rubbery cloud that forms in the liquid and activates the transformation from wine into vinegar—was descended from an original mother born a century ago in that same house, in that same crock.

At this point, Papa, with the glass door clattering shut behind him, confirmed all of this in a distracted way while he set two slim, unlabeled bottles on the checkout counter. One was half-corked and full of a rusty red liquid, and the other, sealed with a cap of scarlet wax, held a stalk of greenery suspended in a viscous golden syrup.

Maman sifted noisily through the drawer behind the counter, murmuring, "*Voyons, voyons,*" and then found the spoon she had been looking for. She uncorked the vinegar bottle and poured a dropperful onto the spoon.

I sipped.

I wouldn't understand until later that my life—not dramatically, but permanently—had just changed. All I knew at the time was that the liquid on my tongue, filling my sinuses and wringing my salivary glands, changed the definition of whatever I had previously understood "vinegar" to mean. It smelled like wine, and it had a fragrant, gentle acidity that, as Maman had predicted, had nothing to do with the harsh sourness of every vinegar I'd ever previously paid attention to.

I swallowed and looked back and forth between them.

"*Vous voyez?*" asked Maman.

"Yes, I see," I said.

"*Voilà,*" she said, collecting her spoon and recorking the bottle with a matter-of-factness that showed how little doubt she had ever had on the subject.

Papa lifted the other bottle by the waist.

"In the freezer," he said, tapping the bottle with a thick fingernail and looking me in the eyes. "One hour before dinner."

"In the freezer," I repeated, nodding.

"You drink *un petit coup* as an aperitif." He pinched *un petit coup* between his thumb and middle finger to show me. "Very cold."

He nodded solemnly. "*Verveine,*" he said. "You will see."

"It is very good," agreed Maman. "You will see."

The only *verveine* I had ever drunk was herbal tea in Madame Villatte's living room, which was not stored in the freezer or drunk as an aperitif.

"*Une . . . tisane?*" I asked.

"*Une liqueur,*" said Papa.

"It comes from where?" I asked.

"Oh, I make it," said Papa, as if his making it were obvious and slightly boring—a necessary prelude to the sumptuous culmination of drinking it straight from the freezer, *en apéritif*, ice-cold.

"Next time, you'll try the Vin d'Orange," he added, and smiled through a bundle of fingertips that he then kissed open.

"Listen," I said. "I don't even know where to start. Can I at least pay—"

"Oh!" Maman said, and rang up three endives, as a way of expressing how out of the question any payment was. As a sort of exclamation point, she took a bundle of parsley stems from the glass of water at her wrist, and pointedly dropped them into the bag with the endives.

Not knowing quite what to do with myself, I said thank you, and shook Papa's hand, and then before I could think too much about it, I leaned across the counter, and aimed my left cheek at Maman's soft left cheek, and made a smooching sound into her left ear, and then into her right.

"*Oh, il est gentil,*" she said.

"*Allez,*" said Papa. "Bring the bottle back to me when you have finished."

I rang the tinkle bell above the door on my way out, carrying a plastic sack in each hand—one containing ninety centimes' worth of endives and a bouquet of parsley, and the other, slightly heavier, holding something my money couldn't buy.

I got home and began the post-supermarket-vinegar phase of my life by tipping a tablespoon of rusty liquid into a bowl with some salt.

They would be on duty for another hour or so at Le Jardin de Marie. Papa stocking shelves. Maman on the stool beneath the humming double fluorescent tubes. She would be sitting with good posture. Waiting for the next customer. Aware, but perhaps not entirely so, of her great value.

51

The easy part of the morning consisted of my saying, "Hey, let's try a coq au vin," and Mary Jo saying, "Yum."

The local Intermarché was not open at all on Sunday. Marie might or might not have everything we needed. The *tabac* almost certainly wouldn't.

In the end we left the kids in their jammies, and, half an hour later, we pulled open a door to the central covered market—the Halles Centrales—in Béziers, without any settled idea of what went into a coq au vin.

At a busy vegetable stand, we took a wicker basket and started guessing. We grabbed carrots (good guess), celery (yes), potatoes (no), mushrooms (yes), and then asked the chatty proprietress what else went in a coq au vin that we might be forgetting.

She thought for a second or two, then her face lit up as if she'd just remembered something, and she chirped, "Don't know!"

She turned to another customer in line.

"Jeannette, what goes in a coq au vin?"

Jeannette stood rooted beneath her wispy henna perm as if the market bags in each hand were slowly pulling off her arms. She thought about it and then her bags lifted in an apologetic shrug.

"Check with Anne-Marie at Selvo. Oh!" said the vegetable grocer. She picked out a mesh bag of pearl onions. "Those I know you'll need."

Anne-Marie was no more helpful than Jeannette. I explained that we were trying to assemble a coq au vin, but didn't have a recipe, and Anne-Marie nodded, waiting silently to receive my order. In the end, we picked out two beautiful legs and two beautiful breasts with wings attached from among her offerings of *poulet fermier.*

Anne-Marie stood at the chopping block in her dressy wool jacket and silk scarf, using a rubber mallet to hammer a meat cleaver through the rib bones of a quarter chicken.

We also took a lucky guess and bought some salted pork belly to be sliced into *lardons,* reasoning that, among other things—*lardons.*

Anne-Marie then met us at the other end of the counter for the cheese half of the Selvo butcher/cheesemonger twofer, where we bought a salty Roquefort and some of the nicest, smelliest runny Camembert we had seen since we'd arrived. So 0 for 3 on coq au vin advice at the Béziers market, but batting 1.000 in our search for butchers in *foulards* who would also sell us excellent cheese.

We left with everything we thought we might need for coq au vin except the evidently critical *vin.* And it was still Sunday.

But then we had a noteworthy bit of good luck. Across the street from the Halles was the Caves Paul Riquet, and the sign on the front door said, of all things, "*Ouvert.*"

Inside, a delicate, earnest woman wore glasses that made her look as if she were constantly frowning in concentration. I told her about our coq au vin, and wondered if she had any advice.

Oh, she believed that something might be arranged. Was I looking for a wine to cook the dish with, or was I looking for a wine to drink with the meal?

I explained that we were living in the Faugères region and that we had several bottles of good but expensive Faugères, but we didn't think we wanted to cook our chicken in quite so many euros.

She agreed that it was important not to exaggerate.

She placed an index finger against her lips and surveyed her wall of reds. The silence lasted just long enough to begin to be awkward.

Then, as if continuing a thought that had begun inside her own head, she said, "Because of course with coq au vin you would want something more in the direction of finesse."

She relapsed into silence, then came back and faced me, before launching into a remarkable monologue.

"The problem with Faugères is that it is too powerful when it is young, and you don't want to overwhelm the delicacy of the coq au vin. You could get away with an older Faugères in which the tannins have softened with age, but even then many of them would have too much oak. Coq au vin really should be cooked in a Burgundy, but of course it is not so easy to find a Burgundy that one is willing to pour into a *cocotte* onto the thighs of some chickens. On the other hand, you don't want to cheat such a dish. Let me ask you, are you willing to spend, let's say, five or six euros on a bottle of cooking wine?"

She looked at me apprehensively, until I reassured her that I did not plan to cheat my coq au vin over five or six euros. Her face softened with relief, and she grabbed two bottles and held them out to me in her two fists, then hesitated and glanced over her shoulder. A thought seemed to occur to her, and she put the two bottles back and then crouched to pull a third bottle slowly from its cubby as if not quite daring to think what she was thinking, yet not quite able to resist the inevitability of this most recent choice.

She stood up. "Monsieur," she said pensively to the label of this new bottle. "Might I ask." Then she paused before giving voice to her folly. "Would you, in fact, be willing to spend as much as eight euros?"

I confirmed that I was willing even to spend eight euros.

"Because, truly, with this wine," she continued, before I had even finished, "you and your wife, you will . . . I can assure you." She smiled with a mix of shared anticipation at what the evening would bring and relief that nothing had intervened to prevent this supremely correct choice from being made.

She set the right choice carefully on a stack of wooden wine crates.

"Now, what do you plan to drink with this coq au vin?"

At this point, I had to admit that the only wine we had in the house was the Faugères I had mentioned earlier—bottles that, six or seven minutes previously, I would have felt proud to serve with coq au vin to anyone who cared to sit at my table, but that now struck me as something so potentially jarring to the palate of a coq au vin eater that I might as well set out a carafe of freshly squeezed orange juice.

I asked Madame what she might recommend.

Madame rushed to assure me that she was not proposing to talk me out of our excellent Faugères. She was quite sure they . . .

"But," I suggested, "you are thinking perhaps of a certain wine."

She stopped herself and looked directly at me. High on her cheeks, two rose-colored points flared. "*Oui,*" she said, with that strange emphasis the French sometimes place on the word by whispering it with a sharp intake of breath.

She disappeared around the corner of a display, and came back cradling a bottle in the crook of her left arm that she also held by its neck in her right hand, as if to make doubly sure she wouldn't mar, with a dropped bottle, an occasion that was about to unfold into a kind of perfection.

I had time to register the words "*Côte de Nuits*" on the label, and then she was asking for my attention again.

"Monsieur," she said, "it is important to serve this at sixteen degrees. You must not serve such a wine at ambient temperature." She paused to make sure that I was staying with her. "This would be a catastrophe. *Vous comprenez?*"

I nodded.

"I suggest that you open the bottle one hour before you serve your coq au vin."

I made a gesture toward agreeing with this, too, but she held up a finger. "When you open the bottle," she resumed, "you will pour a finger of the wine into a glass to assure yourself that the wine is good. This will also reduce the volume in the bottle, and open more of the surface of the wine to the air." She paused. "Do you understand?" she asked again.

I nodded.

"It is easy to spend some hundreds of euros on a bottle of Burgundy," she said. "This is not one of those bottles, but I think you will appreciate it very much."

"I think that you are right," I said.

Only then did she allow herself to transfer the bottle, and the burden of responsibility that went with it, into my hands. "Bon appétit," she said.

"Thank you," I said.

She nodded crisply. Looked at the bottle and then back at me. "It will be necessary to come back and tell me how it was," she said.

"Oh my God," said Eva, chewing her first bite of coq au vin and staring disbelievingly downward, as if she couldn't quite accept that the flavors flooding her mouth had come from such a mundane and earthly source as the plate in front of her.

"Oh, shit," said Mary Jo as she and I simultaneously came to terms with the implications of our first sips of really good Burgundy.

The implications in both cases were dire. Eva would crave coq au vin not only for the rest of the trip, but, as it turned out, for the rest of her adolescence, which is like developing a youthful craving for beluga caviar or Julia Child's full recipe for boeuf bourguignon. There will never be enough occasions to satisfy your craving. Nor, Mary Jo and I were silently concluding, would we ever probably accumulate enough wealth to spend some hundreds of euros on enough bottles to satisfy our own newfound craving for the wine of Burgundy.

"This is French?" asked Eva.

Eventually, the coq au vin was reduced to piles of bones. Eva's plate displayed the swirling brushstrokes left behind by her desperate sauce-sopping.

The kids excused themselves for the greener pastures of a Sunday night movie on the iPad, and we poured the last Burgundy we would drink for a while into our glasses. A steady breeze through the open terrace door bent the candle flames, and built several romantic-looking wax stalagmites on the olive-wood cutting board beneath the candle-holders.

Occasionally my gaze fell upon André's wine in the kitchen, and I had an instinct to feel sheepish about how hard we had just fallen for a wine from faraway Burgundy. But in the end, I couldn't convince myself that André, or Jean-Luc, or Thierry for that matter, would find any blame in our having taken Madame's advice tonight, serving our Burgundy at sixteen degrees, and giving ourselves over to this new way in which wine could be pleasure, and pleasure, in turn, could be a bond that linked you to people who were then always with you, whether in body or spirit, when wine was poured.

52

At seven a.m., I heard Jean-Luc's tractor backing out of his garage. I tipped back an espresso with a lump of sugar and tore a saggily ripe fig in two and ate it, before clopping down the front stairs and out the door.

Nicole emerged from her garage, and we touched cheeks briefly.

"Where's your coffee?" she asked, a little mordantly, and I protested—like a teenager for once falsely accused of a crime he was regularly guilty of—that I had already drunk my whole coffee upstairs.

Nicole had caught me in the act repeatedly with a ceramic mug in my left hand and the steering wheel in my right. It was a perfectly normal American activity that was viewed as both bizarre and dangerous here, and Nicole's warnings had become increasingly dire, quoting, most recently, the French *Code de la Route*, whereby I could be sanctioned by the gendarmes if found insufficiently in control at the wheel.

In any case, this morning, despite my reckless tendency to sip coffee at twenty-five kilometers per hour through village streets, I had been entrusted to act as her chauffeur.

She distractedly talked me through our route with references to signposts that only someone familiar with the village could possibly follow—head straight to the Virgin (the statue of the Virgin Mary at the village entrance), take a left up the hill past the Christ, then left again after the almond tree next to the AOP sign.

The *fourgonnette* was a sprightly senior citizen who bore her minor aches and pains good-humoredly. The worn black steering wheel made harmless little *eep* sounds as I hauled it right and left, and we rocked a bit on the truck's boggy suspension.

The final few cicadas of the season were cheeping sluggishly as, about four minutes later, we climbed out into the morning air. Without preamble, Nicole and I began the now-familiar morning routine of sliding stacks of buckets from the back of the truck, grabbing the thermos of coffee and some thin-walled plastic cups, and selecting a handful of clippers.

Nicole mumbled to herself like someone prone to forgetting things, though I had not yet known her to let a single loose end slip in any context. We loaded each other's arms, and descended the narrow path, the bucket handles clanking softly.

The growth that lined the path was as thick as an alder swamp. I edged around the toothy cane of a wild rose, speaking its name silently— *églantine*—such a beautiful name for the nightmarish hooked thorns that had lain in wait for me.

The whole morning had proceeded with such a sense of routine comfort and familiarity that I was not prepared for what happened to me when our path turned a leftward corner and, over perhaps twenty jolting, clanking steps, a curtain was drawn wide, the ceiling of the sky was lifted, and I was faced with a hundred miles of hills, lit slantways by the morning sun, rolling away in perfect stillness behind a vineyard that sloped away from my feet through broken light in parallel rows of trellised, chest-high vines. A red tractor and its black cabin sat halfway down the third row, tires hidden, looking like a boat riding low through green swells. I stood still for a minute at the edge of the path, hugging a stack of buckets to my chest, with a coffee thermos hanging from one hand, looking around me with a confused aesthetic hunger, as if I couldn't quite pull enough of the scene into view at one time. My stomach felt light.

It wasn't just a pretty view. Something about the shapely, orderly, proportional vineyards and agricultural land sitting peacefully in the distance amid the boisterous and comically ragged wild *garrigue*, all watched over by the dark hills, was so satisfying in such a multitude of ways that I found my eyes darting from one thing to another, not just for the visual pleasure, but because I felt an aching spasm of desire.

"We are where, here?" I asked Nicole, who was tromping away from me across the tilled furrows of soil at the upper edge of the field.

"Les Espinasses, he is called," said Nicole, without looking back.

And with one more furtive look toward the horizon, and then another, more lingering, that sent me lurching over the angled metal stake at the end of one of the rows, I made my way clumsily after her.

53

Out of a growing fascination, I had shown up nearly every Friday for Monsieur Sauzet, the fishmonger. I had learned, if not mastered, at least one way to cook everything he sold, with a few remaining exceptions.

I had even convinced Mary Jo and the kids, perhaps 30 percent of the time, to actively look forward to what I set on the table, which I considered a dazzling batting average.

Joe had particularly come to crave fried monkfish tails, sometimes called poor-man's lobster. We had learned just how fine-fleshed were fresh sardines, cooked hot and fast over vine-wood stems and seasoned with lemon halves squeezed in cascades onto their charred and salted skin.

And I had spent a happy afternoon beheading and gutting two slippery fistfuls of anchovies, laying the silvery remains on a bed of salt to dry before stacking them in Le Parfait canning jars between layers of coarse Camargue sea salt. I thought of them as treasures.

They lived on my refrigerator shelf in the spirit of those dusty jars in Jean-Luc's garage that I so admired. Jean-Luc had grown and processed those fig and apricot preserves. Had made and bottled those cordials and liqueurs. Had engaged with the plenty of the local seasons and set some of it against a future need, or a future pleasure, likely shared with people he cared about. I, in my turn, had dried and salted my first batch of anchovies pulled from waters almost within sight of my pantry, which now stood ready.

The predicted rain came on a Friday, and, for the first time, I saw why a village that spent much of the year flirting with drought had such a comprehensive civil infrastructure in place for the channeling and evacuating of water.

Rainwater poured down the two gutters flanking Avenue de la Liberté, creeping in under our garage door and sending up continuous geysers as it sluiced against the tires of our parked car.

I stood in this downpour at the appointed time, under an umbrella that bucked and threatened to leap from my hands into the branches of the plane trees overhead.

When M. Sauzet arrived, I was the only one there to greet him. He didn't even unload his truck.

"Where are they?" he asked, without seeming to need an answer. "They all complain about prices, but a little rain falls . . ."

He opened the back of his van. "I have a beautiful *loup de mer*," he said, and pulled out a lead-gray sea bass the length of my forearm. I paid him as the wind slammed the door shut behind him, and he ducked back into the driver's seat and accelerated out of town.

The next week, one of his elderly customers would attempt to convince him that she had paid less for her *merlan* only the week before, and he would inform her that that was not possible, because the previous week it had rained, and the only customer was his friend the American over there, and, more than that, the American had not complained about prices.

In the courtyard that evening, under the protection of the terrace overhang, as rain poured off the edge in a silver curtain, I kindled some vine twigs into flame with a crumpled page of the local newspaper, *Midi Libre,* arranged an interlocking layer of *ceps de vigne*, and was soon staring at a roaring little fire working its way through the twisted, knobby stumps.

I cut diagonal slits in the fish's sides, and stuffed the slits with minced fennel fronds, garlic, and lemon peel. I stuffed the abdomen with lemon slices, parsley, sea salt, and lengths of wild fennel stalk from Jean-Luc and Nicole's Espinasses vineyard. I roasted the fish, unscaled, over the vine embers, which breathed orange and red in the swirling wind, hissed occasionally when droplets of rain were blown onto them, and sent shifting clouds of that sharp smoke into the air that could not be compared, as Jean-Luc had rightly insisted, with charcoal.

When the skin was thoroughly blackened and the fish's eyes milky, and an exploratory knife slid into the meat of the shoulder found little resistance and released a tendril of aromatic steam, I moved the fish onto a cutting board and carried it to the table.

By all rights, the near perfection of the fish's preparation and presentation should have been enough for anyone. The stiff, crisped skin helped to pull the meat cleanly from the spine, and a cutting board featuring two steaming boneless fillets amid flakes of char was presented to the family. Fennel had unquestionably been the correct choice—aromatically, culinarily, aesthetically. The fact that it had been brought home just days earlier from a vineyard within walking distance, where I had picked grapes and admired everything around me, added a layer of romance that by itself would practically have required its use. And none of that, in the end, managed to convince my children that they did, after all, appreciate the smell of wild fennel, which lightly infused every delicate white flake of the fish's flesh.

I had known this in my heart. Had known I was pushing a stone that would roll right back. Had not even found a line of magical thinking that could convince me that the moment of my kids' conversion from fennel skeptics to fennel lovers would correspond exactly with the day I happened to possess foraged fennel stalks hanging from my ceiling, vine stumps in a sack next to my grill, and a particularly beautiful sea bass to cook up. I simply had not been able to resist creating the moment that these elements made possible. I had acted in service to the moment, not to the people I would share the moment with, and at least this time I recognized that it was not their fault, but mine, that they had not fully appreciated my beautiful grilled fish.

I didn't understand how much I had internalized the village-wide pre-occupation with the drought until it finally rained. Rolling out our garbage bin that evening, I ran across Jean-Luc, and we stood inside his garage doorway, watching the downpour. I felt a swelling sort of relief, as if the repo man had been called off because some beautiful stranger had just paid off my car.

But as it turned out, rain was sometimes a good thing when you grew vines, and sometimes it was not. According to Jean-Luc, a hard rain during the harvest, especially after a sustained dry spell, was often as bad as the drought itself.

The thirsty roots guzzle. The water reaches the grapes in less than twenty-four hours. It bloats them, dilutes their flavor, undoes all the careful measuring for acidity, sugar content, flavor concentration—for that moment of perfect, fleeting ripeness.

So now it was time to wait. To see how many millimeters would fall, and then to rely on experience, intuition, and a little science to determine how much damage had been done, and when it would be possible to resume picking grapes.

There was a minor but meaningful redemption amid the catastrophe of rain that had been the opposite of, yet not undone, the catastrophe of the drought. And that was a small, warty, green-and-brown-spotted frog about the size of a teaspoon that Joe discovered on the shoulder of Avenue de la Liberté.

"It's a parsley frog!" he announced after some urgent research.

Several subsequent announcements traced the progress of his investigations.

"They're kinda rare!" he said.

Then: "It says they only breed after heavy rain."

"She's less than four centimeters long. I think she's a female."

"They're called parsley frogs because of the green spots on their backs."

"You guys, I'd never have seen her if it hadn't rained!"

He presented his new frog, named Parsley, to Jean-Luc, who had never seen one—information that Joe received with intense and badly hidden joy.

And that evening, Parsley joined September in the terrarium next to Joe's bed, where they both consumed their prey alive, September slowly and in pieces, Parsley instantaneously and whole.

54

Eva had taken on the morning bakery run, mostly out of a refusal to begin school days with a breakfast someone else had chosen.

She would set out her change the night before, arrive just as the bakery opened, and then walk home in the predawn gloom, splashing through a chain of yellow sodium lamp pools with a bag of pastries, a baguette under her arm, and a handful of gummy candy in her sweatshirt pocket.

By the time she got back, a plate of sliced fruit and a tub of Président butter would be waiting on the table and I would be groggily making tea. She would mine far into the interior of the halved baguette, pulling the flaky white *mie* (interior) from the crusty golden *croûte* (crust), and then applying a thick frosting of salted butter. We would munch together in silence, and leave in time to beat the school bell, but not so early that she would have to socialize extensively among her schoolmates waiting for the gate to open.

This frequently involved crawling past the gate, allowing Eva to reconnoiter, then looping back through Murviel-lès-Béziers to approach the gate again under more favorable interpersonal circumstances.

"Have a good day, honey," I would say when we had arrived, and the

woven armor of her nylon jacket would shush against itself as she shoul-
dered into her backpack and sheared away for another day spent, as I
imagined it, among friends who weren't quite friends, in a language not
her own, in a temporary city, on a quest she hadn't chosen.

Flickering through the ancient plane trees that lined the exit to Murviel, I would switch the radio station. At exactly 7:57 a.m., the host of
France Culture's morning radio program would say, "Bonjour, Philippe,"
introducing the lettered and eloquent daily reflections of Philippe
Meyer, *le Toutologue* (the Everythingologist). To this day, even the
thought of Meyer's voice places me behind the wheel of a Renault Scenic, on a narrow French country highway, with golden morning light
washing over passing vines, enveloped in the bittersweet feeling of loving a child you do not, for the moment, understand.

I waited at noon, across the street from Collège le Cèdre, pulled tight to
a stucco retaining wall so the cars of the other parents could squeeze
past me.

An old-fashioned rotary school bell rang, and in the mirror I
watched the lunchtime dam burst, discharging a river of teenagers who
poured downhill toward me, swallowing every object in their course—
streetlamps, concrete sidewalk pylons, bikes, cars, and eddying groups
of one another.

I caught a splash of coral sweater and blue jeans walking with what
looked like Eva's walk, in the pale halo that surrounds daughters when
they walk toward their fathers, even in rearview mirrors.

"Here is my daughter," I said to myself. "Walking as if it's no big thing,
among her French classmates, down the street in Murviel-lès-Béziers."

Fifty or so splay-footed steps, with a just-noticeable hitch, brought
her up alongside the car. She sat, and unzipped a compartment of her
backpack to pull out a stick of gum. She wore a blue mohair scarf, which
she had bought at the Pézenas market a week ago, and which she
wrapped high on her shoulders like a cowl, in much the style of the
many scarves that had just flowed past my window, but unlike anything

she had ever worn before coming to France, and this was one of the things that we agreed not to talk about.

With my heart full of things that the father of a teenager sometimes either needs to have said already or needs to wait and say later, I asked, "How did school go?"

"Good," she said, and took a first bite of her Hollywood (pronounced oh-lee-WOOOD) chewing gum.

"Bad, fair, good, great, or fantastic?" I asked, glancing in my rearview mirror and easing into the single line of cars that passed for a traffic jam in Murviel.

Eva changed the radio from France Culture to the Top 40 station NRJ (pronounced, in French, *en-air-ZHEE*).

"Good," she said. And someone named Carly Rae Jepsen sang us most of the way home, filling the silence of the car with invitations to call her, maybe.

"I'm losing her," I told Mary Jo that night.

"Who?"

"Eva."

"You're not."

"I try to talk to her and there's nothing."

"It's normal."

55

In Paris long ago, *merguez*, a skinny North African lamb sausage, had been one of the most satisfying street foods that also fit into my monthly budget. The vendor around the corner in his kufi skullcap would stuff a couple links of *merguez* into a split length of baguette and lay a tongful of French fries on top of that.

Monsieur Congnard made our favorite local version.

I looked around the shop as he wrapped the brick-colored bundle of sausages and rang them up. How interesting would it be to spend an afternoon behind the counter with him, I thought. I had no idea—other than cutting large sections of animal into smaller cuts on demand— what it meant to be a butcher in a French village.

It occurred to me that I could simply ask Monsieur Congnard if he would allow me to join him someday in his shop. There was not a rule out there prohibiting such a question, even if I had no real motivation for asking, beyond an interest in learning something I did not know.

"*Ecoutez*," I began, before I had had time to think it through, and then I was launched and there wasn't a natural way to turn back. "My family and I are in Autignac until the end of the year." Here I tossed my head in the direction of Autignac, which was information he didn't really need.

"I know," he said.

"I don't know how many times in my life I will have the occasion to see a butcher shop like this. Do you think it would be possible for me to pass an afternoon with you sometime, to watch how you do your work?"

I looked across the counter at his blank expression. He stood leaning on his cutting board, weight resting on one hip. He had no idea how to answer. All he wanted was to go home to dinner after a long day.

He scratched one of his sideburns skeptically with the same hand that held his knife, and there was silence in the shop. My heart pounded. I opened my mouth to launch an apologetic retraction.

"This would be a great pleasure," he said.

He thought about it. "I receive my deliveries on Wednesdays. It would be good if you came on a Wednesday."

56

That several of Eva's classmates took riding lessons was not a surprising phenomenon in an agricultural region. But horse lessons didn't appear anywhere on any list at all of things Eva seemed likely to ask for.

She was not afraid to take action, even if she might later decide it was mistaken. But that wasn't enough explanation for her voluntarily taking on the double challenge of learning to ride a horse and learning that skill in French.

She had been experimenting with her camera for weeks, trying and failing to conquer a hill she could plant her flag on and call her own. It wasn't in her nature to accept the role of apprentice to Mary Jo. She had to, if not necessarily win her semisecret competition with her mom, then at least differentiate herself so that whatever she was doing remained unblurred by how much their interests and creative instincts overlapped.

In the end I think horseback-riding lessons were a way of saying, maybe to herself, maybe to Mary Jo and the rest of us, "OK, here's something I'm going to do that is mine."

So we found a stable, and Eva and I went to a farm supply store to pick out riding boots with heels, and cushioned stretch breeches, and a visored helmet.

Twice a week, I would pick her up from school and wind along country back roads while she changed clothes in the rear seat.

Her instructor, Aurélie, made exactly zero concessions to Eva's being an American girl learning English riding style in the French language, and would hurl exasperated instructions from the middle of the arena at all of her students, but—it seemed to Eva's father—at Eva especially.

She called her Ay-VAH.

"Ohhhh! . . . Ayyy-VAAAAH! . . . No, but why don't you do what I'm saying to yoouuuu?"

Eva didn't understand half of the technical expressions that Aurélie delivered to her like cracks of a whip, and as Eva struggled to focus on the unfamiliar terms, her rhythm would get out of step with the rolling of the horse beneath her and her helmet would bounce around on her head with the syncopated saddle impacts. She would climb back into the car stony-faced and tired, after walking her horse back to the stable and struggling to unbuckle the saddle, too frustrated or stubborn to ask for help.

Her face had a familiar, clench-jawed set to it.

"What is this about?" asked Mary Jo.

I didn't know. But this was Eva. And I was willing to follow where she led, hoping she would not leave me behind.

57

I had just returned from an afternoon at André's when our doorbell rang. Nicole stood next to Jean-Luc on our front stoop, gingerly cupping a bird's nest in her two hands.

"When the vines are pruned in goblet form, the birds make nests in the hollows," explained Nicole. "Mary Jo, she might like to take a photo, no?"

"For *le blog*," clarified Jean-Luc.

It was the first of what would grow into an extensive private museum of the nests of local birds.

Word had spread among the crew of grape pickers that Mary Jo was a photographer who published pictures of interesting bits of nature.

Some days she and I picked grapes together, and other days, the sky would be overcast, and the flat light perfect, and there was simply too much material around for her to squander the morning with clippers in her hand.

"*Regardez*," Jean-Luc would say, approaching Mary Jo with a bouquet of white *rouquette* flowers, or the barred wing feather of a raptor called *buse variable,* or the unruly head of a late-season asparagus.

"*Mah-ree ZHO!*" our teammate Valérie would call, pointing to a particularly elegant *vrille,* or vine tendril, spiraling from the top of a trellis wire.

Richard would announce he had found a *cousin* (coo-ZAN)—a cartoonishly large and colorful grasshopper-like bug that sings the word "*cousin*" when its belly is stroked. And big, bearded Richard would tenderly escort the stripe-suited passenger on his finger to have its portrait taken in Mary Jo's studio at the end of a row of vines.

Suddenly the call would go up, "*Knee! Knee!*" And somebody, or often several people, would be pointing at an abandoned *nid* (bird's nest) in the center of a vine, where the fingers of the branches joined the palm of the trunk. Someone would extricate the nest and hand it to Mary Jo, whose delight was so transparent that finding nests became a point of honor among our crewmates.

Nests began lining our bookshelves and the half wall separating the kitchen from the living room.

Jean-Luc and Nicole would act as the delivery service on days we couldn't go out into the vines, and when we had all found a place for everything, I would, if I could possibly negotiate it, slip the stems of wineglasses into their hands and encourage them to stay and talk.

I served them Papa's Liqueur de Verveine one evening, and Jean-Luc analyzed it at length, saying that perhaps Papa Casties used Fine Faugères, the esteemed barrel-aged local brandy, whereas Jean-Luc used high-proof *eau de vie.*

I showed them the bottle of vinegar I had been given, and they looked at each other.

"Steve," said Jean-Luc.

Several years ago, he had attempted to make a white vinegar from sweet Muscat wine. "A good Muscat is . . ." Here he looked heavenward.

"I waited for more than a year until finally it turned, and, Steve . . ."

Here again he tried to express through gesture and expression just what effect a vinegar made from sweet Muscat could do to a man.

"I will get you a bottle," he said.

58

It was on a bad vocabulary day that I asked, at a garden store in Béziers called Baobab, where I could find *"des herbes,"* and been shown first a collection of ornamental grasses, and then bags of grass seed, before I described exactly what I was looking for and was told that I was not looking for *des herbes* (grasses), but for *des aromatiques.*

The resulting purchases, once transplanted, sat just outside the terrace door, against the two-foot-thick heat sink of our courtyard wall. There was a bouquet of aimless-looking basil, one bristly dome of thyme, one copse of parsley divided among the A students standing attentively in the center and the delinquents looking over the edge of the pot. There was a stalk of lemon verbena. A scruffy tangle of winter savory. And, finally, a spare laurel tree that I would forever remember for giving me my very first smell of fresh bay leaf.

Passing by the breakfast table one morning, prepping for a soup, I broke a laurel leaf in half, releasing the smell of cloves and bitter citrus.

"Smell," I said to Eva.

She held it to her nose. "Mmm," she said, without looking up from her list of vocabulary words for that day's *dictée.*

Mary Jo's grandmother used to proclaim that she loved all of her grandchildren just exactly the same, except she loved Mary Jo's sister, Dee-Dee, just a little bit more. In that same spirit, I loved all of my herbs just exactly the same, except I didn't love them all the way I loved crushing a small handful of thyme, and smelling the humusy, balsam woodiness that was so much a part of this landscape, and yet was so reminiscent of home that

I might have been holding a torn-up handful of sphagnum moss in a Minnesota cedar swamp. And that didn't take into account what happened in the air above the stovetop when a mound of silver-green arrowheads got swept from the cutting board into a warm bath of olive oil and garlic.

59

School lunch in France meant something quite entirely different from what it meant in the States. No pizzas, hamburgers, French fries, Diet Cokes, or Italian dunkers.

French students were expected to expand their palates as well as their minds, and our two kids, whether they liked it or not, were now French students.

In Autignac, Joe's weekly menu was posted outside the school gate, and the offerings rivaled the prix fixe menu at most decent local restaurants. To take an example from a random Thursday:

Le Déjeuner *(Today's Lunch)*

Salade de tomates (Tomato salad)
Bouchées de poisson pané (Morsels of pan-fried fish)
Risotto aux champignons (Mushroom risotto)
Bleu d'Auvergne (Blue cheese from the Auvergne)
Pâte de fruits (Fruit jellies)

The following days would include a *courgette clafoutis*, mutton stew, chickpea salad, wilted spinach with béchamel sauce, an onion omelet, and aged goat cheese.

And the rule was "No vegetables, no dessert."

Among the complaining we heard, we would also receive a positive review now and then of such exoticisms as chicken couscous, *pâté de campagne,* and lentil soup, which now came recommended by hungry friends and classmates, not devious parents with an agenda.

Eva might even take a cheese knife some early evening, and, perhaps thinking her father wasn't watching, reach past the easy wedge of mild and buttery Brie to scrape up a puddle of salty, heady, odorously ripened Camembert, which she might well proceed to spread on the thin slice of baguette in her left hand.

According to the original plan, a lot of mornings spent in southern France with short stacks of cookbooks were going to result in a lot of well-prepared evening meals from an entirely new repertoire of recipes around our French table.

The logistics of this—the precise steps leading from the morning armchair to the evening's splendor—had been glossed over, in the same way that it is relatively easy to imagine starting a business, and also to imagine a million dollars, but less easy to start an actual business that makes a million dollars.

I had always loved the feeling of tying on an apron around three in the afternoon and settling in with a chef's knife and a cutting board. But I had not ever acted as the daily cook for a household of four, which I had somewhat cluelessly thought myself capable of doing here, mostly alone, and the relentless dailiness of it was making itself felt, and was further, it could be said, interfering with the kind of cooking that tended to contribute to the greater glory of Steve Hoffman.

"Do you want some help?" Mary Jo would ask.

I didn't want help. I wanted to overwhelm the family with dinners that they craved, and that made them love France, and that made them appreciate the exquisite calibration of my caring for them, as they relaxed and enjoyed their evenings. I wanted to introduce a few Mediterranean staples into our regular Midwestern dinner rotation, and I wanted to self-educate my way into quiet domestic mastery.

That's all I wanted.

60

"*Pissaladière*," I announced a little defiantly, and dropped a cutting board in the middle of the table.

I had spent the afternoon caramelizing a skilletful of sweet yellow onions with a fresh bay leaf from my new laurel tree, until the onions were the color of a field of barley and softened to somewhere between a marmalade and a puree, while next to me, under the warm halogen lights above the kitchen countertop, a yeasty dome of pizza dough had risen in its ceramic bowl.

In my efforts to achieve the perfect round-cornered rectangular shape, I had spent enough time rolling out the crust to receive a mild warning from Mary Jo about overworking the dough.

"What you making?" she asked.

"None of your beeswax."

I had minced half a dozen of my salted anchovy fillets and stirred these into the onions, then stripped several dense ruffs of thyme and savory into the mix. I had spread this *garrigue*-scented onion jam onto the rolled-out crust, and baked it for twenty minutes.

The dish checked every box—an authentic southern recipe, using Mediterranean ingredients, in the familiar and well-loved form of a pizza. And at the same time, I knew it had no chance.

Once the pizza had finished cooking, I decorated it with the requisite finish of anchovy fillets laid out in a diamond crosshatch pattern and, in the center of each diamond, one glistening black olive.

"Do I only have to try it?" Joe asked—his standard opening bid when preparing to negotiate an unwanted meal.

"It's a pizza," I said.

"Are those anchovies?" asked Eva.

"It's a pizza," I said. "It's a famous and authentic southern French dish."

I rocked a chef's knife back and forth, cutting it into squares.

Truly. It was perfect.

"It's not a pizza," said Mary Jo. "A pizza has tomatoes and cheese and some kind of meat."

"Yes, in Minneapolis and Naples," I said.

"I wish you'd learned Italian in college," said Eva.

"But, here's the thing. I learned French," I said. "So we're all going to eat southern French pizza in southern France. Which I think is wonderful."

"It has the word *piss* in it," said Joe.

"From *pissalat*. Occitan for 'salted fish.' Nice try, young grasshopper."

"I'm going to go buy a baguette," said Eva.

"Stores are all closed," I said. "And I know for a fact, young lady, that you had *soupe de poisson* this week for school lunch and had to have eaten it or you wouldn't have gotten dessert."

"Fish is different from anchovies," she said.

"That might be convincing if you had ever eaten an anchovy."

"I don't need to eat one. Just smell it."

"I will, thank you. Mmm. Salty and bready."

"And fishy and olivey and oniony," said Mary Jo.

"Yum," I said.

"You're turning into a food bully," said Mary Jo. "No one likes a bully."

"I like being a bully," I said. "I eat better when I'm a bully."

Eva started to say something.

"Hey, Eva!" I said, and rose from the table.

"What?"

I returned from the oven with a second pizza—round, not square, and bubbling with mozzarella.

"Shut up," I said.

I took another slice of *pissaladière*.

It was perfect.

61

Concerned that overfeeding had led to, or at least hastened, the death of April the mantis, Joe was doling out crickets to September and her roommate Parsley once in the morning, once after school, and once before bed.

He was upstairs giving them their after-school meal one day when he called to me.

For a split second after I arrived by his side, I didn't fully understand what I was looking at, and then I did.

September the mantis was grooming herself, like a cat cleaning its front paws. She was licking—or whatever the mantid equivalent of licking might be—tiny droplets of blood from her front pincers.

Beside her on the carefully smoothed sand of the terrarium were Parsley's long legs, extended as if in mid-leap. They ended just above the roundly muscular thighs, from which emerged two delicate femurs attached to a pelvic bone. Other than that, there was nothing left of Parsley.

Joe's face was puffy, and he wiped a wrist across his eyes, hurriedly, as if frustrated with his own tears. He cleared his throat. "I think I underfed them," he said.

When Joe was about three, we went on a spring vacation to the Atlantic coast of Florida, and on a windy morning beach walk, we came upon a dead but completely intact loon, delivered up by the surf. This was during Joe's "What do dinosaurs do for danger?" period, and he stood shivering in the raw wind, staring down at an actually dead creature, within touching distance of his sandals. He listened in silence to our theorizing about whether the loon may have migrated from Minnesota—where we heard them call all summer—and what might have befallen it, whether it had been injured internally somehow, whether it had been caught under the water and drowned, whether loons were susceptible to hypothermia.

On the way home, Joe embarked on an extended, speculative monologue, in which he put together for himself, and for us, an iterative, accumulating narrative explaining exactly how the loon had died and why. The story contained elements from children's nature books, and from the conversation we had had while huddled around the dead bird. The story involved a dangerously deep dive underwater, a shark of some kind, cold winds, and eventually a deadly case of "pipertheramia."

Something like that happened now, as we sat together on his bed, watching September the assassin dispassionately clean the tools of Parsley's destruction.

When he finally talked, he talked his way around the central event, wondering why the legs had been left behind, expressing his surprise that a mantis could predate a frog its own size. He grasped at the word "predate" like an intellectual life ring holding him up at the surface, where science and rationality could distract from the depths of guilt and sadness and horror below. Where he didn't have to imagine the stalking; the strike; the squirming; the elegant, kicking legs; the bloody, agonized disappearance, bite by bite, that had resulted from his placing two beloved creatures in a glass box together, one of which had possessed everything it needed for danger, and the other, not nearly enough.

I felt overmatched as a father. I figured there were fathers who would know what to say, but I didn't. I couldn't bring myself to minimize what had happened. To talk about Parsley like a goldfish flushed down the toilet. To try to desensitize this too-aware boy, grieving beside me over the death of a frog the size of a half-dollar. I didn't want him desensitized. I wanted him as he was. I wanted to let him know there was no one to blame. That he got to be a boy. He got to make mistakes. There was no lesson to be learned here, except that I loved him and always would.

And yet, I knew Joe in all the ways he was like me, and I knew by whatever instinct that knowledge gave me that trying to share his sadness with him was not the answer. It might make me feel better. But he didn't want that.

I was pretty sure I understood something that I couldn't express to him. I understood that he had let himself love Parsley in a way that nine-year-old boys weren't supposed to. He had opened himself up, as he was still so beautifully capable of, and yet he suspected that there was something about the depth of his sadness that he should be embarrassed about. He was caught between the guilelessness of early boyhood and the knowingness of adolescence, and he felt both heartbroken and guarded about his heartbrokenness. And I couldn't tell him how much I treasured his ability to love without guile, without also drawing attention to his embarrassment.

So, instead, I just sat there, uncomfortably, theorizing with him, letting him talk it out the way he seemed to need to talk it out, feeling as if I should do more, but also feeling intensely the gift of him—this boy beside me, struggling to hide his pain and grief because they were so powerful in him, who had loved a frog named Parsley.

There was another too-sensitive boy I knew, who had not had enough defenses, who did not know what to do for danger. And though it would take much longer than an afternoon, or a six-month stay in France, to reorient myself to him, to discover ways to offer my acceptance to that other boy, it helped on an afternoon in Autignac to see him—for the first time, to my knowledge—not as my own young self, but as a son like my own son, whom, had we met under other circumstances, I would probably have loved from the beginning.

62

"You know what I just made the other night," mused Maman on her stool at Le Jardin de Marie.

She was pulling another afternoon shift at the till.

"You are someone who interests himself in the cuisine of the region," she informed me. "You will want to pay attention. What I made the other night is called a *macaronade*."

At the moment, I was feeling like someone who had indeed, for a hopeful stretch, interested himself in the cuisine of the region, but sadly the cuisine of the region had eventually broken things off with a letter explaining how it would always love me, but just wasn't *in love* with me.

In such a mood, and with an American's dubious set of associations with the word "macaroni," I was not prepared to take seriously, just then, a description of a dish featuring elbow pasta from a French cook.

"Macaroni," I said. "It is French?"

"They are Italian, the macaronis," she said. "But *macaronade* is Sétois. From Sète. There is a cuisine Niçoise that comes from Nice. And naturally there is a cuisine Sétoise that comes from Sète. Many fishermen from Naples installed themselves there."

She proceeded to deliver the recipe for *macaronade* as decisively as usual.

I could use any meat I liked—loose sausage, beef cheeks, ground lamb, pork.

"But the most typical is perhaps *brageoles*," said Maman.

Brageoles were quite simple, and, yes, after a brief consultation with herself, Maman concluded that I really should make my *macaronade* with *brageoles*, which involved butterflying a thin chuck steak, and seasoning one side with salt, pepper, minced garlic, and parsley, then rolling it up like a sleeping bag and holding it together, if necessary, with a toothpick.

Was I following?

Without waiting for an answer, she led me through the browning of the *brageoles* in olive oil, and the sweating of the diced onions in the same *cocotte* after the *brageoles* had been set aside, and the finely minced garlic added to the pot just long enough to release its *arôme* before deglazing with red wine, and adding peeled tomatoes and a bouquet garni of thyme and bay leaf, all of which, with the *brageoles* now returned to the pot, would simmer for an hour, and this, Monsieur, would be my sauce.

By her tone she might have been describing the precise steps involved in assembling a vacuum cleaner, or sewing on a button. She gave no indication that the quite mechanical steps involved in making a *macaronade aux brageoles* might be having a bodily effect on the American across the counter from her.

A part of my mind, however, was imagining in a vivid way the experience of biting through a slice of *brageole*, tenderized by the acidity of the wine and the tomatoes and by an hour spent simmering in a *cocotte*, and at the same time I was imagining what it might be like sitting for forty or fifty years at Maman's table, the daily beneficiary of her precise and dispassionate kitchen skills.

Finally, I was to cook *des macaronis* in salty water and mix them into the sauce. Everyone should receive two or three slices of *brageole*.

"This is a classic dish in this region," said Maman. "It is also possible to use fish. My grandchildren, they regale themselves."

Maman made a point, when discussing any of the meals she made or recommended, to emphasize how much her family regaled itself with such a dish, and as obvious as this should have been all along, it was clear this afternoon that she did not view her mastery of the cuisine of her region as a kind of diploma to hang on her wall, but a relatively pure means to a particular reward, and that reward was a family's regaling itself day after day in her hands.

I had been stuck on the idea that classic dishes were a higher form of cooking, based on obligation, not pleasure. They were like skill-building exercises developed for culinary schools, rather than meals that the sons and daughters of mothers like Maman had begged for—and sometimes brought with them from Naples to a better life in Sète.

I had been trying to fit into a tradition here and had chosen, unwittingly, something closer to the tradition of (largely male, largely ego-driven) haute cuisine.

But how much more interesting was the daily clamor at Maman's hearth than an attitude that said the chef should be the focus of every meal? What if classic dishes were not, in fact, derived like geometry from theorems and proofs and imposed by culinary ordinance, but handed up from the past? Gifts from previous cooks who had found ways to make things taste good, and who were passing on their treasure maps? What if a traditional cuisine were simply the evolution of all the ways of cooking with what a particular part of the world could grow, refined not by a set of precepts, but by hundreds of generations of cooks answering to the daily wishes of hundreds of generations of family at the table?

If you have chosen to set up camp on the edge of the Mediterranean plain where it meets the foothills of the Espinouse, and if you plan to do a lot of cooking, there is a tradition ready-made to be stepped into, because a lot of cooks before you have worked hard to make the most of just that same situation.

Something like this flood of thoughts was running through me as I watched Maman weigh the two pears I had bought for the kids. She pressed her fingers into their necks and looked concerned. "For today?" she asked.

I said, "For tomorrow," and she nodded, reassured.

Twenty-five years earlier, a slight, bespectacled woman in a Paris apartment, with a similar imperious manner hiding a talent for devotion, had created a space in which I had permission, not to improve myself as I was so relentlessly attempting to do, but to trust that she accepted the person in development before her.

Maman, sitting before me, had been a good mother, as Madame Villatte would have been, had life given her the opportunity. I had often wished I had trusted what Madame Villatte had been trying to tell me, in her teasing but loving way. She had gotten me on track for an eyeblink of time, and when she was gone, I had jumped back off. I wondered now what Maman would tell me, if I promised I would listen, about what it took for a man to be a good mother.

63

I had never cleaned a squid in my life, but they were among the few remaining delicacies that I had not yet bought from M. Sauzet, and so, with two kids standing expectantly to my right, I assessed the arsenal of wide-eyed warheads staring up at me from the sink.

I began by peeling the gelatinous layer of freckled brown skin from the first squid, then, taking my best guess, seized the head in one hand and the body in the other, and, with Joe staring in fascination and Eva looking as if someone were about to throw a bucket of water at her, I pulled, ending up with tentacles and some stringy innards dangling from my right hand, and a slippery matte white dunce cap in my left.

Some mottled shadows inside the body told me I wasn't done, and I scrubbed and scooped under the faucet, each time pulling out something new, including at one point a right hand completely painted with oily black ink.

The end result was an assemblage of six flawlessly smooth bodies like something made out of Kevlar in a lab, and six clusters of tentacles that could only have been organic.

We would never even make it to the dinner table. There would just be a fryer full of hot oil on the stove, a lemony sea smell in the air, and a salty, oil-stained paper towel on the kitchen counter as evidence that there had been any squid in the house at all.

Joe tried his first taste and immediately threw his elbows out like a power forward under the boards, boxing us out until the rings had cooled enough for him to grab a handful.

"Why didn't you guys tell me about squid?" he complained.

To a nine-year-old boy, fresh squid for dinner offered, really, the complete package. There were sea creatures; there was the sci-fi gross-out factor; there was ink, for crying out loud, poured into a glass yogurt pot for all manner of future uses; and there was the breaded, salted, elastic tenderness in his mouth.

Even Eva, once past the swallowing sound of the heads' being removed, was on board, and she and her brother negotiated possession of the last ring by tearing it in half.

Eva had decided not to continue her riding lessons after the first series was complete, and though she had always been willing to quit, without misgivings, any activity that wasn't working for her, the absence of Aurélie in her life seemed particularly to have buoyed her—restoring some of that natural effervescence that was the positive expression of her energetic intensity.

One tangled mophead of tentacles remained on the plate. Joe looked his sister steadily in the eyes, popped it in his mouth, and chewed.

Joe put in his order for squid the following Friday, and I wadded up the mat of paper towels, by way of doing the dishes.

64

"Number three," said Joe.

"Number five," said Eva.

"Number one," said Mary Jo.

"Number seven," I said.

"No way," said Eva. "You can't possibly like number seven."

"He just tries to like weird things," said Mary Jo. "He thinks it makes him look smart."

We were gathered around the terrace table before seven shallow pools of golden-amber liquid. These were the honeys we had picked up at markets, grocery stores, and a farm up the hill called Hives of the

High Languedoc, and we had decided it was time to establish, via taste test, which we each liked.

"Lavender," said Eva. "The rest of you are wrong."

65

We had taken a table at the café for their Saturday pizza night. It was nearing sundown, and the terrace was full but quiet with a soft chuckle of conversation in the cooling evening. Suddenly, around the corner appeared José, in a Real Madrid uniform and flip-flops, with a cap on backward, and a cigarette in the left corner of his mouth. The terrace erupted.

José walked up to the café, shook everybody's hand, kissed Mary Jo and Eva, grabbed a newspaper that was evidently just a prop, because he never looked at it again, and, while accepting with a show of reluctance the glasses of tap beer that appeared at his wrist, carried on a multifront conversation with every group on the terrace, mostly in full-speed Spanish, despite the fact that his neighbors all spoke to him in French.

We began referring to him as the Mayor of Autignac.

Part of his authority among the villagers derived from the fact that he was a local superstar—a prodigy—better and faster than all of them at something they all admired. He was, as Jean-Luc called him, a *machine à vendanger* (a grape-picking machine).

He had joined our crew one day, just as I was getting comfortable with triage and snipping grapes at speed, and I watched him pick a vine clean in the time it took me to move a few branches around and decide where to start. His method involved clearing leaves first, followed by a combination of clipping and ripping that had grape clusters bouncing into his bucket with almost comical speed.

At some point, I found myself across a row of grapes from him. He was working his side of the trellis and I working mine. A competition takes place in this situation no matter whom you're across from.

I peeked across the row to see where he was, taking shortcuts, no longer holding from below, *là,* and snipping from above, *là.*

"*Merde!*"

"*Oh-là-là,*" said Nicole.

And that was the end of the hysterical drama caused by my once again nearly cutting off my thumb.

I went back to work more carefully and assumed the bleeding would stop eventually.

"Eh-STEVE-eh," I heard through the vine in front of me.

José reached under the trellis between two vine stumps, grasped my thumb, pulled it to his side, and squeezed several drops of blood into the bucket of grapes at his feet.

"*Sangre de Cristo.*"

He stood up and, with the edge of his palm, performed the sign of the cross in the air above the trellis's top wire: "*En el nombre del Padre, Hijo y Espíritu Santo.*"

As we continued, one of the Romanian pickers began to sing to herself. Everyone worked in silence as her singing rose and fell in a gypsy minor key. After a few minutes, she finished one of her songs and paused. A nasal Spanish monotone rose from the several vines ahead of the rest of us.

"*Aahh-mennnn.*"

And then he went back to picking grapes, leaving us quickly, and then farther and farther, behind.

66

"Go be a butcher," Mary Jo said at the top of the stairs. I kissed her good-bye, and received a swat on the seat of my pants.

In Laurens, M. Congnard nodded through the plate glass window, and I walked into the distinctive smell of blood and chilled meat, wondering what you talk about on a date with a French butcher.

Preparing tax returns for six or seven hundred Americans a year, ranging from insolvent realtors to decamillionaires, has left me mostly unmoved by wealth and status. But an aura of minor royalty had attached itself to this butcher, and I was not immune to a sense of rank—of being granted an audience—as I approached him across the tiled floor of his austere shop.

I shook the offered elbow of the Butcher of Laurens, whose royal hands were covered in lamb and fat from mixing a tub of sausage.

We smiled at each other for a second, and, not knowing what else to say, I told him the truth: "I don't know what I want to know."

"Maybe you want to know what's in the cooler," he suggested.

"Now I know one thing I want to know," I said.

He led me into the surprisingly small space behind the counter, and pulled the lever handle on a big, insulated door.

It swung open, and there were his wares—headless, hoofless, and, except for the pig, skinned. The bodies hung in an unsettling gloom, suspended by meat hooks that ran between the tendon and bone just above each animal's rear knee. They swung heavily as he wove among them, breath clouding in the chill, to show me what I was looking at.

The timeline he described struck me as breathlessly short—between eight and, at the outside, ten days to sell the meat in some form or another. His cooler was kept at a constant 1°C. He did not have a freezer.

"You don't have a freezer," I said.

"I don't have a freezer," he said.

I looked around the cooler at half a dozen animals, my size or larger. "You're going to sell all that in a week?"

"More or less," he said.

"In Laurens, France?"

In reply, he returned to his workspace behind the counter, dropped a double handful of chopped lamb into a meat grinder, and began cranking. Watching the beginning of a batch of *merguez* fall into a stainless-steel tub, he spoke with a craftsman's pride about what it took to keep the doors of a village butcher shop open for thirty years.

He stressed the distinction between *viande de boucher* and *viande laitière*—beef cattle and dairy cattle—and how a haunch of beef from an older milking cow might cost a grocery store three hundred euros, while the same-sized haunch of steer could cost him three thousand. He twisted the casing in his hand to seal off another link, curved like a cutlass.

Sometimes he needed to cut a shoulder as a roast, sometimes piece it up for stew, and sometimes suggest a different cut or even a different animal.

Cuts of beef that threatened to go unsold could be ground into *steak haché*. Pork into *saucisse*. Lamb and mutton into *merguez*.

I could have listened to him for a week straight. But just then, following the most innocuous and predictable of questions, the day turned in a new direction. "Tell me about your *métier*," he said.

Explaining that you are a tax preparer in America tends to elicit one of two reactions—either coy but insistent requests for free tax advice or jokes such as "How do you make a CPA go insane? Tie him to a chair and slowly fold a newspaper the wrong way."

But here's the funny thing. By the time I had soldiered through my description of life as a pencil pusher, the chain of *merguez* links had stopped falling from the stuffing machine, and Monsieur Congnard was listening quite carefully.

And, with the scales of the conversation thus abruptly rebalanced, we set off anew.

M. Congnard learned that the maximum marginal tax rate in the

United States was a mere 35 percent, a figure that filled him with wonder and desire.

The point of a traditional butcher was to take delivery of animals that remained as nearly whole as possible until the moment he cut individual portions across from his customers. The larger cuts of meat hanging in the locker held on to their flavor and their juices longer, in the same way that a whole apple keeps for weeks and a sliced apple dries out in hours.

I gave a brief guided tour of American labor law as he reequipped the sausage stuffer to handle a batch of pork. I had to repeat several times that, no, truly, American employers for the most part could simply fire their employees, which sent him into a diatribe over the near impossibility of ever firing even the most inept and ill-willed French hireling.

I commented on how much he used his knife, compared to how much American butchers tended to use the band saw, and as he narrated his way through a few cuts, I could see how he was working along seams in the muscles, keeping them intact, rather than cutting through bones and across the grain of the meat the way we make American-style steaks.

By the end of the afternoon, we were both tipsy on bonhomie and the flow of talk.

He was gesturing with a boning knife in his left hand, saying that the small merchants we visitors still revered, if dying, were, after all, worth saving, despite the cancer of high taxes and bureaucracy run amok.

Thanks to the chaotic genius of Midi conversation, a day scheduled to be about an American's love of the French way with food, had turned out to be equally about a Frenchman's love for what he saw as the American way of doing business. Among the things you talk about on a date with a French butcher, it turns out, is the American dream.

I bought a spiral of pork sausage to bring home. There was a mustard taste test ahead of me.

I had also discovered the other evening that mashed potatoes made with salty, high-fat Président butter and moistened with some of their own cooking water, then run through my Moulinex food mill, came out as weightless as beaten egg whites, and the kids were asking for it again.

So, yes, pork sausage and mashed potatoes. Even with Dijon mustard, a Moulinex, and pork from the hills of the Aveyron, it was still the dreaded subsistence fare of Irish and middle European immigrants to Minnesota and Wisconsin.

But my kids were clamoring for it, and they would get it.

67

Nicole had observed, because that's what Nicole was quietly like, that we bought fish from M. Sauzet on Fridays, so just before lunch on this Friday, she brought us her recipe for fish fillets with tomatoes and olives, which she had described one morning in the vines and I had begged her for.

"I wrote the recipe down," she said in her bubbling fast French. "The only other copy is in my head, and I need that for other things." And she set a note card on our kitchen counter filled with the flowing handwriting that she had learned, as had Jean-Luc, as would Joseph, at the École d'Autignac.

Then, with an "Oh, by the way" gesture, Jean-Luc, who had been holding his cap upside down in both hands, set it on our kitchen countertop, revealing a gritty mound of delicate, leggy brown mushrooms.

"*Mousserons*," Jean-Luc explained. "Very small but very perfumed. Try them in an omelet."

Jean-Luc and Nicole reminded me which field of Carignan I should meet them in after lunch, and slipped back outside, with a "bon appétit" over their shoulders.

My occasional contributions to Mary Jo's blog tended to involve a pair of steady hands, and a kind of bovine patience when it came to lining up unstable objects into rows. The *mousserons* happened to fit my skill set perfectly. I got to work, placing mushrooms—which wanted badly to roll along the edges of their caps—in a grid pattern, painstakingly applying my talent, which would not transfer to any future career, for blowing just gently enough to barely clear the page of dirt particles. Mary Jo was on hands and knees beside me, and we reached into the grid in several places to nudge mushrooms and sweep bits of grit. We hadn't showered, and there was the honest smell of body, dried sweat, and mushroom in the air around us. Mary Jo held her breath when she was concentrating, and I could hear the cadence of her thinking in the holding back and letting out of her breath.

When the pattern was in place, she stood up and tried to lean over the arrangement far enough, without stepping on the paper, to take a straight-down shot of the ten frail, helmeted infantrymen all lined up for inspection.

"OK, long arms," she said, "can you give it a try?"

I straddled one corner of the paper, leaning in awkwardly, holding the camera out straight. Mary Jo stood next to me, one hand on the small of my back, rising on her toes to see the flip-up viewfinder.

While Mary Jo photo-edited at the dining room table, I sautéed shallots in olive oil, then added the coarsely chopped mushrooms, which gave off a penetrating, loamy smell.

I heated up a carbon-steel omelet pan (OK, a brand-new carbon-steel omelet pan), flicked water onto it until the droplets hissed and spun, watched a spreading knob of butter melt and spit, tipped three beaten eggs into the pan, and shook it vigorously, creating the little ribs that would brown, while the center arrived at a state just on the liquid side of cooked, and then folded the omelet into a half-moon, with mushrooms and shallot swallowed up inside.

On the terrace, we nibbled some olives and ate our lunch with baguette.

"Good omelet," said Mary Jo.

"I know," I said.

Mary Jo talked about her attachment to grids—simple enough that a viewer could ignore the structure they provided to a composition and focus on the subject. She was happy with the day's photos.

I brought out a remaining wedge of Pélardon from the refrigerator, and we drizzled some honey over it.

Behind the far wall of the courtyard, the breeze made a gentle sighing in the horse chestnuts—the leaves of which had already started to crisp at their edges.

I went back to the refrigerator, and brought out a bottle of Thierry's white wine. I took my time uncorking it, and poured a splashing few fingers into each of our water glasses.

"I read your journal, by the way," she said.

"Is that good or bad?" I asked.

"It's fucking good," she said.

"What does that mean?"

"It means the writing is fucking good, is what that means."

"And what does that mean?" I asked.

She thought about it.

"That you are cursed with too many talents," she said. "And sometimes you forget about the ones that matter."

We sipped Thierry's wine. There was a light sheen of sweat on her forehead and cheeks. A familiar sour smell that I didn't mind rose from my T-shirt when I moved—the smell of physical work.

"What time is it?" she asked.

"Not sure," I said.

"You need to get back to work."

"Maybe. Do you want a cigarette?"

She looked at me. "We haven't had a cigarette in ten years," she said.

"I know. I think I want a cigarette."

"I am fucking dying for a cigarette," she said.

"I'll get a pack of Gauloises when the *tabac* opens."

I could feel her eyes on me as the big canvas parasol lifted and settled, its shadow spilling off the table onto the warm tile.

"Are you making a move, Mr. Hoffman?" asked Mary Jo.

"I'm thinking about it. The afternoon is young."

"Now I really want a cigarette."

I sipped a small, pungent wedge of Pélardon from the tip of a knife and closed my eyes, letting its musk fill my senses.

68

A group of girls had formed a sort of welcoming committee for Eva on the first day of fall semester, and as much as Eva would normally shun the type of do-gooder who would volunteer to welcome the new girl to school, even if that new girl happened to be herself, these companions turned out to be smart and low-key enough not to send Eva running into the hills like a startled *lapang*.

They were Marie, Héloïse, Coline, Julie, and Rachel, and for a week or two after making their acquaintance, Eva described them as "those girls I met on the first day of school."

She must then have allowed everyone in the circle to take one step closer, because the group subsequently became "those girls I hang out with."

Then one crisp fall morning, while Nicki Minaj sang about starships, Eva and I crawled past the entry gate of Collège le Cèdre. I was preparing to shift into second gear for our usual circling spin through town, when Eva said, "Let me see if my *copines* are here."

Copines are not the same thing as welcoming-committee members.

As I knew. And they aren't just those girls you hang out with, either. As I also knew.

Copines are friends. Buddies.

As I knew she knew I knew.

"You can drop me off here," she said. Which would serve as her single, definitive statement on the matter.

"Bonjour, ay-VAH!" they called.

And with her backpack on one shoulder, and a mohair scarf like a cowl around her neck, Eva leaned carefully into the circle of her *copines* to exchange kisses.

With a gargantuan effort, I pulled away from the scene without a single embarrassing parental reverse neck crane. I flickered through plane trees out into the ancient landscape of the *pays d'oc* with Nicki Minaj as my troubadour, singing, after a fashion, about love.

I checked the clock and switched the station.

"Bonjour, Philippe," said France Culture's morning host.

69

I minced a shallot and three garlic cloves and sautéed them in olive oil, while soaking the grit from a bowlful of Monsieur Viguier's *palourdes*. Spaghetti and clams had gone from a once-a-year-if-that delicacy to a heavily requested family staple.

Into the *cocotte* hissed a glass of bracingly dry Picpoul de Pinet, which had begun its life in a vineyard looking over the very water the clams had come from. I threw in a handful of chopped parsley from my terrace collection, and cooked the clams until they had all opened. I set them aside, added to the broth a shake or two of *piment d'espelette*, the juice of a lemon, and a small drinking glass of the starchy spaghetti water. There was no need for salt because the clams had already released some of the Étang de Thau into the sauce.

From the kitchen, I could see the kids curled up on the living room couch, Eva in one corner working her way through Perceval's quest for the grail, asking without looking up what *étriers* were, and what it meant to *chevaucher,* while Joe, frowning earnestly in the couch's other corner, consulted Fabre on his pulled-up knees. And to my right, on the dining room bench, with her back to the warm stone wall, while Stacey Kent sang softly from her iPad, Mary Jo scrolled through the blogs of her on-line sisterhood, looking for inspiration for tomorrow's post.

The kitchen had begun to feel like the center that held this all to-gether, and I craved my nightly aproned shift.

Just the other day, Jean-Luc had stopped by to water the plants and check on the olive tree for Beel the landlord.

I talked with him on the terrace while he worked below, watering the geraniums and the aloe plants, pinching sample olives from the tree, explaining that he either needed to harvest them soon, while they were green, or else wait until they were completely black. All olives, lectured the irrepressible *professeur,* turned black eventually if left on the tree—as all peppers would eventually turn from green to red.

When he was done, he disappeared under the terrace and the hose retracted jerkily across the courtyard as he wound it back onto the spool.

Jean-Luc's voice rose up from beneath me. "Steve," he said.

"*Oui, Jean-Luc.*"

"Steve, I think it would be easier if we called each other *tu*," he said.

The metal nozzle at the end of the hose clinked out of sight, and I heard his footsteps fade into the garage.

He reappeared below me, carrying a pot-shaped glass jar.

When he had climbed up to the terrace, I could see that inside the dusty jar, obscured by cloudy, whiskey-colored liquid, was a half liter of small green olives.

"From our tree?" I asked.

Last year's. I was first to wash them in fresh water, and I was not to use my fingers to remove them, because of *les microbes,* unless we planned to eat the entire jar at one time. If they were initially too salty, I was to soak them for several hours in fresh water. I received these instructions amid a gentle hailstorm of second-person singular pronouns.

Tonight, a bowl of those olives sat in the middle of the table, with a few raggedly gnawed pits sitting on a saucer beside them.

"Dad!" shouted Eva.

"Eva!" I said.

"Fruit," she said.

And a plate of Marie's elongated, tender Abbé Fetel pears served as a centerpiece amid bowls of glistening, parsley-flecked pasta. The sauce tasted like the Mediterranean with a twist of lemon and a bite of red pepper. Joe filled his mouth in a kind of frenzy. Eva, who had found a way to love these smaller, salty clams in a way that she couldn't manage with oysters, tossed one shell after another onto the discard pile. We drank the last of the Picpoul de Pinet, and allowed ourselves to get a little tipsy and very talkative. We sat in a warm circle of candlelight, comforted by the smell of the sea, as waves of conversation rose and fell.

70

On the terrace, Mary Jo and I were smoking our one cigarette a night, a new-old routine that the kids pretended to hate but often joined us for, while we each sipped a glass of Jean-Luc's Vin d'Orange, which he had delivered along with a bottle of his Muscat vinegar.

I had tried another vinaigrette tonight that—through no fault of the vinegar's—had failed to please anyone, and I had ended up eating the salad myself.

The Vin d'Orange, on the other hand, was an absolute elixir, made of white wine and *eau de vie,* sweetened with sugar and macerated for forty days with slices of orange peel. The volume in the unlabeled bottle between us already showed signs of our nightly raids.

Eva came out from the living room and sat beside us.

I gave her a fatherly smooch on the forehead.

She had a confused and vaguely troubled look on her face. "Anything wrong, honey?"

She was pinching something between the thumb and first finger of her right hand, and here she held it out to us, and carefully lifted her thumb.

There was a tiny shard resting on the meat of her finger.

"This just came out of my foot," she said, like someone reporting a ghost sighting.

"Oh my God," said Mary Jo.

Eva stared at the splinter.

"Is Jean-Luc, like, magic or something?" she asked.

Her limp was gone within a couple of days, and whether it was the removal of that physical affliction alone, or the added consolation of Jean-Luc's having taken her discomfort seriously enough to propose a solution, a subtle change seemed to occur in Eva around this time—a modest slackening, for whatever reason, in the oppositional force of her presence among us.

71

The daily walk to Marie's was increasingly a social occasion as I passed members of my Friday morning fish committee, or fellow grape pickers, or Véronique Balliccioni, André's wife, getting bread, or possibly Yvan or Richard running errands, or Jean-Luc's or André's tractor. Most days, I would pass the bent-over little man on his chair, and would stop for a visit, receiving as a reward the occasional World War II story.

His name was Edmond. Véronique had grown up with him as a village fixture. Those who knew him well called him by the diminutive "Momond" (pronounced Mo-Mo). He monitored the early-morning traffic from behind the lace curtains of his bedroom window, and then descended to monitor the late-afternoon traffic from a folding chair on the street. In between he could be seen in an olive-drab jacket, using his ancient bicycle as a walker, talking about the weather and tipping his cap to passersby.

"Your daughter leaves early," he told me one day as I stopped to shake hands.

"Yes, she likes her morning baguette," I said.

His comment would have landed most men on my paternal, keep-an-eye-on-the-creep list. But this was Monsieur Edmond. He was like the benevolent spirit of the village itself.

"I see her go," he said, pointing up the street. "And I wait to see her come back." Here he pointed first to his own two eyes, and then to our house, and he reached up and patted my elbow reassuringly.

72

We woke to the news that André's *pompe à marc,* the heroic pump that had pushed so many tons of grape skins uphill through a six-inch hose for so many dozens of *décuvages,* was in pieces on the floor of the winery.

"*C'est foutu*" (It's fucked), announced Jean-Luc from the seat of his tractor. The mechanic had officially pronounced the machine kaput about an hour ago.

"*Tu viens?*" he asked. (Are you coming?)

Upstairs in the bedroom, I pulled my work shorts from the laundry basket, and, hopping into them, brought Mary Jo up to date.

"Sounds like they could use you," she said.

"Steve Hoffman, from Shoreview, Minnesota, is needed at the winery," I said.

The crisis atmosphere in the Balliccioni *cave* was palpable. Thierry was sipping a coffee and looking over some notes from his oenologist. André was staring at the ground in front of him, holding a cell phone to his ear and walking lazy circles around the courtyard. And Jean-Luc was methodically shoveling a damp pile of pressed *marc* into his trailer.

I raised an arm as I stepped through the gate, and received three acknowledging chin lifts, more welcoming in their offhandedness than trumpets and a parade.

André shut off his phone and announced that a new pump would cost seven thousand euros, and if all the universe could come up with were solutions in that price range, then the universe could go to hell.

He said this with fatalistic good cheer, and I noticed, despite so many premonitions and dark warnings, that when the dreaded and long-predicted event finally did come knocking on his door, André refused to treat it, or even refer to it, as a *catastrophe*. We would haul the stuff up in buckets.

I couldn't tell how Thierry was feeling about the big middle finger André was thrusting at fate and the market for wine pumps. For someone trying to make a wine like Rarissime, seven thousand euros for a pump that would move wine faster and expose it to less oxidizing air might well have looked like a bargain.

While André figured out how to replace his *pompe électrique* with a *pompe manuelle*, consisting of buckets and volunteers, I joined Jean-Luc at the grape press. We worked in slow and steady rhythm, and when his trailer was full, he drove off to the distillery, where the humble *marc* would be purified into *eau de vie*.

Then it was time to open vat number five, on Thierry's side of the winery, which released that great sour alcoholic cloud of fermented scent.

Véronique was summoned, and showed up in gum boots, mascara, and a tank top. She went gamely to work with plastic rake and pitchfork on the densely packed *marc*, visible through the open trapdoor of vat number five. Each filled bucket got carried up to the grape press, lifted about head high, and dumped into one of the open hatches up top. Then André, Thierry, and I each tromped back down to Véronique at her station, where she would rake another three or four gallons of purple mush into our buckets.

"*Doucement*," warned Thierry as I found my rhythm and accelerated my pace.

When a fifty-hectoliter macerating vat is emptied of its juice, there are probably still twenty hectoliters of *marc* left inside. Carrying that in four-gallon buckets means about 150 round trips to empty a single vat. It was wet, sticky work. The buckets were quickly covered in juice and they dripped on the way up to the *pressoir*.

The humor was teasing and pointed. I found myself visually checking in with Thierry as material destined to make fifty-dollar bottles of wine slopped around in buckets and coated the concrete floor, until our boots slapped in the spilled juice with each step.

Because the rake is not a precision instrument, about as much *marc* was spilling into the overflow tote as was spilling into the buckets themselves. Every sixth or seventh bucketful required a pause to scoop the spilled *marc* out of the tote and into a waiting auxiliary bucket.

The American instinct for efficiency is strong, and at some point I couldn't hold it in any longer.

"Why don't we just fill the totes and carry them directly up to the *pressoir*, instead of trying to fill buckets inside the totes?"

André paused to find a reason that this wouldn't work, failed, and remarked that the American wasn't perhaps so *bête* (stupid) as he looked.

Thierry appeared taken aback that we would now be carrying more weight on each trip.

"We're not in a hurry," he remarked.

The day was not going his way, and I saw him begin to protest.

And then I watched him hold back.

We tried carrying the totes up in rotating teams of two, and it was more effortful, but much faster and more efficient.

We finished the morning doing *décuvage à l'Américaine,* and I reassured them that there was no need to thank me. That's just what we Americans did: save the French.

By noon, the *pressoir* was filled and turning, with rich cloudy juice raining into the catch basin.

It would have been a perfect morning for emotions to simmer over. André asked to do more work on behalf of his friend than his friend's rent would probably cover. Thierry asked to indulge his friend's pennywise-pound-foolishness that threatened to undo, or at least coarsen, a year's worth of exquisite vine tending. Technically, it was André's *cave,* and André knew a bit more about how to pull this off, logistically, but

Thierry was aiming to make a more ambitious wine, with a lower tolerance for delays and missteps. The stakes were high on both sides, at the most critical time of the year.

But it hadn't simmered over. André had reached deep and found some charm to deploy, and Thierry had swallowed his objections and let André do things André's way. Down where their opposing needs met and wore each other a little raw, both men must have been chafing all morning. But then, as had surely happened hundreds of times before, they both chose once more, as members of a tiny, interdependent village, not to rattle the structure that had supported their personal friendship—and effective working partnership—for twenty-plus years.

There had been a place for me all morning, and up on the terrace, I saw that there was a place for me at the table, too. My being a part of things appeared to strike everybody as unsurprising. If anything, my absence would have created a conspicuously empty chair.

André clapped his hands together and turned to Thierry. "So what are we going to drink today?" he asked.

And the two of them discussed which of their own wines they would serve for lunch.

73

A few days later, in a field of Grenache, a sharp callout from Véronique brought me up out of a sore-kneed crouch to see what the matter was. She was not a particularly rigorous taskmaster, but neither did she care much if her occasional haranguing bruised feelings.

Jean-Luc, on his way to the tractor, turned and raised his arm in protest, a gesture startlingly out of character both for him and for this increasingly tight-knit group of grape pickers. He was still grumbling to himself as he climbed into the cab.

I moved my bucket and bent to the next vine. I hadn't been close enough to interpret exactly what had happened, or how serious it was, but I felt a woozy kind of seasickness at the thought of a fault line dividing any member of this new family from any other.

José drove me home that night, gripping the wheel tightly with eight fingers, and holding a Chesterfield between the other two. We communicated just well enough to catch up on each other's history, and understand each other's simple jokes.

When I asked what had happened between Jean-Luc and Véronique, he got serious, with a worried, submissive expression.

"*No sé,*" he said. "But if *Juan-Luca* does not pick for Véronique, then I don't pick for Véronique. *¿Entiendes?*"

"No, I don't understand," I said.

"Eh-STEVE-eh," he said, looking out the windshield with his sunken, chronic-smoker's eyes. Jean-Luc and Nicole, he explained, they saved his life every year.

He could not possibly make enough money in the olive groves of Andalucia to live decently—picking olives, or, worse, picking capers on his knees. It was only by living with Jean-Luc and Nicole that he could piece together something closer to living a life than living out an existence.

"They are like parents," he said. "For me," and he pointed quickly to his own chest before clutching the wheel again.

He paused, still looking out the windshield, as the uneven ground jolted the car.

"For me, they are my saints."

74

The Soulenque is the traditional celebration of the end of the *vendange*.

When she had first invited us to join the Soulenque at Domaine Balliccioni, Véronique had explained, "*Oui, La Soulenque—où l'on se saoule!*" Which translates roughly as "Yes, the drunk-fest—where everybody gets shit-faced!"

To feed thirty-six of us, ten kilos of mussels were opened and debearded, stuffed with seasoned pork sausage, and placed back in their shells. Each shell was individually tied with twine, and the stuffed mussels were then slow-cooked with cuttlefish rings in a tomato-garlic sauce.

You can't really bring a bottle of wine to a winemaker's party. So Eva had curled up on the couch for two long afternoons with a laptop on her knees, which somehow resulted in a perfectly edited six-minute video, with musical accompaniment, of footage from the *vendange*—both in the vines, and in the winery.

"How did you do that?" asked Mary Jo.

"I'm magic," said Eva.

We peeled and chopped apples and mixed them with cinnamon and sugar. We pinched cold butter into a short *pâte brisée*, and rolled it out, whisked confectioner's sugar into water for frosting, and improvised another Apple Delight, which descends from Mary Jo's Romanian grandmother, not coincidentally named Eva. The Romanian and the American grape pickers, we felt, had earned some culinary representation at the Soulenque.

We received a knock on our door, and I found Jean-Luc on our stoop.

He wanted to wish us a good afternoon, and let us know that he and Nicole and José would not be at the Soulenque. Did I understand?

I said I understood. Then I said that I understood nothing, but I understood.

He nodded at me with an uncertain half smile.

Was this about the dispute with Véronique?

It would be less complicated, he said, if the three of them did not go, and he wished all of us bon appétit.

We arrived to the sound of subdued conversation in the crowded Balliccioni courtyard, and handed the still warm *Délice de Pommes à l'Américaine* to our hostess, Véronique.

The kids were aloof, but they kissed and shook their way through the reception line before retreating to a neutral corner and trying to avoid eye contact with their schoolmates.

After that, the crazy drunk-fest continued with one or two fingers of Thierry's rosé poured into everyone's wineglass, which people swirled, sipped, talked about, and then mostly held in front of them while they indulged in that other powerful local intoxicant—conversation.

Without our next-door neighbors, there was a melancholy void in the day that could not be shaken off. The iPad sat on the lunch table, shuffling through a slideshow of Mary Jo's images from the *vendange,* and if the photos were to be believed, I had spent about half the time bent double, looking for bunches of grapes, and the other half upright with my arms crossed, leaning backward, agreeing with whatever Jean-Luc had just said.

André played host and spoke to everybody in his intentionally awful English, when he wasn't trying to speak "Romanian" to the Romanians, which also came out as English with a French accent.

We had a chance to speak to Thierry at more length, about his ambitions for Mas Gabinèle, and about the *assemblage,* or blending of the wines, which was the next big signpost on the road from ripe grapes to wine in bottles.

Yvan, standing next to me, talked about his years in California "working black" (without papers) on construction sites that would empty at the first appearance of a government vehicle. He remembered *les clams* dug up on California beaches, for which there is no equivalent French word, and wondered if I thought they were more like *coques* or more like *palourdes*.

"This American," said Yvan to Richard, placing a comradely hand on my shoulder, "works the *vendange*. Works in the *cave*. Then, did you hear? He goes to Laurens and spends an afternoon behind Jean-Pierre's counter." He gave my shoulder a heavy slap. "He is a better French than we!"

André stopped by with round two, Thierry's top-of-the-line white, called Rarissime Blanc, aged in brand-new casks of French oak. In his best English, André made sure we understood that the wine had been "*ele-VAYTE. een. auk. bahrell.*"

We toasted André, Thierry, the wine, and all the *auk bahrells*.

At some point, an hour or so into the proceedings, a low-level stirring began to make itself audible.

Soon the general hum was punctuated by more emphatic vocalizations, until someone offered the observation that we were in France. This wasn't Spain, "where one lunches at four hours of the afternoon."

We approached Véronique to see if this wouldn't be a good time to watch Eva's movie. She said yes, and, in fact, better before lunch than after, because . . . Here she extended her thumb toward her nose and twisted her fist—the universal French symbol for impaired drunkenness.

Mary Jo set André and Thierry in front of the computer as the movie started, and soon all thirty-six revelers had stopped talking and complaining and were crowded around the fifteen-inch screen of Mary Jo's laptop, watching composite footage of the three weeks they, or their family members, had just spent. The courtyard fell quiet except for occasional interjections of "Look, it's Valérie!" or "*Oh, oui, Mah-ree ZHO, elle adore les vrilles.*" (Oh, yes, Mary Jo adores vine tendrils.)

By the time the credits had rolled, no one was talking at all. There was a brief ovation, and everyone drifted back to their places talking about the movie.

André approached us, unabashedly moist-eyed.

"*C'était magnifique, ce truc-là.*" (That was beautiful, that thing.)

We explained that it had been Eva who put the footage together, and she received her first artistic feedback from a live studio audience as André bent to kiss her on both cheeks. "*Merci*," he said, and, seeing that her hands were empty, rushed to get her a glass of white wine so he could toast her properly.

Thierry came up to us, a little red around the eyes as well, and talked about how most of the *vendangeurs* had not seen any of what had gone on at the winery, and how the winemakers had seen little of the work in the fields, and how nice it was for everyone to see the whole process.

"You have made a real exchange with us." He clinked our glasses.

For weeks, we had been enthusiastic participants, but we had mostly, of necessity, been takers—of images, of experiences, of recommendations, of stories, of gifts. We had been given a level of access that we couldn't have dreamed of before we left, and that there was no real way to repay. It felt very good, for a few minutes, to have contributed something, and to be thanked for it, among people who, in different circumstances, would have been props in a two-week French idyll, but who that afternoon were coworkers and neighbors—André, Véro, Thierry, Nicole, Yvan, Richard, Valérie, Dédé, Gabi, Chrystelle.

All afternoon, there would be a sadness inside the celebration, as people we would now see less often drifted away. As the wine, and then the coffee, and then the *eau de vie* flowed, arms were thrown around shoulders, cheeks kissed, and people opened up about how much they loved this place, or this process, or being involved with something that was done so carefully and well.

This felt to me like the end of many things. The end of the harvest. The end of the daily closeness with this team. The end of early mornings in vineyards. The end of entire days of Jean-Luc's company, and the accelerated learning that resulted. The end—could it be?—of the relationship between Jean-Luc and André, which had started all of this in André's tasting room when Mary Jo and I had first learned that we had located ourselves in something called the Faugères appellation.

Jean-Luc had referred several times to the twist of destiny that had somehow landed two such strangely compatible families next door to each other in, of all places, Autignac, France. Equally unlikely had been our dumb luck in landing among three members of a tiny wine community, who all knew each other, and who represented nearly all of the important strata of the world of local wine, and to a great extent, of French wine as a whole—Jean-Luc, the *viticulteur,* with his encyclopedic knowledge of vines and their care; André, the *vigneron,* making the traditional wine of the region in the traditional way; Thierry, the *vigneron* and *négociant,* striving to make some of the highest-rated wine in the entire region. It had given us, in a matter of months, a remarkably complete grasp of all that was involved in making French wine, with the accompanying French vocabulary to talk about it competently with almost anyone involved in wine, almost anywhere in France.

I felt in a way that I had fashioned myself into a tool that could find an important purpose in this very place, and it was another of the day's sadnesses that these new abilities would likely go to waste among the woods and lakes of Minnesota, assembling tidy piles of government forms into submittable American tax returns.

Eventually, Véro's booming voice, grown familiar over the last month, called us to lunch, and we sat under the eaves of the *cave,* and ate mussels and cuttlefish, and Cantal and Roquefort, and *mousse au chocolat* and Apple Delight. Bottles of Thierry's red Rarissime, his jewel, came out and were opened and sampled.

I swirled and inhaled for a long time before taking a thoughtful mouthful. Mary Jo and I leaned toward each other, on this, our twenty-third wedding anniversary, on a day that ended up having nothing to do with wedding anniversaries and that was at the same time the expression of so much that had been so good about being married to each other for twenty-three years. We compared notes about the wine in voices that no one could have heard, but with expressions that could not have been misunderstood.

I looked up and saw that Thierry had been watching from the other end of the communal table. I lifted an imaginary cap and lowered it toward him. He nodded solemnly, and swallowed hard, and looked away.

And that was another way of giving back.

75

What Jean-Luc mostly taught us was what he knew best: the growing and tending of wine grapes. And over our conversations, I had come to understand how each variety of vine—not the grapes it produced but the vine itself—had a character. It did well in certain soils, with certain exposures to the sun; was more or less susceptible to specific illnesses; budded, flowered, and ripened earlier or later; grew upright or sprawled; had round leaves or lobed leaves; was thirsty or didn't like wind; required lots of heat; couldn't stand the damp; needed its exuberant growth to be disciplined; or needed to be encouraged to come out of its shell.

There is a theory that one part of terroir is not simply the soil, but the fact that the sun releases volatile aromatic compounds from summer vegetation, and that the waxy skins of grapes are capable of attracting and holding those molecules, which contribute, in aggregate, and however minutely, to the eventual flavor of the resulting wine. In the case of the Languedoc and Faugères, this would be the scent given off by the *garrigue* surrounding most of the vineyards in the region. It is a scent that anyone would recognize who has spent a late-summer day in the Midi, wandering the prickly edge of a vineyard.

If wine is a human body, then tannin, alcohol, and acid are the skeleton, the bones that hold it up and let it grow old without collapsing. Syrah might be said to be big-boned, and Mourvèdre and Carignan more birdlike. Fruit and texture are like the flesh on the bones, and Grenache and Mourvèdre are particularly voluptuous, while Syrah is maybe a little more muscled. And aroma is like the skin—the point of first contact, with hints and promises that can only be fulfilled once you engage with the body. Sometimes the whole ends up beautiful, and sometimes it's awkwardly limbed and ill-proportioned. And sometimes when it is beautiful, it is also something else—charming, or stern, or shy, or generous, or vivacious, or exuberant. Sometimes it has a personality.

Languedoc wines tend to be deeply and darkly fruity, because the grapes have a long Mediterranean growing season that lets them reach a level of maturity that other regions with less sunlight can't attain.

In general, "jammy" is not a compliment in the wine world. It is the biggest knock against the style of California wine that Robert Parker made popular, and that became ubiquitous and eventually a bit despised: a big, alcoholic, overripe, understructured wine with a ton of oak. That effect is generated by leaving grapes on the vine very late, when they are very sweet, extremely ripe, and have begun to lose acidity. In other words, by intentionally pushing California grapes in the direction of how Mediterranean grapes mature naturally.

A good Faugères wine does not reach that level of soft, cloying jamminess. It is picked at peak ripeness, but not past it. It has structure in the form of alcohol and tannin, but it is nevertheless a ripe wine, based on fully mature grapes.

The winemakers we spent the most time with called that kind of flavor *fruit confit,* which means "cooked fruit."

That extremely ripe, dark, luscious quality is vastly more appreciated in southern France than in America certainly, and to a certain extent even than in the rest of France.

Figs are not picked "ripe" here but saggy, sticky, half-dried—not juicy, but jammy.

Prunes here are a true delicacy, with their own *Appellation d'Origine Protégée,* called *pruneaux d'Agen,* made from a specific variety of plum called the *prune d'ente.*

For a long time, I could not appreciate this.

But what happens when you live here long enough is that you start to adopt the richness, the darkness and ripeness of Languedoc wine as your baseline wine—your home team—and begin to compare all other wines to Languedoc wines, or more generally to wines of the Midi, which mostly share this quality of what French wine drinkers call *rondeur.*

Rondeur means "roundness" and it is a word you will hear often when winemakers from this part of the world talk about wine. It is a positive characteristic. It means a kind of corpulence, a generosity. One way to think of it is in the language of shapes, where roundness is the opposite of squareness and sharp corners. But in the specific language of wine, at least in French, *rondeur* is not the opposite of squareness, but the opposite of *tension.* A wine can be *rond*—round, agreeable, full, reassuring—or *tendu*—tense, vivacious, nervous, fresh. A round wine is structured on alcohol. Alcohol provides the bite that keeps it from being flabby or viscous or flat in the mouth, but alcohol also gives round wine something the French refer to often—*onctuosité* (unctuousness). A tense wine, on the other hand, is structured not on alcohol but on acidity— a sharp, green-apple underripeness.

And in the end, what we are really talking about (at least in the Northern Hemisphere) are the differences between southern wines and northern wines generally. Southern wines tend to be rounder, and northern wines tend to be more tense, which is simply the result of what sunshine does to grapes when there is more or less of it. But the two words also, somewhat wonderfully, are a shorthand for the Languedo-cian view of life itself, lived under the round, relaxed generosity of the Mediterranean sun, in contrast to the anxious, driven neuroticism of northern life.

Understanding all of this led, in my case, to one further reordering of my thoughts about wine. And that involved a shift away from think-ing about wine as primarily coming from particular regions, to think-ing, instead, about wine as primarily coming from particular latitudes. The first sorting I do when I take a sip of wine I'm not familiar with now, is not to try to decide whether it was made in Bordeaux or Burgundy or Napa, or more broadly whether it is French or Italian or Chilean, or even more broadly whether it is New World or Old World—but whether it is made closer to, or farther away from, the equator. Whether it is, in broadest terms, round and alcoholic, or tense and acidic. This evolution of my thinking about wine, specifically, was part of a larger process of internalizing something I had accepted intellectually before, but never felt quite so deeply: that in a world of increasingly limitless possibilities, some things still can be done in one place on earth that cannot be done in another. And I learned to love our round Languedoc wines, despite their lingering reputation for excessive strength and richness, as one of the things that we could do here that others couldn't, and I began to feel my love for André's and Thierry's wines as a part of me. Part of my identity as someone who had a relationship with this small corner of the world. And, in turn, it might be said that I began turning incrementally more round myself, and perhaps incrementally less tense.

76

A man arrived at the Balliccioni *cave* one morning carrying a plastic mesh crate full of sample jars. He entered the courtyard without announcing himself, but with a briskness and purpose to his stride that drew everybody's attention.

This was Jean Natoli, Thierry's oenologist.

An oenologist is like a consultant on retainer, although the relationship often turns warmer than that, with the oenologist evolving into a trusted consigliere, even a co-creator of sorts, and, not infrequently, a friend.

An oenologist offers advice and, when necessary, intervention through every phase of the winemaking year from planting to bottling. During the harvest and the intensive winemaking months of September through December, they will consult as often as every other day.

Jean and Thierry were particularly close—intimately entwined in each other's professional and personal lives.

Jean shook hands with everyone present, taking the time to square himself briefly in each of our directions.

As André drifted back toward his half of the *cave*, Thierry approached with three wineglasses in his hand, giving one to Jean, and one to me, without commentary.

We proceeded into the yellow industrial light of the *cave*, and Jean, like the schoolmaster he resembled, asked Thierry about the state of his to-do list from their previous meeting, which Thierry, with an apologetic schoolboy look, admitted he had . . . almost . . . completed.

They went to work immediately. Thierry filled his glass from vat number one, Syrah, smelled it, and tipped some of the wine into each of our glasses—a young, raw, powerful, tannic wine. It was like holding a small hedgehog still against the roof of my palate with my tongue.

The flavor, or rather the combination of flavor and aroma, contained something that my wine vocabulary would call spiciness or maybe pepperiness inside the fruit. When I swallowed, there was a pleasant sandpapery feeling left on my tongue and gums, and the dark berry flavor, tasting mildly infused with herbs, lingered for a while, fading slowly, leaving a coating behind, like the residue left by wiping oil from a surface with a cloth.

The ability to say even that much about the experience of consuming a mouthful of wine, already vastly more than I could have said a month earlier, pleased me, yet it still felt elusive and insubstantial, this collection of sensations that gestured toward something I could barely make out, but that appeared, if I squinted hard, to be Syrah-shaped.

Thierry's assessment began where mine left off. He didn't need to identify this as Syrah. Of course it was Syrah. He would have known it even without the whiteboard hanging from the vat.

What he was wondering to himself, and simultaneously prodding Jean to help him conclude, was what kind of Syrah, exactly.

He walked into the courtyard and returned with a plastic grape bucket, which he placed on the floor next to us with a clank of wire handle. We took turns leaning over the bucket and spitting, then we all brought our glasses back up to our noses.

"He is rich in the mouth," Thierry suggested.

"*Mmmoui*," said Jean, noncommittally, and took another sip, then swished, inhaled air up through the wine in his mouth, and spat.

Jean asked several technical questions. Which vineyard again? This had finished its malo (its malolactic fermentation), correct? How many hectoliters?

They bounced impressions off of each other in the half-knowing, half-speculative tone of sports fans arguing the playoff prospects of the Vikings versus the Packers.

The wine was long on the palate.

There was a density to the color.

The tannins were ample, tightly wound.

There was pencil lead and black licorice and confiture of black currant.

Jean took notes throughout, and would interrupt himself by tracing filigreed patterns in the air with his pen hand as he elaborated a particular opinion.

In the end, he pronounced the contents of the vat "promising," recommended leaving the wine in place for now, on what are called the lees, the sediment that falls to the bottom of vats and barrels as a wine sits still, and which can add a heft or fullness to the body of a finished wine. He held out a glass vial from his crate, which Thierry filled from the spigot.

At each stop, we repeated our routine.

Jean embraced his role as scientist, but relished opportunities to add a little poetry to his descriptions. The feel of the Grenache Gris in the mouth was not just refreshing, it was *tonique*. A Syrah wasn't peppery, it tasted of *poivre de Madagascar*. The Grenache-Mourvèdre blend in vat number five was beginning to *pinoter* (resemble the Pinot grape).

We moved fast, and there was a lot that I didn't catch. As the two of them discussed not just what was happening in their glasses, but in some sense where each vat was headed, the first phase of the assembly of that year's wine was taking shape. Was this Mourvèdre worthy of a starring role in Thierry's most expensive and ambitious wine, called Inaccessible, or should it play a bit part in a lesser *cuvée*? Which wine would the fleshiness of this Grenache best soften?

And this conversation, added to all the others that I had lately overheard and participated in, helped to sketch in further the profiles of these grapes, which all had characters. Some of their traits were true everywhere, and some of them only expressed themselves, or best expressed themselves, here in the south.

After creating a nine-point to-do list, including a demand that one vat of stalled Grenache be reactivated with NH_4 this morning absolutely without exception, Jean tore the carbon from his checklist, handed it to Thierry, and grabbed his plastic milk crate full of test bottles, now filled with samples for analysis.

He turned to me and said, "We will soon be assembling Thierry's wines from last year. I think it is the fifteenth, yes?"

He turned to Thierry, who lifted his head from a slightly dismayed perusal of all the work that lay ahead of him, and confirmed with a distracted nod.

"In my laboratory," said Jean Natoli. "If you would like, please bring your wife. Her name is . . . Marie . . . ?"

"Mary Jo," I said.

"Yes. Mah-ree Zho. I think you will both find it passioning. And of course we will find your opinions interesting, too."

And off he went after two crisp handshakes, stepping briskly over several hoses on his way across the courtyard.

I looked a little dubiously at Thierry.

I felt I understood my relationship with André. We were amiable companions and comfortable coworkers and soon it would not be surprising to hear one of us refer to the other as a friend.

Jean-Luc . . . Jean-Luc was Jean-Luc. Already like a part of me—a mixture of father, brother, mentor, and friend. I would carry him with me for the rest of my life, I felt sure.

What to make of this Thierry Rodriguez, who remained faintly intimidating, yet was so much like me in so many ways? Thierry, who hid himself behind politeness and social polish? Whose perfectionism appeared to arise out of an anxiety that resembled my own? Who was caught in midlife between the comforts of bourgeois success and the temptations of ambition? Who was just a little bit awkward in a way that made him slow to trust?

I sensed in Thierry a softness beneath the hard shell, and a corresponding need to vet anyone who might eventually be invited into that precarious place, as if he, too, were susceptible to a kind of hurt that only intimates could inflict.

We had been conducting, I was increasingly convinced, a preliminary, fraternal sort of flirtation, with each of us recognizing something of his own strengths and weaknesses in the other, but neither feeling confident enough to make whatever the first move would be.

The gate crashed shut behind Jean Natoli.

I watched Thierry rinse our three glasses in the sink.

"The *assemblage*," I said, uncertain that he had heard, much less approved of, Jean's invitation. "Mary Jo and I, we are, in fact—"

"Mmm? Oh of course," said Thierry, drying the final glass. He held it up to the light, wiped the rim once more, and placed it carefully back on its shelf.

77

In Autignac, the rhythm of the *vendange* was breaking up into something else.

We heard hunting season arrive before we saw any evidence of it. Jean-Luc had explained that there was no annual opener on a particular date. Hunting season simply followed the *vendange,* whenever it was concluded, whether early or late, so that hunters with guns and pickers of grapes did not cross each other in the fields. From the terrace early one morning, as I sat in the glow of my laptop, the season announced itself with the pop of shotguns, and the occasional boom of a boar rifle up in the hills, accompanied by the ancient sound, simultaneously mournful and thrilling, of baying packs of dogs.

Tractors no longer pulled trailers full of grapes past our front door. Some yellow and red appeared at the edges of grape leaves in a few fields.

We had spent recent weeks painstakingly stirring ourselves into the community, and Autignac's pot-au-feu was now lightly but noticeably seasoned by the four Americans at 42 Avenue de la Liberté.

Joseph asked to walk home from school one day with his new friend, improbably named Steve.

A certain Ludovic, with long sandy bangs and big brown eyes, came asking after Eva, who calmly rebuffed the stricken young man in our doorway.

On a cool morning, as the north wind carried traces of smoke down from the stumps they were burning in the hills, I passed Jean-Luc on my way to the bakery.

"*Salut, Steve,*" he said. "*Comment vas-tu?*" as casually as if we had grown up together, and we talked for a while in front of his garage.

Dinner at the café now required a quick round of handshakes and cheek kisses among neighbors, merchants, fellow *vendangeurs,* and, of course, José, before the family was allowed to sit. I was making it a point to approach the café owner and shake his hand. Offer a bonsoir. And he would nod to us as we arrived. He called me "Monsieur," and at least once I thought I saw his stubbled cheeks contract into a proto-smile as he took our orders.

78

Our backs hurt, our brains sagged, our mouths were sore. We had just spent a morning on our feet in the headachy fluorescent glare of a window-less laboratory.

Mary Jo pulled the passenger door shut, still holding it in.

"Was that possibly the best morning we've ever spent in France?" I asked.

"Holy crap," she grinned, displaying pretty blue teeth.

At about nine thirty that morning, we had been shown into a consulting room at Jean Natoli's Laboratoire Oenoconseil, and found ourselves surrounded by perhaps seventy years of winemaking experience divided among three of the attendees—Thierry, Jean himself, and Jean's assistant, Claire. The two remaining participants, representing the great state of Minnesota, boasted wine careers spanning perhaps three score and ten days apiece.

We felt ourselves to be in almost painfully intimate surroundings. This felt less like a lab than like a hospital room, where we would spend the morning with a very private man, watching the birth of his child.

Thierry was speaking softly to Jean Natoli about hectoliters and *cu-vées,* while our morning's work waited across the room—twenty-seven clear bottles of wine with sloped, Burgundy-shaped shoulders, arrayed against the back edge of a white laminate countertop.

Thierry looked concerned, as he often did. As, I suppose, would any uncompromising aesthete who had placed an enormous career wager, in late middle age, on a volatile substance subject to the vagaries of weather, temperature, disease, and hired help.

There was a more practical reason as well. He had decided to build his own winery in Laurens, which meant he would soon have a loan to pay back, and this raised the pressure on him to stack the deck this morning at the more expensive end of his gamut of wines, where more profit lay—something he could only do if the quality residing in those twenty-seven bottles across the room justified it.

If all went well, he would make three 2011 wines—his traditional Faugères, his resplendent Rarissime, and, finally, his little folly, called Inaccessible, made mostly from temperamental Mourvèdre, which he proposed to sell for a hundred dollars a bottle.

Jean Natoli described Inaccessible as *un monstre* (a monster). It was the kind of wine that could make a reputation, or sit expensive and un-sold and threaten a career.

Jean made a pouting face, meant to be reassuring. The 2011 vintage promised an adequate amount of monstrosity, he felt.

Thierry looked at him with hopeful, and somewhat anxious, profes-sional deference.

"*Bon.*"

And we were up and across the room, and it was time to blend wine.

Our job: Taste from all twenty-seven bottles, which included all the results, from all the vats and barrels, of all the visits Jean Natoli had made to the winery, and all the checklists he had given to Thierry, and all the previous steps Thierry had taken in the vineyards themselves, from the bursting of spring's first buds to the final harvest. We would rate the contents of each bottle, sort them by quality, and blend these base wines into three distinct, costly, and complex wines that Thierry would bring to market.

In the words of Jean-Luc Vialles, "It is complicated, a glass of wine."

We began marching down the row of stiff-postured little potbellied soldiers. Claire would pour us a quarter glass from each bottle and an-nounce the contents: "Syrah 2011, carbonic maceration, oak casks four-teen through eighteen."

The five of us would tilt our glasses, examine, swirl, sip, suck in some air, consider, and spit into a sink.

Then we would discuss.

Or rather: Then we would all turn to Jean, whose resemblance to a high school English teacher disguised a fearsome reputation as one of the most respected wine consultants in the region. Jean would speak, often at length, after which we would mostly agree with what he had said.

What came as a surprise, however, was that, on the heels of our recent immersion, admittedly brief but intense, in the vines and in the life of the Balliccioni winery, some of the words for what we wanted to say were there when we were asked for our opinions. And, perhaps more surprisingly, these words were solicited and even taken into account, as the group consensus about the contents of each bottle emerged.

The bottles started out in a straight line, but as we sipped, we would either give the wine in question a promotion, asking it to step forward one bottle's width, or we would leave it against the back wall. And occasionally we would come across one of the monsters, or a less powerful *bébé monstre*. These members of the monster family would be invited to take two or sometimes three steps forward.

Carignan, no oak . . . Mourvèdre, barrels fourteen through eighteen . . .

Many of Thierry's wines were not "pleasant" wines to drink. They weren't fruity or light or smooth. We weren't smelling cherries and red fruits. We were smelling roasted coffee, and licorice, and spices, and pepper, and dark jam. The high alcohol content of the big Syrahs and Mourvèdres attacked our mouths, and the hard tannins sucked our tongues dry.

It sounds like a punch line to explain that a morning spent tasting wine was hard work. But around wine number seventeen, barely more than halfway through, we needed a break. Our backs hurt from standing for several hours. Our brains were fried from concentrating not just on the sensations of the wine, but on the rushing current of new information coming at us, mostly in French. Our mouths were worn out from the barrage of strong flavors. And the fact is, no matter how thoroughly you try to spit, a little wine stays in your mouth after every glass and gets absorbed, sublingually, pretty much directly into your bloodstream.

We sat for a minute outside the circle of tasters and took bites of enzyme crackers designed to neutralize the flavors in our mouths.

"I'm going to pass out," I said, "and I haven't swallowed a drop."

The amazing thing was Jean and Claire's endless stamina—their ability to recognize that wine number eight was *réduit* (reduced) and that number twelve had a pleasant aroma of toast, while relentlessly rating and retaining each wine in the context of all the others, and in the context of the three products that were the final goal.

After a brief respite, Mary Jo and I grabbed our picks and shovels and headed back into the cold, dark mine that is wine tasting and *assemblage*. We worked until the whistle blew at bottle twenty-seven, Cinsault, no oak, which Jean found *élégant,* and which Claire pulled forward to join the contenders.

At this point, perched on his stool in lab coat, jeans, and suede chukka boots, Jean began acting like a scientist in a lab, which, of course, he was. He poured winning bottles into a narrow glass beaker, and that beaker into a larger beaker, until the larger beaker eventually contained 100 percent of one imaginary bottle of wine. He put his palm over the open mouth of the beaker, shook the contents vigorously, and poured us each a quarter glass of his concoction.

I don't pretend to have access to all the reasons the blend accomplished what it did. Sipping earlier from the row of samples, I had thought in several cases, "OK, stop right here. Here's your wine. No need to blend anything." But a mouthful of Jean's prototype made most of the individuals seem simplistic or exaggerated. The peppery spikiness of the Syrah got smoothed out. The hard tannic darkness of the young Mourvèdre softened. The blend had more flavor. It filled your mouth differently.

We are used to varietal wines at home: Cabernet Sauvignon, Pinot Noir. But winemakers here talk about blending as lying close to the heart of what they do. They don't often use the word "art," but when they do, they are usually talking about blending.

Our morning in the lab made clear what they meant in a way I couldn't have appreciated until I had sipped my way down a row of single varietals, and then tasted, minutes later, their individual contributions to a blended wine.

Jean found this first effort "pleasing enough," but he wanted to deepen the color with more Syrah, and use that one luscious Grenache to add a bit of silkiness.

This was what he could do that the rest of us could not. He was not reacting to what was there, but building something that was not there. Claire appeared to be close on his heels, but Mary Jo and I were now mostly cheering from the sidelines, lost in the thrill of witnessing a tour de force. Even Thierry, a wine man his whole life, nodded to the beat of Jean's improvisations more often than he contributed his own riffs.

Jean could use words like "unctuosity" and "muscled" and "vegetal"—a litany of eye-rollers that would normally have me smiling glassily and edging toward the door—and get away with it, because each variation he presented to us all day long was manifestly a better wine than the previous one. He was using these words to generate tasteable differences in the wine he was constructing, not to display the sort of tight-sphinctered knowingness that places a certain kind of wine lover on the sociability scale somewhere between English majors and *Star Trek* conventioneers.

Four permutations later, we all agreed that Inaccessible 2011 had found itself. It spilled over with excess as it was supposed to, but—and here Jean got to use one of his favorite words—the final blend was nevertheless remarkably "consensual."

As we worked on the remaining two wines, Jean allowed himself, finally, to lift Thierry from the tenterhooks of suspense he had hung from all morning.

Without intentional flattery, Jean talked to us about Thierry's achievement—about levels of flavor concentration and complexity not often seen in the region. About a uniformity of excellence to Thierry's wines that was almost hard to believe.

Thierry held a glass to his nose, accepting these compliments with the serious expression of a man trying not to show how very, very pleased he is.

And just like that, Jean was reading out formulas, and Claire was turning labels toward the wall, as the contents of each were accounted for.

It was the birth of a vintage, and we had left our mark on it—as diluted, perhaps, as the blood squeezed from my thumb into José's grape bucket, but still, it could be said that a part of us now made up a part of a vintage of Mas Gabinèle. It was going to be an extremely good year, and our sense of elation came from sharing in Thierry's triumph, and having had a stake in it.

The proud father did not hand out cigars. But we did have the privilege of watching him, a man of often impenetrable courtly reserve, spend ten minutes quietly corking his baby monsters with a smile of the purest fatherly delight.

Later, in the parking lot, as a kind of love song, or possibly just intoxicated by the general euphoria, Thierry kissed us each on both cheeks, and thanked us for being there with him, as one might thank a supportive friend postcrisis.

I had spent months coming to grips with what Thierry meant to us—believing that the benefit traveled primarily in one direction, from him and all he had to offer, to us, who were so receptive.

His giddy post-*assemblage* mood raised the question of what we might also mean to him.

His *négoce* clients knew him as a businessman, but in most cases did not see the artist-aesthete beneath the veneer of consultant-professional. His workers and crew knew him as a winemaker of great finesse and devotion, but beyond that he existed almost monolithically as someone of a different class: "someone with money."

Mary Jo and I, through the luck of our shared past and our natural inclinations, were able to see the winemaker, the businessman, the husband, the aesthete, and the friend.

If wine, per Jean-Luc, is pleasure, it is also fundamentally something that is shared. As you choose a bottle from a shelf, whether in a wine shop or a dusty basement, the delight—the delicious anticipation—never derives from the question "When am I going to drink this bottle?" but always from the question "Who will be sharing this bottle with me?"

When Thierry had invited us to the blending, and more broadly into the world of winemaking in which he lived, he was telling us that he had picked something a little bit special from the shelf of his life, something he felt we would particularly appreciate, and he wished to set time aside in order to share it with us, not exclusively for our benefit, but because it would give him such great pleasure to do so with people who understood.

Before letting us go, he offered us a mostly full bottle of Inaccessible 2010, recommending its remaining eighty or ninety dollars' worth of wine for dinner.

79

I saw Nicole on the street for the second time in a single afternoon, having just returned from Marie's only to run back up to the *tabac*.

"He climbs, he descends. He climbs, he descends," she said as I hurried past her.

"I forgot the milk," I said.

"*Eh bien, faute de vache . . .*" she said. Which was absolutely true. Lacking a cow, one must go buy the milk.

On my homeward leg, I came upon Jean-Luc, loading a big jerry can of water into the back of his truck.

I pointed my chin at the water as I passed. "For the dogs?" I asked.

"*Eh non,*" he said.

"For the garden?"

"*Eh non,*" he said, with a sheepish smile.

"Guess what he does with the water," I said at the dinner table.

"He puts it out for the wild birds and animals," said Joe.

"Because of the drought, yes. How did you know that?"

"I've seen him. Up by the Christ. When I check my ants."

"I thought he was trapping songbirds to eat, but no. It turns out he's Saint Francis of Fricking Assisi."

"I'm literally going to cry," said Eva.

Later, Mary Jo and I sat and watched the sky darken, just the two of us and the owl who had been calling most evenings around sundown.

A rustling at the woodstove next door sent a wistful pang through me.

Since the end of the *vendange,* our household had been awakened most weekend mornings by idling diesel pickups below our bedroom windows, and the deranged sounds of crated dogs who knew they would shortly be released into the wild to follow their noses for a day.

As a lifelong hunter, I had spent some time imagining what hunting must look like in an oak and chestnut forest rising up out of rolling vineyards, and I also wondered what the midday lunch might be, seated among Frenchmen, in a clearing looking over the Mediterranean plain. And I must confess that, though I expressed it in a quieter way, I felt a little bit like those dogs.

Once or twice, I had so arranged my weekend mornings as to be exiting or entering our front door as Jean-Luc and his hunting partner gathered their gear. I had made clear to Jean-Luc, up to the limits of tactfulness, that should the two of them ever feel like company on one of their excursions, they could rely on me with absolute confidence.

Jean-Luc's repeated *"Bien sûr"* was never less than warmly reassuring, but the weekends came and went, and there was no knock on our door, and this deferred invitation had the faintest whiff of estrangement about it.

"God, I miss them," I said to Mary Jo.

"Who?"

"Jean-Luc and Nicole. We had such a good thing there, for a while."

We had by now nearly depleted the bottle of Jean-Luc's Vin d'Orange.

I took a sip, and held my glass up in a toast to our neighbors on the other side of the wall.

"Invite them for dinner," said Mary Jo.

"Yeah, like I'm going to cook for Nicole."

"Why not?" asked Mary Jo.

80

I caught Jean-Luc in front of his garage and invited him and Nicole to dinner with my usual attitude of apology, prefacing my invitation with protestations that I understood how busy they were, that I understood if they couldn't afford the time, and on and on, until he interrupted me with a trademark finger raised in the air between us.

"Steve," he said. "*On a le temps qu'on prend.*" One has the time one takes.

José showed up with them, and after kissing his way through the rest of the family, he paused briefly to take in Joseph's Barcelona jersey, bent to plant a kiss on each of Joe's cheeks, then looked him in the face and hissed, "*¡Catalán!*"

He had brought with him a bottle of Rioja, sleeved in the traditional gold-wire netting, which I was sure he could just barely afford, as well as an unlabeled bottle of green liquid, and as I fussed with cutting boards and plates of olives, and filled glasses with Grenache Gris, he told us, with some translating from Jean-Luc, the story of the liquid.

It was olive oil from his hometown, but it wasn't just olive oil.

"*Jamais à vendre, Eh-Steve-eh. ¿Entiendes? Pas possible.*"

It wasn't possible to buy this olive oil.

It was made in a public square, where they set up a wooden press each year, stacking Arbequina olives in layers separated by straw mats, and at some point, the weight of the upper olives would begin gently to crush the lower olives, and—of the olives' own weight—the first press of slow, pure green oil would seep from between the slats. The village children would have hunks of bread ready and would wipe the olive oil directly from the press, and eat.

I remember the evening not as a single unfolding event, but as a series of discrete moments that would shimmer back to life in my memory for weeks afterward.

My pumpkin soup. A disaster. Chunky and tasteless. Just shy of inedible. Nicole joins me in the kitchen, a paramedic of sorts, working to resuscitate the patient. We add some crème fraîche. A pinch of nutmeg. Some more salt. She asks if I have a food mill, and I am able to reply in the affirmative. The soup does not get much better. We all laugh about it. And the supposed worst-case scenario becomes a story to be told. The story of Steve's *soupe de potiron.*

Eva showing Jean-Luc and Nicole her splinter-free foot, and Nicole volunteering that Jean-Luc is gifted with some sort of healing touch. He asks me if I have any warts, and, in fact, I do. I hold out my right hand, which he takes in both of his, wiping his right thumb several times over a grainy spot on the back of my hand. "It will go away," he says, and blinks both eyes at me, to confirm.

Jean-Luc's joke: Guy goes up to the boss. Says he needs oil for the wheel of his wheelbarrow. Boss asks what it sounds like. Guy says, "Squeak . . . squeak . . . squeak." The boss says, "You're fired." Guy can't believe it. "Why?" he asks. "I just need oil for my wheelbarrow so I can keep working." Boss says, "Your wheelbarrow isn't supposed to go, 'Squeak . . . squeak . . . squeak.' It's supposed to go, 'squee-squee-squee-squee-squee-squee!'" Jean-Luc, gasping for air, his hand on Joseph's shoulder. Repeats the final line to Joseph, the two of them roaring like drinking buddies.

José filling several gaps in the conversation by shaking his head and repeating, wonderingly, as if in the presence of madness, *"Minnesóta . . . meno treinta."* Minnesota. Thirty below.

Stan Getz wreathing out through the patio doors to join the candle-light and the conversation as Jean-Luc, beside me, samples his first mussel from a heaping bowl, with steam rising from the white wine and saltwater broth. He names the aromas of thyme and laurel leaf, and sighs with pleasure.

I tell him how sad it makes me that he and Véronique have argued. How I feel almost ill at the thought of a rift with the Balliccionis. But he says it will pass. This is how small villages work. There is no choice. Autignac is a family of eight hundred people, as it has been since he was born. One doesn't abandon one's family over a disagreement in the fields.

Nicole asks her husband if he might stop talking long enough to pass the bread. He turns to me and says, "Steve. Do like my father. Never get married. You see where it leads." Then he repeats it for the table.

But mostly what I remember is Mary Jo, who gave off a kind of light all evening that joined with the candle flame to show all of us the best of ourselves. She was boisterous and ardent and at ease. She was Mary Jo, as she had been, as she was, as she would be. The table was beautifully strewn with the stems, tendrils, leaves, and dried blooms of vineyard and *garrigue*. The wavering light moved in tiny glints along the rims of wineglasses and the edges of mussel shells. She communicated directly, in her own language, which was English and French and Spanish and all the rest of her. I couldn't imagine a fluent speaker of French who could so completely have commanded and seduced this table of French-speaking friends and family.

Late in the meal, Jean-Luc got up from the table and disappeared down the front stairs. Several minutes later, he reappeared with several bottles. They were the last of his *prunelle* liqueur, a bottle of Vin de Noix (walnut wine), and the gallon jug labeled "Poire 2003" from his dusty apothecary. The jug was about a third full of pear brandy he had made almost a decade ago, and which had been aging in his cellar ever since—except for a rare few evenings like this one, he said, that merited a finger or two of *eau de vie de poire* à la Jean-Luc.

PART IV

81

Given how little I was hearing about school, I was ready, when the time came for teacher conferences, to listen to a muted variation on the same school conference we always had when it came to Eva: She would be an observer, a slow joiner, cautiously friendly, a rule follower, a good and disciplined student. But we would certainly hear that she was also, in this new setting, extremely shy, if not downright withdrawn, and understandably handicapped by a language barrier and a number of cultural hurdles.

On conference night, Mary Jo and I walked through the chilly darkness of the courtyard to her first classroom, where a circle of local parents talked familiarly with each other about what they were likely to hear, good and bad, over the course of the evening.

"Are you the parents of Eva, *l'Américaine*?" asked one of the mothers standing against the wall.

We assured her we were.

"I'm so glad Eva can come to Héloïse's birthday party," she said.

"We . . ." I looked at Mary Jo. "We also!"

"Eva has been such a good friend."

"*Ah bon?*" I asked. (Really?)

The door opened and Eva's homeroom teacher, Mme Gomez, ushered out a grim-looking couple, who trudged down the hallway toward what looked like another round of solidly bad news.

We introduced ourselves, and sat across the desk from Mme Gomez, prepared to make the best of whatever we were about to hear.

Mme Gomez picked up a folder from the top of a stack, hinged it open, and spread some papers in front of her. She scanned them for a few seconds, and then looked up at us. She hesitated as if searching for the right words. Then she shook her head and smiled.

"*Eva m'épate*," she said, which translates roughly as "Eva blows me away."

She proceeded to deliver a five-minute tribute that ran out of steam only because she appeared to have used up every superlative extant in the French language. Eva was friendly. She was popular. She worked hard. She turned in all her homework and participated in class. The friends she had made were the right kinds of friends, good students and good citizens. She helped everyone—students and teachers alike—with their English.

"*Tous les professeurs l'adorent*," we heard. All the teachers adore her.

"Do you know," we heard, "that she refuses to let us evaluate her on a different scale from her classmates? She insists that we grade her as if she were a native speaker. Do you know this?"

"Do you know," we heard, "that she is ranked in the top five in her class with no allowances for French being her second language?"

"If you have more children like her, will you send them to me, please?" requested Mme Gomez.

"You will continue to hear this all evening," she said.

And we did.

"*Elle est super-chouette*," gushed her math teacher, a dour Humphrey Bogart whom Eva said she saw smoking between classes.

"There are no concerns. No concerns with Eva," mumbled her *sciences vie et terre* teacher, poking through her work as if trying helpfully to find something to be concerned about and failing.

"I hear more English spoken in the hallways these days. I believe that is partly Eva's influence," said her English teacher.

"The pupil has nothing to learn from the teacher," said her art teacher.

"She is magnificent," said the music teacher who had made her sing a solo on her first day in his class.

After each meeting, I did my best to translate for Mary Jo, although the attitude of each teacher could not have been confused for anything other than what it was.

By the time we had completed our circuit through Eva's typical school day, we felt battered by good news. It had been a relentless shelling.

"Are you still pretty worried about Eva?" asked Mary Jo, with her hand resting inside my crooked elbow.

"That little shit," I said.

82

It was midmorning, and we found ourselves in another carefully pruned corner of Thierry's domain, our low voices muttering against the chalky stone walls of an eleventh-century priory.

We sat not in pews but on barstools, and our host had just poured a finger of Mas Gabinèle 2011 Grenache Gris into each of three glasses on the counter between us.

He had invited us to visit him here at the Prieuré Saint Sever, a miniature medieval hamlet isolated by a 365-degree expanse of vines and hills, where he maintained his business headquarters, two donkeys, and—in the priory itself—his tasting and salesroom.

Our celebrant swirled his glass and tasted with quick double sucks that had grown familiar over months of standing with him next to vats of wine and laboratory spitting sinks.

Mary Jo and I were aware of sipping the distillation of a field we had come to love, several miles distant, where a lithe cypress stood next to a vineworker's hut. The fact that the wine was in perfect balance, brightly dry, breathing grapefruit and quince, was almost beside the point.

When we had finished swooning at the ludicrously seductive surroundings, Mary Jo drifted off across the stone pavers, and soon her camera was saying, *shaweek, shaweek, shaweek.*

Thierry and I sipped and talked, enjoying with an offhand sense of normalcy a morning that would have been the big headline news from any previous trip abroad: "That morning we spent in Languedoc, honey, remember? Sipping those wines in that medieval church? By private invitation? Just the two of us, alone with the winemaker? Remember that?"

In this case, the winemaker wasn't done yet. He poured a finger of Rarissime Rouge into a new glass, slid the base toward me, and then dropped a bomb into the middle of our lives.

The bomb, as it went off, sounded like this: "You know, this would be quite possible for you and Mary Jo."

Mary Jo heard her name, and grasped enough of the rest of it to head back toward the scene, in order to assess the damage.

I was looking at Thierry over the rim of my wineglass, with rich, spicy black-currant fumes crowding up at me. I held his gaze and sipped, and then carefully set my glass back on the bar.

"What do you mean?" I asked.

Thierry glanced at Mary Jo, and so did I. She was leaning on her elbows with an amused expression that said, "Yes, Thierry, tell us exactly what you mean."

"I mean to buy hectares of vines, to make wine . . . this," said Thierry, gesturing around himself at "this," which is to say, at world-class wine on the bar, at cases stacked for shipment, at an office just across the way, and, beyond, at the groomed and gorgeous grounds, vine-encircled, that stood for a particular life, mixed of comfort and professionalism and artistry. A life the pieces of which he was setting in place with some pride and satisfaction. A French life, spent doing one of the things that France did best. A life he could see we understood and admired.

Mary Jo looked back at me, and we had a short but very busy exchange that after twenty-three years didn't need to be spoken. My blank deadpan was saying, "This is, of course, a fantasy proposal that would be ridiculous to take seriously, and I refuse absolutely to take it seriously, although I am, at some level, in spite of myself, taking it extraordinarily seriously."

Her wry look, with chin resting on right palm, was saying, "You are shortly going to have to deal with a tremendous amount of guff from your wife about that look on your face right now."

"A hectare of vines in Faugères sells for about fifteen thousand euros," continued Thierry pitilessly. "It is a region that is still quite affordable.

With your French and what you have done just over the last few months, Steve . . ." He trailed off. The conclusion hung obvious and unspoken above the bar.

One of the donkeys brayed in a far field.

I nodded several times, and took another sip of wine. I could end this easily. It was preposterous. Which I could simply say, politely, and that would end it.

Because it was preposterous.

I shifted on my barstool. "How much . . ." I began.

And the morning stretched into early afternoon as Thierry ran the numbers with us, with a patience and generosity that, until recently, I would have felt unworthy of to the extent of refusing to intrude on his time.

Eventually we moved to his office, an environment that we all found comfortable. The draw of the office was something we intuitively recognized in each other.

He pulled spreadsheets and a profit-and-loss statement, showing what yields of twenty to twenty-five hectoliters per hectare amounted to at Mas Gabinèle's average price per bottle. Looking at *ébourgeonnage* (debudding), and *vendange verte,* and summer pest control, and the *vendange* itself, and the *mise en bouteilles* (the bottling), and *la taille* (pruning) as numbers in a column leading inexorably downward toward a bottom line. Estimating that an investment of perhaps 100,000 euros, spent with care, would set one up with enough good acreage and enough annual hectoliters to, over time, operate a Faugères wine label at a small profit.

"How would this be possible while we live in Minnesota?" we asked.

This would be a reason to visit each fall, suggested Thierry with a smile. And Thierry would help. And the Ballis would help. And Jean Natoli, certainly, would be interested in such a project.

As he and I loaded two cases of Mas Gabinèle into the back of our car, he said, "My wife and I would like to invite you to dinner. Can you email me with some dates that would be convenient? The children are welcome."

Mary Jo and I drove past donkeys that might once have slept in a *gabinèle,* and an ancient olive tree producing its particular number of liters of harvestable olives.

Behind us, Thierry waved from the gate.

"What do we do now?" I asked.

"Maybe the universe is trying to tell us something," she said.

"Doesn't it feel that way?"

"And maybe it's tempting us to do something really fucking stupid," she said.

83

I pulled away in first gear.

"How did the party go, Evie? Bad, fair, good, great . . . ?"

"We cooked," she said.

"That's it?"

"Pretty much. Cooked and talked. We were there for two hours before Heloïse even showed up. We all just hung out in the kitchen and cooked her a five-course lunch. That's apparently like a middle school party in France. We baked a chicken. We made pasta with Roquefort sauce. We made a salad with vinaigrette."

"Evie, that's—"

"Oh my God," she said. "*Tarte aux poires* for dessert. So good."

"Did it all turn out?"

"Everything. I mean . . . perfect."

"It's what you grow up doing here, I think."

"It's crazy. They just, like . . . know. I still can't do goat cheese by the way."

We turned off the Route de Béziers toward Autignac.

"Then they start talking about how I was going to leave soon. Rachel starts crying and I'm like, 'Rachel, you can NOT cry.'"

84

The frenzy of the grape harvest was well behind André. Much of the work now left to do in the winery involved the deceptively complex act of moving liquid from one container to another. A game of musical chairs, with a fixed number of vats—never quite enough—all holding liquid in various states of completion. To empty one meant finding room in another, or, in some cases, if the wine showed promise, its contents might be transferred from a vat into oak barrels.

That's what André was preparing to do this morning as he fitted inlet and outlet hoses to a pump with the rattling clink of threaded brass that was part of the music of the postharvest winery.

A Mourvèdre in the back corner had excelled since its arrival in September. He had pushed it hard ever since, the way a coach will sometimes work over a particularly gifted athlete, knowing he or she can take it.

Now it was time for all of that raw power and dark, rough-hewn exuberance to be finished—its edges rounded, its loud voice modulated—by spending some quiet time in oak. If all went well, it would emerge in a little more than a year with the same physique—muscled and imposing—but with its adolescent wildness polished and channeled into a young adult maturity.

This idea of coaching or education is part of the French conception of how wine develops. In English we talk about aging wine in oak, but in French, they refer to it as "raising" wine. The word they use is *élever,* and it is the same word they use to refer to raising a child. A young student is called, in French, an *élève*—someone in the process of being elevated by education. And a wine aged in oak barrels is a wine *élevé en fûts de chêne,* meaning raised—with connotations of discipline, improvement, and education—in oak barrels.

The barrels sat on their sides in the flat light from the open doorway with a stillness that looked like patience, bungs like round mouths open and facing upward. The oak was French, most likely from one of those hallowed forests that everyone who makes red wine in France knows about—the Bertranges, up near Burgundy, or possibly the Tronçais, where sessile oaks planted by Louis XIV for navy ships grow tight-grained aromatic wood on twenty-five thousand acres of shallow-soiled hillside.

Before the barrels had been sealed, their interiors had been toasted by a brazier set inside them. The lightness or darkness of the char, called *la chauffe* in French, opened up or closed off the pores of the barrel to varying degrees, and gave different flavor profiles, from vanilla and licorice, to coffee and caramel, to tobacco and tar.

This was a medium-heavy char, meant to contend with a powerful wine, and emphasize some of its darker moods.

André fed the end of the hose into the first barrel, and asked me to hold it in place. He pressed a button, and the pump hummed. I felt a slight recoil as the first jet of wine splashed into the bottom of the barrel, which had earlier been filled with water to make the joints swell, and ensure that it was watertight.

As the barrel slowly filled, the rising wine inside pushed a gentle exhalation out of the open bung, and, standing beside it, I was gradually aware of an aroma that grew more persistent and more familiar the fuller the barrel became. There was the sweet-acrid burned-syrup smell of toasted wood, like the smell of a smoldering fireplace. There was the unmistakable perfume of red wine, made up in this case of alcohol fumes and the particular dark, fleshy, almost bloody fruit of young Mourvèdre; and, finally, there was the smell that hangs in the air after a plank of wood has been freshly sawn—something dusty and a little spicy—which was the smell of the oak itself.

All of this would end up in a bottle someday, recognizable but never quite this raw, and the individual scents never quite so distinct and separate as at this moment, while a splashing stream of wine whisked the three elements into the air of the barrel, and pushed them out at me.

It was like an inoculation—a once-for-all-time imprint of what oak and wine smell like when they have interacted with each other—and a source of comparison that I would draw from ever after.

André reemerged from the back room, and, with the hand that wasn't holding my hose, I scooped some of the aroma above the barrel up toward my nose and looked reverently skyward.

He grinned, and made his way out into the courtyard, the tops of his rubber boots shivering around his shins with each step.

A few minutes later he was back beside me, shining a flashlight into the barrel at where a broad purple pond had formed, churned by the thin waterfall of wine from the hose, while droplets splashed against the dark cinnamon char of the rounded walls.

Then André was gone. The pump behind me shut off, and I was told to follow him.

André grabbed two wineglasses and a glass siphon, like a basting tube bent at an angle with a glass trigger grip at one end—an instrument called a wine thief in English, and a *pipette* in French.

He thumbed open the door to the *chai*, or barrel room, and made his way down one of the rows of barrels, crunching pebbles as he walked, and when he found what he was looking for, he coaxed a white plastic stopper back and forth out of one of the barrels, and dipping the tip of the wine thief into the barrel, he placed his thumb over the other end and lifted it back out, half full of an inky dark liquid that he then let flow into each wineglass by lifting and replacing his thumb.

Standing in the dim and monastic half-light that angled in from the door, surrounded by stone walls and a pebbled floor and wooden barrels, André looked like a part of something very old. Although the sounds of diesel engines, hydraulic lifts, and electric pumps had sometimes drowned it out, this was at the heart of what he loved about all this—the hands-on, low-tech, artisanal wrestling with stubborn raw materials that were capable, in the end, of transcending themselves into the beauty of a glass of wine, or a scene like this.

He handed me my glass.

"This is a Mourvèdre from last year," he said. "It was of very high quality. As good as what you were putting in the barrel in the other room. This one will make my next vintage of Orchis."

We half raised our glasses and each took a sip, then looked down to suck air up through the liquid in that always-serious-seeming posture that leads naturally to a state of reflection.

"Since one year, it is in the barrel," he said. "But . . . brand-new oak, like in there," and he gestured with his wineglass toward where I had just been working.

It was an explosive mouthful. The wine still tasted smoked from long, airless exposure to the charred barrel, and the spicy woodshop smell was as present as the fruit of the wine itself. It was not something I would have taken a sip of in a restaurant, and asked for more.

"He is very structured, very carpentered," André said. "Very powerful."

"Too powerful?" I asked.

"Yes, too powerful by himself," he said. "But he is the spine, and we will add the flesh when we blend.

"Now, here is what will be interesting," he said.

Taking my glass back, he removed the stopper from a different barrel, one row over.

"This is a three-year barrel," he said as he dipped the wine thief and withdrew it again.

"The wine has been there for three years?" I asked.

"No," he said, concentrating on filling two glasses held complicatedly in his left hand with the *pipette* in his right. "This is the third wine this barrel has held, and it is the same wine we just drank—the Mourvèdre from last year. The same batch, from the same vineyard, just a different kind of barrel. And we will see what that gives."

Despite my mild disorientation, I was able to wonder at the difference between this glass and the last, which were fundamentally the same wine—the same grapes, the same year, the same vineyard and soil—but with effects that made this seem almost impossible. Where the first glass had been—despite the supposed mellowing of a year's worth of oak education—full of extremes, this second glass was tamed. Strong and flavorful with Mourvèdre's tannic sting still intact, but seeming to flow more thickly over the tongue, and not tasting as if the oak had flavored the wine, but as if it had melted it, giving it more density, somehow.

He was thinking about it.

"You know," he said. "A Bordeaux, when it is first bottled, it is undrinkable."

He must have read something in my expression. "A small Bordeaux, yes, of course. You can drink him. But the great ones. They are not made to drink now, but in ten years. Fifty. They are not a pleasure. But all that tannin is like strong bones. It permits them to stand up straight, even when they have turned into old men.

"My Orchis, he is not a great Bordeaux. But he has bones. And he has something that Bordeaux does not have. He has heat in him, and *garrigue,* and blackness. Even that wine in your glass right now has those things, yes? But he is polite. He is round. That one over there." He nodded toward the first barrel. "He is not civilized. He will fight for many years inside the bottle. We will marry him with some other wines when we blend him, but it will not be a marriage in which one gives a little *bisou* on the cheek at night, you know?"

Back in the winery, André said he'd take over on the pump, and asked me to top off a smaller line of barrels, the 225-liter *barriques* that are the most common form of barrel to age wine in.

The whole point about barrels is that they are closer to being alive than vats. They have pores, and they, in some sense, breathe. They don't just store wine but exchange part of themselves with it. This means that a small amount of wine is constantly evaporating through the pores of the barrel—a form of petty larceny that the French affectionately call *la part des anges,* or the angels' share.

He went to fetch what I thought would be another hose, but instead returned with what looked like a watering can, made of a brilliant, polished stainless steel, with a long, straight swan's neck of a spout that, just at the very end, hooked downward.

He opened a valve and ran wine into the can, like filling a bucket with a garden spigot. He showed me how to insert the end of the spout into the hole, and then stop the stream of wine inside the hole before it could drip on the outside of the barrel.

"When do you leave?" he asked.

"Near the end of January," I said.

"You and Mary Jo must come to dinner," he said.

And with that I was set loose. My job for the rest of the morning would be to work up some body heat, carrying my elegant new tool back and forth between wine vat and wine barrel, taking care not to let any drops fall on the porous, breathing wood. Now and then, I would lean forward to inhale a partial noseful of French oak and Faugères wine as I methodically restored to the barrels their stolen angels' share.

85

My copy of *Je Sais Cuisiner* had begun to move around the house. I found it on the couch, and then on the kitchen table.

"Dad!" Eva shouted from the hallway bathroom.

"Eva!"

"What's a *moule à madeleines*?"

"A madeleine mold."

"Get me one," she said, and the toilet flushed.

On a Sunday morning, she set out flour, sugar, and eggs and was grating the zest of a lemon beside her *moule à madeleines*. OK, her brand-new *moule à madeleines*.

"What you up to?" I asked.

"Making something I want to eat," she said.

"Can I see?" I asked.

"Out!" she ordered.

Evicted from our own house, Mary Jo and I took a walk out of town, up past the Christ.

"Do you want to see the most beautiful vineyard in the world?" I asked.

Winter sun was shining on the slope of the Espinasses's Syrah and Mourvèdre. The leaves had all fallen, and there were wisps of smoke in the distance.

I thought of this view as somewhere we belonged now. It wasn't something we were borrowing for the length of a vacation. It had joined those few patches of the world that, taken together, added up to some important part of who I was.

There was the view from our rear deck in Minnesota, over wooded yard and cattail bed to Turtle Lake in the distance. The view from the Gunflint Trail looking down at Grand Marais Harbor, fragile and tiny on the edge of the endless expanse of Lake Superior. The rocky north shore of Pine Lake in the Boundary Waters, in January, in total silence, surrounded by snow and ice and evergreens.

And now this, of all things. Scrubby Mediterranean *garrigue*, unimposing, thorny-hearted, and generous. And connected, I felt now—whatever else happened hereafter—to who we were.

"Seriously," I said. "Look at this place. What are we going to do?"

"I think the question is what are *you* going to do," she said.

"It's what I've always wanted."

"What?"

"This."

"Owning a vineyard? Making wine?"

"France. Belonging here. Not just going off on a plane and coming back to your old life. This is a commitment. This actually changes things."

She put her arm in mine. "We could do it," she said. "I know we could."

"Let's."

"Is it what you want? Not what you think you should want? Not what people will give you affirmations for?"

"I think so. I love this place. I love these people. I feel understood here."

"So what do you say no to?"

"What do you mean?"

"I mean we can't just add this. We're at capacity. This is a big, huge fucking yes. So where do all the nos come from? To make room?"

"I don't know yet," I said.

86

"That will never work," declared Marie flatly.

I had just described a roasted cauliflower dish I intended to experiment with that evening.

"No," agreed Maman.

"With cauliflower, either you cook it in water to tenderize it, or you make a gratin with a béchamel sauce," said Marie.

"The problem—" began Maman.

"Yes, the problem," continued Marie, "is that either you will *cramer* [incinerate] the cauliflower, which is not good, or else—"

"Or else it will not cook enough," said Maman.

"Exactly," said Marie. "And if you want crunchy cauliflower, then—"

"Then you might as well eat it raw," said Maman.

"Voilà," said Marie.

"But on the other hand," said Maman. "Perhaps Monsieur should try it, and who knows?"

"No, but, Maman," said Marie.

"Marie, let the man make his cauliflower and we will see. He will make a reporting to us."

"I will," I said. "I will tell you tomorrow."

"Voilà," said Maman.

"By the way, how is it," asked Marie as I was stepping through the door, "that Joseph is getting *zéro fautes* [none wrong] on his *dictées*? When his French *camarades de classe,* according to my nephew Baptiste, are having difficulties? This is not too polite, I think."

I said I would talk to Joseph seriously about this.

As the door swung shut, I heard her say, apropos of my cauliflower, "*Non, Maman, ça m'étonnerait.*" (No, Mother, that would astonish me.)

I went home, poured a healthy stream of olive oil over a bowl of cauliflower florets. Added sea salt. Stripped five or six stems of thyme into the bowl, and rubbed a few seeds free from the bouquet of wild fennel hanging from the kitchen beam. Spread all this onto a baking sheet and put it into a 200°C oven. After about ten minutes the florets were softening but not coloring. So I lit the broiler and took them out just when a few points of gold had begun to spread.

They were, with all due respect, tender, unincinerated, and mouthwatering.

Marie looked dubious the next day, and asked me to repeat my methods as she wrapped my baguette. She informed me that I must open a restaurant because evidently I had much to share with the people of the region.

87

Several times at the winery, during the *vendange* and its aftermath, we had brought up with André the possibility of importing Domaine Balliccioni to Minnesota.

He had waved us off, and we had assumed he either didn't want to be bothered with the red tape involved, or had been approached like this before, by foreign visitors proposing schemes in the heat of their visits that always cooled once they got back home.

But then we received an invitation to an evening of Champagne and coquilles St. Jacques chez Balliccioni, and, as we sat for the first time at their dark wooden dining room table, negotiations were opened.

"The wine is made," said André. "It is time to sell the wine."

Looking like a scrubbed-up schoolboy in his unaccustomed button-down shirt, André began like this: "I don't want to sell so much wine in the United States that I have no wine left to sell to my friends over here."

As if to illustrate his point, he washed down a mouthful of Nicholas Feuillatte Brut, acquired just last year in an exchange with a friend in Champagne.

Then he continued: "I'd like to sell wine in America because the idea pleases me," he said. "And because I can tell people that I export to the USA, which would be very sympathetic. And, of course, because it would be a connection to our American friends." Here, he half raised a crystal flute into the candlelight between us.

But he had heard stories about pallets of wine destroyed by New York customs over a single labeling irregularity.

And how would they deal with the language barrier, he wondered. His *Ing-GLEESH was verrhy goood,* he assured me, but *not so verrhy VERRHY goood.*

I found myself, for the first time, in a position to offer reassurance to the unflappable André Balliccioni. The language barrier was nothing. Mary Jo and I were always an email away. If the Hoffmans had to register themselves with the FDA, we would register. We would get exact labeling instructions. And then, Véro had always wanted to go to New York. Now it could be a business trip. We would meet them there.

The Champagne bottle nosed toward Mary Jo's glass, and then found its way to mine.

There was one final concern.

"We will pay you how?" asked Véronique, who kept the Balliccioni books.

Bof.

We tried our best to explain, over some reflexive objections, that the Balliccioni account *chez off-MAHN* had been, if anything, overfunded, and would remain flush for many years to come.

I'd like to think that, at this point, Mary Jo and I came into focus for them. That they understood what we had been asking for, and it was not something they might originally have suspected from two eager Americans with a proposition. They looked at each other and paused. They could easily have resumed their insistence on a plan to pay us. But they didn't insist. They shrugged and smiled back at us, and André got up to open another bottle of wine, and Véro mentioned the bedroom upstairs that could be ours any time we came to town, and it was as if they had picked up a couple of pens and scribbled their names side by side at the bottom of the new set of terms we had all just agreed to.

The topic turned to Thierry's winemaking proposal. We mentioned that we and the kids had just had dinner with Thierry and his wife, Nicole.

Véronique acted taken aback. *"Chez eux?"* (At their house?)

"In Béziers," I said. "Yes."

She and André exchanged a look.

"He does not invite people to his house," said Véronique. "Almost never. Only those . . . He would only do that if he considered you to be friends."

"He is very generous, Thierry, but very discreet," said André.

"This is something you should know about him. In his way, he is like André. With André it happens more quickly, but I mean to say, when he accepts you," said Véronique, *"c'est pour de bon."* It's for keeps.

We walked together through my litany of winemaking concerns, and how many of them Thierry had answered for me, except that Thierry, as both a winemaker and a *négociant*, probably couldn't make the wine itself for us.

"I'll make your wine," André said, in a tone he might use to offer us a ride home. "You two give yourselves pleasure deciding what kind of wine you want to make, and as long as I'm making wine, I'll make your wine, too. A couple of hectares. It's nothing. Don't think about it."

That's how he said it: "Give yourselves pleasure." In an evening filled with talk of business, it was the importance of pleasure, its trustworthiness compared to the fickle rewards of money, that had been the theme.

The evening ended a surprising number of hours later, at the front gate of the winery, under the yellow sodium streetlamps, with cheek kisses all around.

When all other permutations had been exhausted, André grabbed my shoulders and gave me one, loud, smacking kiss on each cheek before sending us out into the night.

88

I received a Tuesday morning phone call from Jean-Luc, informing me that my son had Wednesdays off, and didn't I think it was time that we spent a morning in the field with Monsieur Joseph and some hunting dogs?

Joseph had not entirely recovered from the loss of Parsley, and had retreated into a fragility marked by Asterix comics, and asking me not to leave his bed at night until he had fallen asleep. I was not certain whether he was quite ready to watch hunting dogs chase innocent wild animals.

"You don't have to go, Joe."

"I want to."

At eight the next morning, Jean-Luc's garage door clanged open, and his white truck eased out backward. Through the side window of the rear compartment, three hairy and slightly mournful faces stared at us.

Joseph climbed in to be sniffed, licked, wagged at, and generally welcomed into his pack of fellow hunters.

The idea was not to carry a gun with a nine-year-old around, but to watch the dogs work, and maybe give him a chance to see a hare, or a deer, or a wild boar break free during the chase.

The three dogs got louder the farther we drove. By the time Jean-Luc and I got out, at the end of a bouldery trail, Joe sat amid a chaos of ginger projectiles hurling themselves from window to window, barking deliriously and occasionally throwing their heads back to howl. Jean-Luc opened the door, and I stood ready with a camera to take a picture of Joe with his packmates.

But the dogs just disappeared. They tumbled out of the truck, nails scrabbling, and by the time I had raised my camera halfway to my eye, they were out of sight in the *garrigue,* and all we heard of them were their *grelots* (gruh-LOW), the brass bells they wear around their necks, which chimed softly in the brush.

What became clear right away was that pack dogs do not follow the hunter; the hunter does his best to follow the dogs, or at least stay within earshot of them in order to sense their progress and anticipate their direction.

We hiked up gravel roads, and followed the edges of vineyards, the tinkling bells fading in and out of our hearing, punctuated by an occasional raucous *woof.* At one point, as I was gazing onto a still landscape, a tuft of brush shivered violently, then its neighbor, and then a flash of brown at ground level announced that Gitane was at work.

Soon enough, one of the dogs started barking furiously, and within seconds the other two had joined in. Jean-Luc raised a hand and we listened.

"*Ça y est. C'est parti,*" he said. The dogs had found something, and we stood still, trying to sense where the baying chorus was headed. We found ourselves looking over a bowl of a valley, where the dogs were suddenly close again, shaking the brush below us, darting into the open and back into the vegetation, and barking over each other—Gitane's raspy tenor, Dolly's clear alto, and Daisy's shrill soprano.

"You OK, Joe?"

"Yeah."

Somehow, Jean-Luc could tell they were on the trail of a rabbit. He pointed out the tight arc their barking was following. A hare would have run in a much wider circle, and a boar or a deer would have taken off over the hills.

The morning's rabbit managed to lead the dogs on a nearly one-hour chase. The dogs' barking grew ragged and infrequent, and after a time stopped altogether, replaced by the sound of the north wind rustling in the brush, and the jingling of *grelots*.

Joe had followed most of the chase with rapt attention, but it is the right and obligation of nine-year-old boys to get distracted in the presence of sticks and branches, which, swung across the tops of heather and broom, managed to slice off their tops in an extraordinarily satisfying manner. And there were cade junipers in blossom, full of so much pollen that a nice, fist-sized stone, shaped like, say, a hand grenade, could be lobbed into one of them, generating an explosive burst of pollen smoke that would hover dramatically before drifting off on the north wind.

There were worms, ants, and spiders to observe, as well as one mutilated grasshopper missing both back legs and part of its abdomen, yet still indisputably and gruesomely alive.

"Can you kill it, Dad?" he asked, and turned away as I brought a merciful foot down.

As we walked along, Joe and I would call to Jean-Luc and ask about what we were looking at, or sometimes hold out a treasure. Jean-Luc would turn our specimens back and forth in his hand, or bend to peer at the plant that Joe was pointing to, then stand up and begin, as always, "*Alors, ça . . .*"

Eventually we found ourselves in a grove of parasol pines, and Jean-Luc slowed.

"Oh-ho," he said.

89

"*Tiens*, Joseph," he said, pulling out an ancient pocketknife and handing it to Joe. It was a Laguiole jackknife, loose on its hinge, with the grip coming apart and the blade worn thin.

I knew this knife's story. It had been the pocketknife of a shepherd in the hills nearby, who had still been watching his flock at age ninety-five, and who died happy another decade later. Jean-Luc owned several better knives, but he preferred to carry this one, because it could still slice an apple and a *saucisson,* and because, about forty years ago, he had married the shepherd's granddaughter.

He pointed Joe toward a mottled reddish dome about the size of a hamburger bun barely visible beneath a litter of pine needles on the side of the trail.

Joe took the knife and squatted on the heels of his tennis shoes. He peered into the brush and announced that it was a mushroom. He looked up uncertainly, holding on to his oversized orange cap, not sure whether he was being useful or being humored.

He was instructed to slice the mushroom off at the ground and then look at the stem, which he did with an agonizing slowness and precision.

"Does the stem look like it's bleeding?" asked Jean-Luc.

"*Oui,*" confirmed Joseph. There was a reddish-orange liquid coming out of the stem at the cut.

"*C'est un lactaire,*" Jean-Luc said with an excited tension in his voice, gesturing toward the canopy of pines hovering over us.

"They grow under parasol pines," he said. "One calls them also *sanguins,* because of the *sang* [blood] that drips from the stem when you cut them."

"And, Joseph," he said.

Joe looked up at him, ready to follow any command.

"We will cook them tonight on the grill," said Jean-Luc. He opened his eyes wide and kissed his fingers in a way that managed, in a single gesture, to bring Joe very privately and securely into their little mutual conspiracy.

As the dogs continued their work, we got to work ourselves, hunting a new prey among the pine needles. Now that we'd seen one, they popped up everywhere. Joe turned out to have an especially good eye, which Jean-Luc made much of, and together the three of us collected enough to cover the inside lining of Jean-Luc's hunting jacket, pressed into service as an impromptu collecting basket. There were a few locations that only Joe could reach, and he would crawl into tunnels of greenery and then crawl back out full of leafy debris, holding orange-red trophies in one hand.

His joy rose to a peak of happy giggling when his father tromped on one particularly beautiful specimen and Jean-Luc turned to Joe to commiserate, in a torrent of outraged French, with all appropriate hand gestures, over the hopeless clumsiness of the third member of their party.

The dogs had now run for the better part of four hours straight, and none of the morning's chase had offered enough promise to keep them working into the afternoon. We found our way back to the truck, carrying our spoils and souvenirs.

Five or six hours later, a vine-wood fire in our courtyard jumped across the faces gathered around it—Jean-Luc's, Nicole's, Mary Jo's, Joseph's, and my own—while Eva tried taking long-exposure photos from the terrace above.

We had not washed the mushrooms—heaven forfend—we had just swept the dirt and moss from them and set them upside down on the grill.

Nicole was dripping olive oil with precision into their gills so the oil would be absorbed but not well over onto a flaring fire that might char the caps. Mary Jo dropped a suspicion of finely minced garlic onto each cap to avoid any risk of distracting from their delicate, meaty flavor.

Jean-Luc and Joe sprinkled pinches of sea salt and pepper onto Nicole's oil and Mary Jo's garlic, and I had the great joy of seeing Joe joyful again—animated and laughing and serious by turns, but fully immersed in every minute. All the important elements of his recent life—family, and play, and nature, and food—had come combustibly together in a single day, and seemed to have exploded his mournful constraint.

Jean-Luc hadn't known about Parsley. Whether he was just intuitively good with boys, or whether a particularly fine-tuned sensitivity had alerted him to Joe's tender state, what was clear was that Joe had needed exactly what Jean-Luc had to offer that day, which had been both a flavor of adventure, and the company of men who loved boys enough to protect them from those parts of life they were not yet ready to face.

Nicole tested the mushrooms' tenderness with a knife and eventually split a couple of the bigger ones so they would lie flatter.

When the mushrooms were cooked, we all sat around the candlelit table, drank red wine and Orangina, told stories, laughed, and ate our kill, which had felt no pain, and had only bled a little.

90

The most common definition of the Mediterranean region is, simply, "where olives grow."

In Autignac, olives appeared in serving bowls at most meals, and made increasingly frequent appearances in what we cooked, including, quite regularly now, Nicole's simple recipe of fish fillets simmered in a sauce of tomato, white wine, onion, thyme, bay leaf, and whole green olives.

The olives she preferred, because their firm flesh stood up well to cooking, were called Amellau. The Amellau tree they owned was a venerable loner, rising up from the corner of a fallow vineyard, and Jean-Luc was anxious to pick it because the tree happened to stand immediately beside a gravel road, and roadside trees full of ripe olives, he said, "risk changing proprietors abruptly."

On a crisp, sunny morning, we found Jean-Luc's ladder beside the tree's knuckled gray trunk. He made muffled sounds of greeting from somewhere up among the silvery foliage, before climbing down and unbelting his improvised collection basket, fashioned from the bottom half of a plastic tub.

With the courtesy of every dirty-handed worker we had encountered, he offered his elbow to shake: "*Salut, Steve.*" And then the obligatory double kiss for Mary Jo.

Nicole returned from their truck with an empty bucket, which called for another round of kissing. Several months in a cheek-kissing culture had begun to spoil me for other greetings. I could handshake and bearhug with the best of my compatriots, but neither combined the formality and the intimacy of the cheek kiss. I loved the fact that, in order to perform the gesture, you had to step out of the stream of your life for a couple of seconds and acknowledge the importance of the person across from you. You would know, by the time you pulled apart, whether someone had had coffee for breakfast, whether he had shaved, whether she was wearing perfume.

On the way home from Murviel one morning, I had watched two trucks approach each other from opposite directions and each pull off onto the shoulder of a narrow highway. The two men who emerged from the trucks were bearded, one dressed in work clothes, the other in camo. Both held cell phones to their ears, and without interrupting either conversation, they met in the middle of the road, leaned toward each other over the dividing stripe, kissed on both cheeks, and returned to their trucks, still talking.

Nicole placed her empty bucket on the ground, and Jean-Luc poured a thudding stream of fat green olives into it.

Olive picking, even more than grape picking, falls short as an intellectual challenge. There, quite obviously, are the olives. You just pull them off with fingertips, or in cascades by milking the branches with your cupped palm. They are so hard and dense that there is no risk of injuring them if a few happen to hit the ground.

The challenge is purely physical. You have to be tall enough, or you need a ladder. This was good news for the six-foot-one American who had spent the better part of September folded in two.

"*Il est doué*" (He is talented), remarked Nicole as I reached several feet above her head to pull a branch down.

We worked in silence for a short time, to the sounds of rustling leaves, snapping stems, and our own breathing.

But it didn't take long.

"Steve," began Jean-Luc, with just a slight strain in his voice from reaching high for a branch.

And we passed the rest of the morning deep in conversation.

That afternoon, in a dim stone garage, we brined the olives in a lye solution, regularly cutting sample olives in half into the evening, to track the progress of the brine toward the pit. In eight days or so, he and Nicole would can them in salt water and there would be olives to eat.

A week or so later, we were on one of Jean-Luc's hunting trails, negotiating the cruel nest of spikes within a hedge of blackthorn, also known as sloe, also known as *prunelles*. We filled our buckets with the sky-blue berries, which had endured enough cold weather now to sweeten, moderately, their summer astringency. When we had picked all the *prunelles* that it seemed prudent to reach for, we drove to a spot Mary Jo and I had found farther down the hill.

Later, just before we were to leave in January, we would taste the two liqueurs side by side, and discover that the berries picked closer to the plain had made a sweeter liqueur than those picked from Jean-Luc and Nicole's spot, farther up the hill. It would bring us full circle to the fig tree of our first conversation in their orchard, and the effects of rocky hills and lush flatlands on fruits and the liquids made from them.

A jar of Amellau appeared in our larder beside José's olive oil. The *prunelles* that Mary Jo and I had found as part of our STILL blog wanderings were enough to make two bottles of liqueur. One bottle sat on our kitchen shelf. The other, it was agreed, should remain next door, in Jean-Luc's apothecary.

What none of us was willing to acknowledge for now, was that we were provisioning for a future in which Mary Jo and I would not take part.

And then came December. Which is not to say the month after November, but December—the third and final praying mantis to join the Hoffman ménage at 42 Avenue de la Liberté.

December was party to two rather wonderful events during her life with us.

The first occurred on the day she was found, when Joe removed her from a hedge and stood for a while, contemplating the beautiful and remorseless predator walking impersonally up his arm. What I watched in that minute or so, I like to believe, was Joe remembering the fear and anger and revulsion that had become associated in his experience with mantises, then letting himself remember his love of insects, of ecosystems, of interspecies connection, of, I want to say, the world that Jean-Luc and his dogs had opened up to him just a few days earlier. And then he let his love, however tentatively, outweigh his fear. Whether or not that was exactly what happened, he did bring her home, and, possibly because he had had to overcome something in himself before he could accept her, she became his favorite.

The second event occurred shortly before December died. We woke to find her clinging to a branch of fennel. Just below her, enveloping the same branch, was a loose, foamy mass that looked a little like a caterpillar and a little like another emergency.

When Jean-Luc stopped by to consult, we learned that December had not lost most of her insides in the night—or perhaps she had in a way, but those insides were made up of hundreds of mantis eggs, soon to be protected for the winter as the foam hardened into a cocoon around them. In the spring, hundreds of miniature mantises would emerge, spend several days gleefully devouring one another, and then the strongest of them would disperse.

Yes, of course, said Jean-Luc. He would watch over them until then.

And this made explicit what we had not said until then. That we would be leaving. And we would miss them—miss this. So much that it was difficult to talk about.

"*Il y aura un trou*," said Jean-Luc. There would be a hole when we were gone.

91

I made my *daube* with beef, although the stew can be made with veal, or lamb, or mutton, or wild boar, or octopus. What was not in question was that the weather—raw, windy, and below freezing—called for just exactly this dish. The *tramontane* was paying us a visit, and cold air shed from the snowy flanks of the Pyrenees shrieked down Avenue de la Liberté and pried at windows and doors.

I built my *daube* on Paula Wolfert's recipe, supplemented with advice from several other trusted culinary experts.

Nicole didn't particularly like the orange zest, but conceded that it qualified as a classic ingredient.

Marie said serving it over mashed potatoes made her gag, with the soupiness, and the softness, and the . . . well . . . in a word, *beurk*, which is the onomatopoeic French exclamation for disgust. Rice or egg noodles— and this was just her opinion, of course, but it was intended to be definitive—rice or noodles was what you served with a *daube*.

There was one subject of universal agreement, however: If there is a perfect wine for making a *daube*, it is the rough-and-tumble, earthy sophistication of a good bottle of Faugères. No prissily elegant Burgundian Pinot Noir, thank you very much. This is not a coq au vin.

I explained to Monsieur Congnard that I was making a *daube de boeuf*, and then, concerned that I might be acting fussy, I explained that I needed about a pound of meat from each of three different parts of the animal. One thing I will always love about our months in Autignac is the moment just after this, when he simply nodded, and waited for me to tell him which parts.

I tested my translations of "shank," "short ribs," and "chuck," and, to my relief, he disappeared without a quibble and came back from his cooler with *jarret, poitrine,* and *paleron,* which he trimmed and cubed for me, before weighing each cubed mound on his scale.

"When do you leave?" he asked.

"Too soon," I said.

"I won't be here when you come back," he said with a strange smile.

"You're not retiring!" I said.

"I'm not retiring," he said. And he told me of his plans to build a new shop just on the outskirts of Laurens. It would allow him to expand his own shop, and also house, perhaps, an artisanal bakery and a small *épicerie* (grocery store). He would be bucking the creaking French system, building something new on the faintly American notions of hope and confidence in the future.

"When you come back, I will show it to you," he said, and waved me out of his shop, with three pounds of unpaid-for beef from three different parts of the animal.

Back home, I sautéed carrot, celery, and onion in olive oil, then added some garlic until the garlic released its scent, and then went to the terrace for some bay leaf, thyme, parsley, and winter savory.

"How's Daddy doing?" asked Mary Jo as I walked past with kitchen shears in one hand and a mixed bouquet of greenery held to my nose.

The recipe's instructions said to use a local wine from the same area that the beef and vegetables came from, and we had that one licked.

A classic *daube* is layered before it goes in the oven. I arranged the cubed beef mixed with the wine sauce in the bottom of the *cocotte.* Then I sprinkled sliced onions over the beef. Then quarter-inch *lardons* of pork belly. Then chopped tomatoes. Then a coin of orange zest, a bay leaf, and several whole sprigs of herbs. I cut a circle of parchment paper the size of the mouth of the pot, and laid it over the top of everything, pressing out any air so almost no evaporation would occur. Finally, I sealed the lid with a rolled rope of dough. This was an attempt to re-create the original *daubière*, which is a completely sealed clay pot that shepherds used to set in the coals and let cook all day.

In our case, everything would cook for an hour at 350°F, and another four at 250°F. It would have to do. There would be time later, perhaps, to track down a real *daubière*.

As soon as I had vacated the kitchen, Eva occupied it, making a grapefruit ice by pouring a thin layer of sweetened grapefruit juice into a sheet pan and freezing it, later to be scooped up as spoonfuls of pink crystals.

All afternoon, while the wind howled outside, the house filled with the winey, herby, garlicky smell of *daube de boeuf*. At the center of everything—there in the dark of the oven—pumped the beating heart of the family *cocotte*.

By the time dinner rolled around, we could barely stand it anymore, and when the *daube* was finally served in pasta bowls over mashed potatoes, because the food mill made them so beautifully, and because that's what the family liked, the big, almost black chunks of beef fell apart at the slightest touch of a fork. We took our first bites and thanked Monsieur Congnard, André Balliccioni, and whichever Occitan shepherd first had the idea of cooking one of his lambs in wine over the remains of the prior night's campfire.

Dessert would be grapefruit ice and another glass of André's Kallisté.

The leftover *daube* would taste better the next night.

And then we would leave the *cocotte* behind, where it belonged, a gift to 42 Avenue de la Liberté.

92

A wicker picnic basket sat open at one end of the stone bench next to Thierry's *gabinèle*, and Mary Jo and I sat at the other.

Behind us, the kids combed the rows of Thierry's Grenache Gris vines, looking for the mini bunches of *grapillons* that, though Thierry considered them unacceptably underripe for winemaking, ranked among the sweetest grapes the kids had ever eaten. This was their evening's chosen dessert, and I did not quite know what to do with the feeling it gave me to hear my two kids foraging comfortably among French vines like veteran *grapilleurs*.

We heard the sound of an engine, and tires on gravel. Over the hill behind us, an SUV approached along the edge of the vineyard, eased in between our vehicle and the *gabinèle*, and stopped.

Down out of the front seats of the SUV climbed Thierry and his wife, Nicole, petite and well, if casually, dressed.

Mary Jo and I played host, inviting our two visitors to join us for the sunset, gathering them around the stone bench that they had designed, and pouring them each a glass of their own wine.

They had swung through to gather some almonds to feed the family of squirrels in their yard before driving home for the night.

"Your husband wants to turn us into winemakers," I told Nicole.

"Well, he is sometimes correct," she said. She treated her husband with a fond sort of skepticism that was as ready to acknowledge his strengths as to puncture his occasional pomposities.

I outlined my list of objections to Nicole, who volunteered her husband's help, as if they had already discussed this. One didn't need to start large-scale. There were *micro-cuvées*, devoted to small production and high quality. Vats. Oh, vats could be purchased. New or used. Vats were not a problem.

Thierry emptied his glass, and lingered over the same view he had showed us early on, when we'd met as near strangers. He looked satisfied, and, for Thierry, unusually calm. "*C'est une belle aventure*," he said, confirming something to himself, it seemed, as much as trying to persuade.

It was, indeed, a beautiful adventure.

I felt that acquisitive rush to hurry and make this happen. To, figuratively, get something on paper, signed. A contract, something that would pin me down, would pin all of us down, and not let us renege. I wanted to make a commitment that would not let me forget this moment and all that it meant. Would not let this—all of this—slip through my fingers.

Thierry raised his glass, and for a brief dissociative moment, I was back at the Balliccionis' table in the candlelight, and Véronique's voice was saying, "*C'est pour de bon.*" It was for keeps.

And what if it were?

What if I didn't have to earn this over and over? This moment, this place, this friendship? What if there were no threat of expulsion, whether we did buy vines or did not? What if there were no further doing required, but simply being whatever Steve Hoffman meant to Thierry and Nicole Rodriguez? What if this were—all of it—simply enough for now? What if it were *pour de bon*?

93

In some ways, after months of acting like the least receptive French villager in the household, Eva turned out to be possibly the most intuitively French of all of us. She was, for one thing, unafraid to be herself, to be inscrutable, to be infuriating, to be unapologetic. For another, she assumed, like the majority of French citizens, that life's problems were generally caused by people not adopting her worldview.

But she had also figured out, in the midst of the overwrought identity crisis that is every adolescence everywhere in the world, that she needed to shore up the walls around what it meant to be Eva before she could allow herself to participate in an experience so foreign and challenging that it threatened to change her before she even knew what it was that was changing.

What her performance in school had built were the walls that, for the purposes of this trip at least, defined Eva's territory. It was hers because she had constructed the walls all on her own. She was, in one identifiable and satisfying corner of her life, unassailably of her own making.

Establishing that meant she could now come back and join us. She had picked her own battleground and won on her terms. And now she could negotiate the peace.

She had even returned to her camera, spending an afternoon with Mary Jo, ordering her around the kitchen, setting up shots, dismissing Mary Jo's ideas impatiently as they created a video of Eva, in an impeccable white apron, creating a batch of homemade yogurt to post online. The music she chose to accompany the video was not sampled, in the end, from NRJ's Top 40, but from the family's dinner soundtrack.

On a Friday, Eva stopped me as I reached for the second of two cuttlefish we were proposing to fry and serve for lunch. My hands were slippery with ocean slime, and covered to the wrists in cuttlefish ink and innards.

"Let me clean the next one," said Eva, who had established what was hers and what was not. I stood behind her, but not too close, as she pulled off the head and, squealing with delighted disgust, plunged her hand into the pungent mess of the cuttlefish's body.

94

We walked Joseph to school on a chilly morning not long before our departure.

His buddy, Steve, hollered, "Bonjour, Joseph!" as he sprinted past us, appliquéd hoodie flying.

Monsieur Edmond paused his afternoon walk to tip his hat. He rubbed one upper arm and aimed a sour grimace up at the sky. "It makes not warm," he observed, then continued his slow progress toward his front door.

Joe ran up the steps of the school courtyard and folded himself gigglingly into a game of *chat*, a form of tag that involved a lot of mop-haired children, and a safe zone if you were touching the trunk of the mulberry tree, now leafless and violently pruned back to a knotty head of bare branches.

I realized with a start that this was the same game we had witnessed beside the village well nearly six months ago, when failure had appeared to hover like a cloud over our entire experiment.

Monsieur Deconchy, in sandals as always, but conceding socks and a loose-knit cardigan to the weather, approached us across the blacktop, looking concerned. He motioned us up to join him.

"Here we go again," I said to Mary Jo through my smile.

Monsieur Deconchy's face was grave and apologetic. "*Il y a un problème*," he said. (There is a problem.)

Mary Jo and I looked at each other.

"You leave when?" he asked.

"In three weeks," I said. "It is what, the problem?"

"I am sorry, but the problem, it is that Joseph is now *quasiment Français*" (practically French), began Monsieur Deconchy.

Mary Jo had now heard the words *problème, désolé,* and *Français.* "Is there something wrong with Joe's French?" she asked me.

"We cannot let him go back to America," continued Monsieur Deconchy. "It is not possible."

And here he allowed his mouth a fractional tightening.

"Ah," I said. "I understand."

"Yes, it is unfortunate," he said.

"We will miss him badly," I said.

"Yes, well, we will take very good care of him. It goes without saying, you are welcome to come visit him often. That, in fact, would be the most wished for."

"It would," I agreed. "It is a thing to be discussed seriously."

We watched Joseph, running toward the time-out tree, laughing.

"Thank you," I said, nodding toward the scene.

"It is I," he said, and held out his hand to each of us in turn.

95

I knew the route in that gossipy old way you use to find places without a map. Past the Virgin, to the olive trees in the triangular park that looked out over the local power lines. A left at the "Autignac" sign, toward the Route de Béziers. A short sprint past Château Grézan, just shy of where Thierry was building his new winery, to Laurens, where Monsieur Congnard would be building his new butcher shop.

Outside of Laurens, the road forked, and then dropped slowly toward a rolling plain of vineyards. On the left, descending steeply, was a field of Thierry's Syrah, where the Romanian boys had practiced their English on me and carried stacks of red totes up the steep hill on strong legs. Ahead on the right was Thierry's Mourvèdre, where the grapes had verged on overripe, and we had had to be especially careful with our triage.

Up ahead, past blackberry-choked drainage ditches, the two cypress trees guarding Thierry's *gabinèle* appeared above a rise of land, and then the *gabinèle* itself. As I passed, I wondered if there weren't perhaps one or two *grapillons* left intact, which, if they were still there, would be just barely juicier than raisins, soft and wrinkled, drooping on their stems, but how sweet they would be.

Just past a dry streambed I eased off the path, over dense grasses, through scraping shrubs, and parked.

There were no cicadas now, and no carpenter bees. The wind sounded like paper sliding over paper as it moved through the trees. The sky was a pale winter blue, with high white clouds. I took my grape-picking *secateur* from the rear of the car, and walked up the trail.

I approached a blurry cloud of low, shrubby plants, looking like something twisted and tortured at the very northern edge of the arctic tree line—something that has been sustaining the blunt force of decades of prevailing winds, and has adopted a permanent leaning posture, with all of its branches aiming leeward.

The plants resembled miniature olive trees, with woody trunks, and scraggly limbs, furred with sharp, stiff, upright leaves more like thorns than leaves, and so silver-gray that there was practically no green in them.

I ran my hand gently up one of these branches, the way you might stroke a cat and then continue all the way out to the end of its tail. I noted with affection that Jean-Luc's healing touch had not in the end rid me of my wart, and felt that this did not diminish, in any meaningful way, the magic he did, in fact, possess. I cupped the palm of my hand below my nose and inhaled, and then I began snipping individual branches, as thick as I could find, without uprooting any of the plants entirely.

I hoped to return to this spot in the future. But, for now, I needed some woody wild thyme to keep a Christmas capon elevated above the bottom of a roasting pan, and perhaps to smolder in the oven and infuse the fine, fat-laced flesh of the bird with smoke, and with something like the scent that my shoes were kicking up right now, and which hovered like a cloud of pollen all around me.

"Thyme procured," I announced when I got home. It was the kids' last day of school before the *vacances de Noël,* and Mary Jo was at her computer.

"Talk me through this," she said. "I'm drafting a year-end STILL blog post. What do I say?"

"You aren't shutting it down," I said.

"That's the question. It was a one-year project."

I dumped an armload of wild thyme on the kitchen counter and broke off a healthy sprig.

"Smell this," I said, sitting across from her.

She rubbed the stem between her palms and then held them up to her nose.

"For fuck's sake," she said.

"And, for the record, no," I said. "You can't shut down STILL."

"It's sort of a pain in the ass," she said. "Every fricking day."

"You love it. The kids love it. I love it."

"Yeah, well, that's sort of what I was hoping you'd say."

"I guess I was assuming that was going to be your wing of the two-winged house," I said.

She looked up. "Be careful," she said.

"OK," I said.

"So, what are we talking about here?" she asked.

"We're talking about the house with two wings," I said. "Which doesn't really have to be a physical house."

She thought about it. "I buy that," she said.

"And as of this year, in my opinion, you have an art practice."

"In your opinion."

"In my opinion. And if that's true," I said, "then you have, let's say, begun construction of your wing of the house."

"Possibly," she said.

I took a deep breath and rolled my head on my neck.

"And part of what has happened here is that, in the course of trying to become a great French cook, I have become a barely half-decent home cook."

"Half-decent is fair," she said. "You can drop the 'barely.'"

"OK, a half-decent home cook. And eating here at this table, next to this stone wall, while you and I drink wine made by people who are, somehow, incredibly, our friends . . . In the course of all that, I have fallen in love with our family. Which doesn't mean I wasn't—"

"Understood," she said.

"So that," I said, "sort of fills in the bottom of the U."

"Of the U-shaped house," she said.

"Of the U-shaped house. The garden will take care of itself, although there might be a few more fruit trees now. You can blame Jean-Luc."

"That leaves one wing," said Mary Jo.

"And we have just been given an opportunity to live the third act of our lives at least partly in Mediterranean France."

"I'm still not disagreeing with you," she said.

"Not only that—to live here not as tourists or visitors or even as expats who have bought a pretty house to retire in. But as people who have some skin in the game. Who have to worry along with Jean-Luc and Thierry and André when there is a drought, or there is hail, or there is *oïdium*, or whether there will be too much heat for the Syrah or not enough heat for the Mourvèdre."

"So, you're saying you want to buy vines and make wine here."

"I'm saying I want to buy the Espinasses vineyard and make Faugères wine with these people, however we might find a way to do that."

She let that sink in.

"That's not the answer I was hoping for," she said. "But I'm happy to have an answer."

"You asked me to step up, to help us be a part of this place. And I have done that."

"Sort of spectacularly," she said.

"And the only reason I say that is because of what it should prove to you. That I can . . . I will . . . do whatever you ask me to do."

I took back the sprig of thyme and held it beneath my nose.

"I'm out of tea," said Mary Jo.

Sitting across from me again, she said, "I'm not a submissive wife."

When we were done laughing, she said, "OK, but seriously," and we both started laughing again.

"What I'm trying to say . . . asshole . . . is that I would rather follow you—set up two homes, buy vats and vines, completely complicate our already complicated lives, work extra hard to make sure we don't mess up our kids, be without you part of every year—I'd rather do all that with the Stevie who can tell me what he wants and is willing to go get it, than do almost anything else with the Stevie who is waiting to figure out what he wants, or worse, waiting to figure out what I want him to want.

"I want you on my team. I want an equal partner to dream with. I don't care what decision we make. I don't mind letting you lead. Just fucking dance with me."

96

I was standing with Jean-Luc on their rear terrace. He and Nicole had invited us for an aperitif before we sat down to our respective Christmas meals. It was the first time I had visited the terrace, and been able to look back from that point of view, over the wall, at the rental home of the Americans next door.

Jean-Luc was grilling the two haunches of a boar he had shot last November. "A little one, sixty kilos," he said. "Not far from La Borie Nouvelle."

What grilling meant, in this instance, was spit-roasting the two *gigots de sanglier* on a rotisserie driven by an old washing machine motor, in front of a hot but nearly flameless vine-wood fire in his wood oven. A stump snapped now and then, emitting puffs of that familiar resinous smoke, which mingled in the air with the porcine smell of sizzling boar.

The blacksmith who had configured the rotisserie for Jean-Luc had also made him a grilling tool consisting of a long cast-iron handle tipped with an iron cone, which was currently lying in the embers, glowing as orange-hot as the wood.

He knocked the cone a couple of times gently against the floor of the oven, then held it suspended over the *gigots,* which spun above a pan of toasted baguette slices. From a plate beside the fire, he picked up a fatty-looking white cube.

"Lard," he said, and dropped the cube into the mouth of the cone, where it burst into white flame and illuminated Jean-Luc's face—his mustache, his glasses, his prominent nose. It caught him with an expres-

sion of peaceful concentration as he focused on the cone and its position above the two *gigots*.

What spilled out the bottom of the cone was not liquid fat but flame.
The cone was hot enough that the lard remained ignited, and fell in
elongated viscous drips of fire onto the rotating flesh of the roasts. The
flame poured down the sides of the meat, spitting crackling bursts of
sparks, and eventually extinguishing itself, so that what dripped onto
the bread was no longer flame but hot, salty fat.

He maneuvered the cone back into the core of the fire and set the
handle down.

The washing machine engine droned.

"So if we stayed here long enough," I said, "would you one day run
out of things like this to show me?"

"There is only one way to discover this," he said.

As he spoke, Gitane wandered out to join us, nose to the ground, tail
waving slowly. "*N'est-ce pas, Gitane?*" he asked her.

"Jean-Luc," I said as we watched the knobs of boar revolve, glossy
with their new lacquer of melted fat.

"*Oui,*" he said.

I told him about Thierry's proposal and admitted—bracing a little at
how audacious it sounded standing next to him—that we had not ruled
it out, in fact, to the contrary . . .

"The vineyard of Les Espinasses," I said. "I do not entirely understand my feelings about it. But that field, in that place, with that view,
that has belonged to you and Nicole . . ."

I waited for a clue as to whether I should continue or not, but he was
expressionless, looking into the fire.

"It pleases me very much. I like to know that it is there. Sometimes I
visit it, just to feel something . . ."

"Steve," he said.

But I pushed on, wanting to finish my statement before receiving his
verdict. "I know you consider your vineyards like your children, and
perhaps it is indiscreet to ask. And of course money would be involved,
which can be difficult between . . . What I want to say is that, if ever the
day came. If ever . . ."

"Steve," he said again. He glanced through the doors at the rest of the group gathered in the dining room. "You can stop talking."

My heart froze. He had promised it to his daughter. It wasn't possible. Of course it wasn't possible.

He gestured with one arm. A short sweep that took in Autignac, the vineyards surrounding it, the hills behind them, possibly a small crescent of the Mediterranean Sea to our south.

"When the time comes," he said. "It's yours."

He put a hand on my shoulder.

"What if," he suggested, "we went inside, and took a little swig?"

Back home, with the capon roasting in the oven on its bed of wild thyme, I opened a dozen oysters—one of the imperative ingredients of a French Christmas meal—and turned to face the two *violets* I had also bought from M. Viguier on a whim, and which resembled nothing so much as enormous lumps of compacted earwax sitting on my cutting board.

You cut them in half, exposing the yellow, mussel-like, fleshy creature tucked in the center like a nut inside a shell. This creature peels up cleanly with an oyster fork, and it's down the hatch, with, maybe, a little lemon juice.

The *violets* were chewy and bitter with iodine. Joe and I were the only takers, and he was able to articulate, as we talked about it, how it was something you could paradoxically enjoy without liking the taste of it.

It was like the stunted scrubbiness of the *garrigue,* or the dark flavor of mackerel, or the oily pungency of anchovies—something that needed time, perhaps, but something you could feel you would learn to love, because you loved the region, and because these things were a worthy expression of the region's rough seductiveness. There was something so unapologetically sea-bottom honest about a *violet* that you wanted to learn to love it, like the broken nose of a beloved husband, or the crooked eyetooth of a beloved wife.

With this improvised aperitif behind us, I set about making the vinaigrette.

Behind me, Eva kneaded dough for a *fougasse,* a Provençal variation on focaccia, slit and shaped like an airy leaf, that she had discovered in her own *New York Times* as opposed to her father's *Je Sais Cuisiner,* and which perfectly matched her taste both for beautiful things and for salty starches.

It was a form of parallel play. Like Mary Jo's notebooks and markers. Or perhaps like a two-dog pack, with Eva as alpha. In any case, it was working.

The vinaigrette was the product of countless prior near misses and outright failures, as I had set plate after plate in front of Mary Jo and the kids, watching their reactions with surreptitious hope and pride, only to be told that the dressing was too tart, or too garlicky, or too oily, or, simply, "gross." I had been told that the salad was overdressed, or underdressed. I had been asked how much mustard I had put in, how much garlic, whether there was anchovy in this one—each question less a question than a sideways accusation.

Tonight, I used half a clove of garlic instead of a whole clove. I used just a few drops of lemon juice, to keep the tartness in check for Mary Jo. I used Jean-Luc's Muscat vinegar, which everybody liked, not Maman's stronger red wine vinegar. I put in a careful little pinto bean's worth of mustard—just enough to emulsify, but not enough to add a noticeable taste. I used the fruity Andalusian olive oil that had dripped first from the press in the square of José's hometown. I used just a little more than two Steve-sized pinches of sea salt. I looked over my shoulder to make sure Eva wasn't looking, then crushed a scant quarter of one of my own salted anchovy fillets into the mix—just the amount, I had discovered, that would do what anchovies are supposed to do, without giving away their presence to my two kids' ever-suspicious palates.

The recipe, if it can be called that, descended from no part of the high masculine art of haute cuisine, and it didn't fit any particular category of local specialty, despite being as steeped in local origins as it is possible to be.

It came by word of mouth from someone named Maman. And had been perfected by trial and error, over days of devotion at the kitchen counter. My carefulness really came from as simple a place as a lot of dinners together, and a lot of trying to make three specific people happy.

Much of the time, cooking is about getting cooking done—getting ingredients off the shelf and out of the crisper, getting at least a minimally healthy cocktail of nutrients into growing bodies, then doing the dishes. But sometimes cooking is about love, and sometimes love can be expressed as a vinaigrette.

"So everything is in place," said Mary Jo as we sipped a finger each of chilled *prunelle* liqueur.

From the bedroom drifted the regular swell of a laugh track.

"Everything is in place," I said, looking over the candlelit wreckage of glasses, plates, bones, and bottles, with the melancholy feeling of a man who has just gotten everything he wanted.

97

The final act of the winemaking year is simultaneously the initial act of the year that will follow.

By late December, we had entered the season of *la taille*, and in the now-leafless vines, pruning crews had replaced hunting parties, inching down the same rows they had visited during the *vendange*, leaving in their wake little graveyards of rough-hewn crosses, all pregnant with next spring's growth.

At 42 Avenue de la Liberté, we were bracing ourselves for our approaching departure. Before that unthinkable event, I would get to spend just a little more time as Jean-Luc and Nicole's crew.

On a bright wintry morning, after a four-minute commute up past the Christ, we were parked and unpacking the trunk beside the Espinasses vineyard. Jean-Luc handed me my one and only tool for the day, a curved-bladed, two-handled lopper.

With the sun just peeking over the horizon, in the most beautiful classroom I've ever set foot in, I commenced the next phase of my education.

"Vineyards look like their owners," said Jean-Luc. "You can tell who an owner is by how he prunes his vines."

Pruning tidies up last year's growth, but also readies each vine for the following spring. It is a way of partnering with the plant, making it exactly as productive as you want and ultimately extending its life. Asking a plant to maximize its production every year is like trying to paint a wall when your roller tray is running dry—you're asking too little material to do too much work, and the result is thin and faded. And so you must shape the plant, constraining its wild instincts, helping it focus its energy into a limited amount of growth.

Jean-Luc is a very practical man. But when he talks at any length about vines and pruning, he sounds less and less like a technician, and more and more like a mystic. What he is really talking about, in the end, is energy flow. The plant is not a plant so much as it is a flow of energy into and out of itself. In spring and summer, the plant expands, pushing sap outward into leaves and fruit, and each fall and winter, it pulls whatever reserves it can back into the stump, which will nourish new growth in spring before the ground has even warmed enough for the roots to begin doing their work.

The pruner's job is to manage this expansion and contraction by routing the next growing season's production in a chosen few promising directions.

The technique is called *tailler court,* which means literally to "prune short," leaving very few buds on the plant. That means fewer grapes, and, in the short term, less revenue for Jean-Luc.

Certainly, if he had his mind on the bottom line, he would be a little crazy to prune quite as short as he does. Each time he snips here, not there, he is snipping off potential short-term revenue in the form of another bunch of grapes or two, multiplied by an average of six or seven stalks per vine, multiplied by one vine every meter, covering a total of sixteen hectares of land. Over a winter pruning season, this adds up to tens of thousands of kilos of perfectly marketable grapes falling to the ground in the form of pruned branches.

But here is Jean-Luc, across the wires from me, fiscally shooting himself in the foot with each stroke of the lopper, remarking on the warmth of the sun this morning, which will add just that extra bit of pleasure to another winter day spent pruning vines with Nicole in their small corner of Faugères.

He works rhythmically and quickly, his clippers pausing only occasionally while he narrates his way through a particular decision. We are in the ranks of Syrah, among vines that have been trained along three parallel wires. Each vine grows up from a central stump and forks just above knee level into two branches that look like arms thrown wide, a common configuration called *cordon de royat*. The arms are trained in opposite directions along the lowest wire, and reach halfway across the space between the stumps, where they meet the reaching arm of the adjacent plant. These arms are the scaffolding from which each year's new growth sprouts upward, to be held loosely vertical by the two additional ranks of training wires.

Our job is to trim last year's sinewy vertical growth back close to the knotted muscles of the horizontal arms.

"*Voyez, Steve*," he says, pointing to the arm of the vine between us. "This *couronne* is getting in the way."

He doesn't like how one of the knots has come to crowd an adjacent knot on the arm of one of the vines, and with a confident snip, he deletes it, leaving three remaining productive growth points on that arm, nicely spaced, then proceeds with surprisingly few swipes of his lopper to remove the branches he doesn't want, and to leave behind one little spur, like a thumb, protruding from each of the three remaining knots that will furnish next year's growth.

The process involves maybe fifteen decisions, and is done in the span of ten seconds or so. We move on to the next stump, and it, too, is reduced, in a sort of leisurely blur, to a gnarled gray crucifix. I ask Jean-Luc why he has chosen to eliminate a fat, healthy-looking branch and instead leave the spur of a more spindly-looking neighbor. He explains that the spindlier branch was closer to the arm, and closer to the nourishment that would flow from the stump.

OK. This makes sense. "Closer to stump better than farther from stump," I repeat to myself, feeling like Frankenstein's monster trying to absorb my master's complex moral system while simultaneously learning to keep my balance in these damned elevator boots.

Several vines later, Jean-Luc stands up to think through a tricky vine that looks lopsided.

Back when he used to work with teams pruning other people's vines, he says, his partner would sometimes ask him what he was doing. "*Je réfléchis*" (I'm thinking it over), he would say.

"You think while you're pruning?" his partner would ask.

"In the books," he muses, "the vines always grow logically."

"*Eh oui,*" commiserates Nicole, bent over her work on the row next to us. She stands up to stretch her back. Nicole has quietly done twice the work Jean-Luc has, while he has been occupied with his role as professor. She removes her glasses, wipes them on her sleeve, and bends to her work again.

Through an accumulation of Jean-Luc's advice, I am starting not just to see a row of stumps sprouting a chaos of growth, but to see with more detail where the arms of adjacent plants meet, and how many knots are located on each arm. But when it comes to making the cuts, he is consistently leaving me scratching my head.

"*Alors, Steve,*" he says. "Since you're here to prune . . ." He smiles at me with one silver tooth winking out from the corner of his mouth.

I tell him that perhaps in a year or two, I will be ready to prune.

"Steve," says Jean-Luc.

And with the apparent non sequitur "There once was a donkey," he begins telling a story. I don't know why we are on the subject of donkeys, but OK, there once was a donkey.

One morning the donkey was left in the pasture to graze. By lunchtime, it had browsed its way beyond the pasture into the vineyard, and the master returned to find the donkey eating his vines. He staked him back in the pasture, believing that the better part of next year's grape harvest was now *foutu*. But the following spring, what did the master discover? Well, of course, that the vines the donkey had browsed were growing better than the vines that had been left alone, and the harvest swelled.

"So you see, Steve," concludes Jean-Luc. "The first *tailleur de vignes* was an ass. Doubtless, you'll do at least as well!" Jean-Luc repeats the joke, and then, under the careful supervision of his *professeur,* the latest in a long line of asses begins pruning vines.

I ask an initial flurry of questions that gradually tapers off into a regular but less frequent "OK, Jean-Luc, tell me what you would do here." I learn to crop the branches *ras,* or tight to the wood, so they don't create ridges that will get in the way of next year's clippers. I learn to avoid cutting my stubs too close to the branch, so the dryness invading from the cut doesn't infringe on the green wood that will nourish next year's growth.

The vertical branches we prune are segmented a little bit like bamboo, and there is a kind of marrow that runs through the center of the branch. I learn to make my cuts exactly on the line where the segments meet, where the marrow is least exposed, and least able to invite disease into the plant.

And finally, after several corrections from Jean-Luc that just don't make any sense to me at all, I finally begin to see the tiny *bourgeons,* or buds, barely poking out from between these segments. These buds will be the branches that grow next year, and it is their location that has governed the cuts that Jean-Luc has recommended. Two branches can be adjacent to each other with apparently nothing to choose between them, yet all morning long, Jean-Luc has unhesitatingly recommended cutting one over the other. Now I can see that the buds on one branch may be pointing helpfully upward, or back toward the training wires, and this makes all the difference.

The buds have been there the whole time, I just haven't seen them. But now that I do, most of the triage that has to be done makes sense. The morning, like our entire stay in some sense, has been a process of magnification, with my vision progressively narrowing from an initial gushing at a hundred-square-mile vista, to focusing on the orientation of buds the size of tomato seeds on one branch at a time. At some point, I find, to my surprise, that for spans of several minutes, I'm mostly just pruning.

Still, about every fourth or fifth stump, I find myself at a loss.

Each call for help brings Jean-Luc at a friendly trot to help me sort through my questions. Sometimes he heads back to his own work right away. But this is the Midi, and after one has stood to stretch one's back, or has heard a partridge call from the adjacent scrub, quite often it is necessary to profit from these brief distractions in order to indulge in conversation, perhaps about the pleasures of a plate of oysters accompanied by a cold glass of Rosé de Bandol.

Nicole is endlessly good-spirited about it, but it must be confessed that when she looks up from her work, she is likely to see Jean-Luc and Steve upright, facing each other across the wires, loppers dangling at our sides, our free hands helping to emphasize a point of agreement.

At some point, Jean-Luc picks up a fallen branch and pulls out his battered shepherd's knife. He slices a bud from the branch, and removes the protective scales from the surface. He carefully slices the bud in two, lengthwise, and explains that all of next year's growth is already contained in the bud.

"*Voyez, Steve,*" he says. "If you examined this bud under a microscope, you could see all of next year's grapes inside already—microscopic, but all there.

"But truly!" he says, as if I had contradicted him. "I have seen it."

Jean-Luc tosses the bud and stem casually to the ground, and grabs his *secateur.*

"*Allez, Steve,*" he says. "*Au travail.*"

And we return to our work, until the next time it becomes necessary to stretch one's back.

By the end of the day, we have completed half a dozen rows of Syrah, with another thirty to go, and the rows of Mourvèdre waiting below.

Over the days that follow, there is a lot of talk. More even than during the *vendange,* when talk among the crew, though nearly constant, was diffused among a dozen workers. This winter crew has been pruned back to three, and the flavor of the conversation is correspondingly richer.

Jean-Luc and Nicole learn about my meandering path from language student to tax preparer. About what feels like a renewal—nurtured in the early mornings on the terrace while Jean-Luc threw grain to the doves—of an old love for writing. And about the strange, stubborn difficulty that exists between my parents and me, despite our both being so happy in so many other ways, and our wishing it otherwise.

In turn, I learn that a lovesick Jean-Luc just managed to wait for Nicole to graduate from high school before asking her to marry him. I learn about their daughter, who is both an oenologist and the mother of their beloved granddaughter. I learn about the second time that *le bon Dieu* attempted to kill Jean-Luc, when his tractor caught the edge of a ditch and rolled onto him.

And then I learn about the third time.

98

They had had a son.

His name was Jérome, and he had grown up here, and gone to the École d'Autignac. He had loved nature and dinosaurs.

"Like your *petit Joseph*," said Jean-Luc.

He had fallen sick at age eighteen, and nobody in Béziers could diagnose what was wrong. They had brought him to the hospital in Montpellier, where he had stayed for a while, and Jean-Luc and Nicole would commute to see him every day after working in their fields. In that hospital room, expert after expert came to visit, and tried everything that could be thought of, but in the end they were helpless to turn back the advance of whatever it was Jérome was carrying in his blood, and he had died shortly after telling his papa and his maman that he thought he was feeling better.

And that was the third time God had tried to kill Jean-Luc.

He and I have stopped pruning and are holding our tools across our chests. He has told the story in his way, and telling it through to the end appears to have soothed this talkative man.

I try and fail to imagine how someone with Nicole's love of innocent things, and her gift for taking care of others, could have borne such a loss.

She's bearing it again just now, two rows over, bent and working. The shepherd's granddaughter. The high school bride. The worker and wife, and partner and cook, and quick-to-laugh mother of dogs and a daughter and one missing son. I wonder how I could possibly have mistaken her forceful watchfulness for anything other than what it was—the intuitions of a good mother who feels a painful duty to watch out for anyone in her charge.

I look at Jean-Luc, who casts an eye in Nicole's direction. I have admired him. Envied him. Wished in some ways even to be him, or a likeness of him. Thought that I had discovered in him the replacement for the man on the street in Paris, except that Jean-Luc was the counterexample—a man who does not need to project invulnerability, because he is happy with his choices, domestically and professionally, and content to live within their confines.

And yet as we stand across from each other, separated by the frailty of a wire trellis, there is no question who would change places with whom.

Jean-Luc would give anything to be Steve Hoffman. Or if not Steve Hoffman, then a man in Steve Hoffman's circumstances. The father of a boy just exactly like Joseph—alive and in good health, affectionate, emotionally accessible, susceptible to the violence of the world, but not immune to its delights, with a sly humor. And, above all, in need of raising by a father and mother who love him beyond words.

The Mediterranean sun warms us from its low winter angle. We stand, American and French, on opposite sides of many things, but in each other's physical and psychic space. Different enough, and enough the same, that we can afford to be intimate.

"Jean-Luc and Nicole," I say. "When I think of the people I feel closest to, when I want to say something to them . . . that they are very dear to me . . . I tell them that I would trust them to be the parents of my children. The two of you, I would . . ."

I pause, in order to get it right, but I can't.

"The French words escape me," I say. "I hope you understand."

"Words are not always the most important," says Jean-Luc.

We resume pruning in silence, and after a long while, the eternal balm of Latin conversation intercedes amid our sadness, and offers its familiar comforts.

Among the minor disruptive favors that Autignac did for us was to offer a new vision of time and how to live in it.

We had always operated on a timeline that moved through days and months and calendar years on a generally rising graph line that might have represented something like progress.

Time in Autignac was more circular than that. It was like moving upward around the spiral of a stretched-out spring. It was based on rhythm, not progress.

It is almost impossible to maintain the illusion of time as a form of forward progress in a place where years are thought of as vintages. There are good vintages and bad vintages. There has never in history been a vineyard whose vintages just kept getting better. No amount of gumption or bootstrapping can undo a year of too much heat, and too little rain, and hail in September.

Instead, what you can count on is the coming back around of the next season, like the family you were a little tired of last Christmas but are looking forward to seeing now that it's Easter.

There is only one opportunity a year to pick grapes in a wine region. When that opportunity arrives, then all you do for that season is pick grapes, with the attendant anticipation as the season approaches, the deep immersion into the season itself, and a weary fulfillment when it's done.

One of Jean-Luc's favorite jokes is that when grape pickers finally get home to their spouses after the *vendange,* their second act is to set down their luggage. Harvest season, followed by mating season.

The grape harvest cedes its place to hunting season, which overlaps with mushroom season, which eventually makes way for pruning season, which everybody will be sick of when droplets of sap appear at the tips of pruned vine branches in March.

And so on—as a lifetime of seasons spiral, with no requirement that any of them be better than the last, simply that they be anticipated and lived through with a certain competence and attention.

Because living this way quite often involved staying in one place, and accepting the mixed blessings of long and devoted commitment, it could be seen as stagnant, and was indeed seen that way by waves of young people moving from the provinces into Montpellier and Toulouse and Paris. And if we had had to decide to raise kids here, and only here, I don't know what we would have chosen.

But you could see it another way, as a kind of eternal contentment, with each new season bringing familiar joys and obligations, and relieving the monotony of the end of the season before. It made sense to us. Who is happier than a fisherman on opening day, a gardener in spring, an athlete on the first day of training? How much more reliable was a life based on the seasons baked into our DNA, and the endlessly satisfying daily loop of hunger and satiety, than a life premised on the precarious notions of accumulation and increase? It was a way of thinking about life that reordered priorities in the direction of happiness and pleasure, and away from the fierce delights—to which we were not immune—of competitiveness and accomplishment.

Do a few things well, and do them in season. And the seasons will reward you with something new, and something familiar, each time they come around.

We had come to notice less and less whether it was exactly August or November, but we could look back with precision on *la saison des figues,* followed by *la vendange, la chasse,* and *la saison des olives,* and now *la taille* would serve as the bridge from one cycle of seasons to the next.

There were seasons of the year, but there were also seasons of a life.

This was my season to be a husband and a father, in the home that our kids would think of as home. To take that lightly in any way was a kind of sin. A sin against Jérome and his parents, to say nothing of Mary Jo, Eva, and Joseph. It was time to finish out my pruning, putting one season to bed, and at the same time preparing for the season to come. I could wish that much of my future life might be spent in the company of these new friends, who had changed so much in me and whose company was such pleasure. But now it was time to give our kids a homeland, from which they could choose someday to set sail.

A long marriage, a long-intact family, eventually become their own kinds of appellations. Irreproducible. Rich precisely in their specificity, their constraints, the depth that comes from commitment to one thing. You couldn't re-create them by starting over in any other place. Under circumstances other than their own, they became something else. I didn't want something else. I wanted the only life that was possible with Mary Jo, with my iron-willed daughter, who had shown me the profits of being oneself, with my tender son, who had reminded me of the costs. My place on earth was that life. It was the ground I had cleared and tilled and planted. In five years, Eva would be on her own. In another five, Joseph. Until then, there was tending to do.

Perhaps someday there would be a vineyard overlooking dark hills, and bottles of our own round black wine in a cool cellar, next to dusty, unlabeled bottles.

And there would be a season for that.

Acknowledgments

Everything starts with my lifemate, playmate, housemate, trailmate, dreammate, couchmate, co-parent, and spouse. My Mary Jo. My all.

My two children, Eva and Joseph, make me hungry for life, so that I might spend more of it with them.

Erik Eastman belongs to a better world, but has consented, for some reason, to remain here with us, and be my friend—for which I am grateful every day.

My agent, David Black, gave me permission to believe I was a writer. Then coached me, counseled me, comforted me, swore at me, and always, always, always had my back. A mensch among mensches, this David Black.

I put my editor, Francis Lam, through hell, including several false starts, two missed deadlines, a bloated first draft, and an unearned and occasionally misplaced stubbornness. He greeted all of this with endless reserves of graciousness, attention, support, intelligence, wisdom, and a quiet insistence that was always patient and never overbearing. He deserves much of the credit for this book's finding itself, at long last.

Jean-Luc and Nicole Vialles, Thierry and Nicole Rodriguez, André and Véronique Balliccioni taught me about the landscape, food, cooking, vineyards, wine, and winemaking of the region they love, and taught me to love it, too. With the gift of their acceptance, they helped me accept myself in new ways that remain with me to this day. I have never been the same.

Chef Alex Roberts, Peter Bian, and the aforementioned Erik Eastman form a group we call the Oyster Shuckers. We play tennis as often as possible, and keep each other sane, inspired, listened to, watched over, and emotionally whole. Thank you, gents. I love you all.

There are many others. But this is the core. These are the ones who get me through.

ABOUT THE AUTHOR

Steve Hoffman is a Minnesota tax preparer and food writer. His writing has won multiple national awards, including the 2019 James Beard M.F.K. Fisher Distinguished Writing Award. His work has been published in *Food & Wine, The Washington Post,* and the Minneapolis *Star Tribune,* among others. He shares one acre on Turtle Lake, in Shoreview, Minnesota, with his wife, Mary Jo, their elderly and entitled puggle, and roughly eighty thousand honeybees.